Peer to Peer and the Music Industry

KC   ey.
             hity

i

Theory, Culture & Society

Theory, Culture & Society caters for the resurgence of interest in culture within contemporary social science and the humanities. Building on the heritage of classical social theory, the book series examines ways in which this tradition has been reshaped by a new generation of theorists. It also publishes theoretically informed analyses of everyday life, popular culture, and new intellectual movements.

EDITOR: Mike Featherstone, *Nottingham Trent University*

SERIES EDITORIAL BOARD
Roy Boyne, *University of Durham*
Nicholas Gane, *University of York*
Scott Lash, Goldsmiths College, *University of London*
Roland Robertson, *University of Aberdeen*
Couze Venn, *Nottingham Trent University*

THE TCS CENTRE
The Theory, Culture & Society book series, the journals *Theory, Culture & Society and Body & Society*, and related conference, seminar and postgraduate programmes operate from the TCS Centre at Nottingham Trent University. For further details of the TCS Centre's activities please contact:

The TCS Centre, Room 175
Faculty of Humanities
Nottingham Trent University
Clifton Lane, Nottingham, NG11 8NS, UK
e-mail: tcs@ntu.ac.uk
web: http://sagepub.net/tcs/

Recent volumes include:

Ordinary People and the Media
The Demotic Turn
Graeme Turner

The Sociology of Intellectual Life
The Career of the Mind in and around the Academy
Steve Fuller

Globalization & Football
Richard Guilianotti and Roland Robertson

The Saturated Society
Governing Risk and Lifestyles in Consumer Culture
Pekka Sulkunen

Peer to Peer and the Music Industry

The Criminalization of Sharing

Matthew David

Los Angeles | London | New Delhi
Singapore | Washington DC

First published 2010
Reprinted 2010

Published in association with *Theory, Culture & Society,*
Nottingham Trent University

SAGE Publications Ltd
1 Oliver's Yard
55 City Road
London EC1Y 1SP

SAGE Publications Inc.
2455 Teller Road
Thousand Oaks, California 91320

SAGE Publications India Pvt Ltd
B 1/I 1 Mohan Cooperative Industrial Area
Mathura Road, Post Bag 7
New Delhi 110 044

SAGE Publications Asia-Pacific Pte Ltd
33 Pekin Street #02–01
Far East Square
Singapore 048763

Library of Congress Control Number: 2009925264

British Library Cataloguing in Publication data

A catalogue record for this book is available from
the British Library

ISBN 978-1-84787-005-6
ISBN 978-0-85702-538-8 (pbk)

Typeset by C&M Digitals (P) Ltd, Chennai, India
Printed by MPG Books Group, Bodmin, Cornwall
Printed on paper from sustainable resources

Mixed Sources
Product group from well-managed
forests and other controlled sources
www.fsc.org Cert no. SA-COC-1565
© 1996 Forest Stewardship Council
FSC

For Mike Presdee (1944-2009).

A great teacher, friend and sharer.

Contents

List of Figures and Tables

Figures

Tables

Key Acronyms and Abbreviations

A&R	Artists and Repertoire
ACTA	Anti-Counterfeiting Trade Agreement
AOL	America On-line
BBC	British Broadcasting Corporation
BMG	Bertelsmann Music Group
BPI	The British Phonographic Industry
BT	British Telecommunications
CCTV	Closed Circuit Television
CD	Compact Disc
CDPA	United Kingdom Copyright, Designs and Patent Act 1988
CNN	Cable Network News
DAT	Digital Audio Tape
DCMA	United States Digital Millennium Copyright Act 1998
DCMS	United Kingdom Department of Culture, Media and Sport
DRM	Digital Rights Management
DVD	Digital Versatile Disc or Digital Video Disc
ECHR	European Convention on Human Rights
EFF	Electronic Freedom Foundation
EMI	Electric and Musical Industries Ltd
EU	European Union
F2F	Friend to Friend Distributed Networks
FACT	Federation Against Copyright Theft
GATT	General Agreement on Tariffs and Trade
HRA	United Kingdom Human Rights Act
HBO	Home Box Office
ICT	Information and Communication Technology
ID	Identification Documents or abbreviation for Identification
IP	Intellectual Property
IPR	Intellectual Property Rights
IT	Information Technology
ISP	Internet Service Providers
ISPA	Internet Service Providers Association
MAFIAA	Music and Film Industry Association of America
MoU	2008 Memorandum of Understanding between BPI and UK ISPs

MP1,2,3 and 4	MP in each case is an abbreviation for MPEG, while the numbers refer to MPEG protocols for digital compression for different media
MPAA	Motion Picture Association of America
MPEG	Moving Picture Expert Group
MPPC	Motion Picture Patent Company
NBC	National Broadcasting Company
OECD	Organization for Economic Cooperation and Development
OPAC	Online Public Access Catalogue
P2P	Peer-to-Peer Distributed Networks
RIAA	Record Industry Association of America
TPB	The Pirate Bay
TRIPS	Agreement on Trade Related Aspects of Intellectual Property Rights
WIPO	World Intellectual Property Organization
WCT	World Intellectual Property Organization Copyright Treaty
WTO	World Trade Organization
UK	United Kingdom
US	United States of America

Acknowledgements

This work would not have been possible without the help of many people. I would particularly like to thank Jodie Allen, Jack Birmingham, Peter Campbell, Tori Durrer, Sergey Erofeev, Betsy Ettorre, Victoria Foster, Gill Gower, Tim Hall, Dan (onions) Hartley, Dave Inker, Paul Jones, Gesa Kather, Devorah Kalekin-Fishman, Jamie Kirkhope, Graeme Kirkpatrick, Andrew Kirton, Lauren Langman, Chris May, Kevin Meethan, Ruth Melville, Steve Miles (the original professor of 'symbology'), Pete ('Mr Incredible') Millward, Dave O'Brian, Sarah Louisa Phythian-Adams (the real undercover economist), Jason Powell, Mike Presdee, Michaela Pyšňáková (queen of the mainstream), Chris Rojek, Imogen Roome, Rebecca Saxton, Jai Seaman and Iain Wilkinson. I would also like to thank Chris, Val, Rachel, Siân, Brennan and Jasmine.

1

Introduction

- Much too much?
- The file-sharing phenomenon
- The structure of this book
- The claim being made

Much too much?

Two wars rage today: one to control scarce 'pre-industrial' fossil fuels; the other to control non-scarce 'post-industrial' informational goods. Global capitalism requires the fusion of energy and information. Managing scarcity in that which is naturally scarce and in making scarce that which is not becomes paramount. 'Corporate power is threatened by scarcity on the one hand and the potential loss of scarcity on the other' (David and Kirkhope 2006: 80). That every networked computer can share all the digital information in the world challenges one of these domains of control. In such conditions, sharing has been legislated against with a new intensity.

Scientists 'manage the horror' (Woolgar 1988) of never being truly sure, with secondary repertoires, circular devices that give a sense of security and closure that is otherwise lacking when confronting a confusing world. This book looks at how parties to disputes over file-sharing 'manage the horror' of having no legal, technical, social or cultural foundations by which to secure their economic interests, identities, strategies and alliances in relation to the production and circulation of informational goods.

Nonetheless, one person's horror is another person's blessing. Henry Fuseli's 1781 painting, *The Nightmare* (see Figure 1.1), was pirated within months of its first authorised reproduction (David 2006b). Fuseli was as upset by the limited payment he received for the authorised reproductions as he was with the pirates, who were distributing his name across the whole of Europe with cut-price editions that made him a household name and his work an affordable household item. Such fame added to the value of the authorized versions. To bypasss contracts already signed, Fuseli simply painted new versions of his original and sold the rights to these. Finally he set up his own printing company. Additional contracts are prohibited today in contracts issued by major record labels. However, the value of free publicity and bypassing bottlenecks through self-distribution are still live

Figure 1.1   *The Nightmare, Henry Fuseli, 1781* The Glynn Vivian
Art Gallery, Swansea

issues. Fuseli's business model might be a nightmare for today's major
labels, but such attempts to 'manage the horror' may benefit audiences
and artists alike.

The file-sharing phenomenon

This book is about file-sharing, the circulation of compressed digital computer
files over the Internet using an array of location and exchange software. In
making their music collections available online, file-sharers create a community of sharing that takes the affordances of network technology in a
radical new direction. Hundreds of millions of networked computer users
and upwards of a billion files made available at any one time challenge the
monopoly power of major record labels, whose ongoing concentration
stands in stark contrast to a free flow of information that threatens to sweep
them aside.

File-sharing software has increasingly migrated from central server mediated forms of exchange to distributed forms of interaction. Each computer
in the network acts as client and server. Distributed systems are a response
to the criminalization of file-sharing software providers, uploaders, downloaders

and even Internet Service Providers (ISPs). Legal moves come from film and music companies who object to material they seek to sell being shared globally. Legal strategies link to wider technical and cultural campaigns to control intellectual property in patent as well as copyright. Currently, dominant players in film and recorded music see file-sharing as a fundamental threat. They may be correct. They may or may not be successful. In the course of conflicts, the very fabric of 'they' shifts, as such file-sharing goes to the heart of contemporary network society, to informational capitalism's discontents, challengers and those that seek to reinvent it.

The economic significance of informational goods increases in network societies (Castells 1996). So the potential to circulate such goods freely through the Internet raises the prospect, as spectre or salvation, of an end to scarcity – at least in the informational realm. Post-scarcity threatens profitability in goods that command a price only as long as demand exceeds supply. Businesses built on scarcity campaign hard to criminalize sharing. Protecting monopoly rights in informational goods, even in suspending market forces at one level, is deemed essential to the maintenance of market exchange relations in general. Suspending market entry is designed to maintain scarcity and hence prices.

Most technologies that undermine scarcity were themselves developed initially by the very companies now threatened. Today's informational capitalist enterprises may be replaced from below or by higher forms of informational capitalism. File-sharing is not simply a product of informational capitalism; it may drive out the old only to make way for a newer, more powerful informational capitalism. Global media corporations are happy to profit from free content where they can. But alternatives also emerge. Castells (1996) suggests that the 'informational mode of development' (forces of production) are not reducible to the 'informational mode of production' (network capitalism), even as critics like Chris May (2002) suggest the two are not so distinct. Telecommunications and information businesses developed the digital recording and storage, along with compression and transfer protocols, that now assist challenges to their monopolies. Hackers extended initial products in new directions. The informational mode of development is not merely extending the dominant mode of production, it is threatening the fetters set in place by property rights regimes.

The structure of this book

The relationship between technical, economic and social networks and the dynamics of change are explored in Chapter 2. Neo-Marxists such as Castells, May and Kirkpatrick are contrasted with the more ethnographic work of Hine, Mason et al. and Miller and Slater, as well as the post-structuralism of Deleuze, Galloway and Kittler.

Chapter 3 explores the history of file-sharing; its first incarnation, Napster, the legal actions which led to its closure in 2001/2, the subsequent generations of software, and the laws that emerged to engage them and which in turn shaped subsequent technical modifications. While Napster's central server offered a technical Achilles heel that allowed legal action against its providers, new generations of file-sharing software adopted ever more complete forms of distributed communication for location and exchange. This circumvented certain legal liabilities on the part of the software providers. The very limits to control have led to the growth of a mass audience for online digital material, and in a standard format that overcame the desire of individual suppliers to control their musical and film content. This created the conditions for a market in download services and MP3/4 players. Suspension of property rights in one domain created the possibility of new markets. Another development, alongside file-sharing, has been the parallel growth (from the same month in 1999) of social networking services. Chapter 3 ends by highlighting the parallel developments of audience file-sharing and the actions of artists reaching audiences by similar means, a theme explored further in Chapters 8 and 9.

A contradiction exists between the location of ideas within an irreducible web of cultural production and the notion of property as discrete units for private ownership. All formulations of intellectual property have recognized that allocation of ownership rights in ideas should only ever be partial and time limited, balancing the private interests of innovators with the general interest of the culture out of which all innovations arise. At a time when informational goods are becoming increasingly economically significant, laws to shore up ownership in ideas seek to sweep aside such balance. Chapter 4 demonstrates that perpetual and strong constructions of intellectual property rights have no assured basis in natural rights philosophy, romantic constructions of creativity or in utilitarian doctrines of the balance of interests. Today's beneficiaries make universal claims to defend partial interests. States, individuals, industries and genres that achieve 'success' claim those coming after should defer to their ownership rights over past achievements. However, those states, individuals, industries and genres now seeking to protect intellectual property rights from younger actors themselves rose to success by disregarding the monopoly rights claimed by those that were dominant before them. Just as the old claim rights over the past, so the young (states, individuals, industries and genres) defend their exploitation of the creative commons on the basis of rights to development and over the future.

Chapter 5 picks up Chapter 3's history of file-sharing, through the prism of legal developments outlined in Chapter 4. After Napster's closure, distributed peer-to-peer softwares emerged and were themselves the target for legal attack. US court decisions in 2003 and 2004 upheld the 1984 'Sony Ruling' which established the principle of 'dual use' whereby a provider of a product with legal applications cannot be held liable for unlawful applications if they are not directly party to such uses and have not actively promoted such uses. The result of the 2003 and 2004 rulings, despite a challenge to the Sony Ruling in 2005, shifted attention from software suppliers to file-sharers. This campaign is ongoing in a set of cross-cutting legal, technical and cultural forms which are explored in Chapters 6 and 7. Chapter 5 examines how legal developments have unfolded across the world. A global intellectual property framework through the World Trade Organization (hereafter WTO), the Agreement on Trade Related Aspects of Intellectual Property Rights (hereafter TRIPS) and the World Intellectual Property Organization (hereafter WIPO) is emerging. However, the growth of 'immaterial imperialism' – global intellectual property rights regime – remains limited by diversity in national and regional interpretation and enforcement. The same legal text can be acted on, or not, or differently. Balance between intellectual property rights and human rights (to privacy and freedom of expression) provides scope for multiple challenges, modifications, exemptions and limitations to a universal and strong form of property rights in ideas, in principle and in enforcement.

Tension between encryption and surveillance in network communication extends long-standing modern concerns over anonymity and regulation. Chapter 6 examines digital rights management, in encryption and surveillance, as a technical mythology – both false and self-contradictory. If 'strong' encryption existed it would be as useful to copyright infringing file-sharers as such systems would be to copyright holders. Strong encryption runs up against the fact that all currently available music in the world is available in non-encrypted format, as CDs are not currently encrypted. Even if every new piece of music were encrypted, it would only take someone to hold a microphone next to a speaker to make a recording of it. But such a digital lock does not exist. Pure technical security is a myth. As long as someone is given the key, it remains likely that it will be leaked. Every encryption system ever developed to protect informational goods has been broken by the global hacking community. The hacker ethic, 'the spirit of informationalism' and/or 'the informational mode of development' itself, routinely upsets the existing mode of production and its regime of intellectual property rights.

Surveillance is used by recording industry proxies to trawl file-sharing networks for copyright infringement. However, similar techniques are used by file-sharers, through add-on software that blocks access to computers whose searching trawls rather than shares. As two sides of the same coin, encryption and surveillance do not in themselves determine outcomes. Rather, it is their use and the success or otherwise of the social networks of such applications that determine outcomes. Whether the resources deployed by hundreds of millions of file-sharers and hackers will prevail relative to the resources deployed by 'content industries' becomes the focus of attention. Such disputes take place at the level of courtrooms and legislatures, research and development laboratories and the global networks of hackers and open source programmers, mass-media storytelling and chat room/blogs, lobby group campaigning and content industry boardrooms, and in the dynamics of musicians and artists deciding how best to reach an audience, make a life and make a living, as well as in the everyday interactions of countless millions of people online. If file-sharing software shows how new technologies create new affordances that cannot be reduced to the existing balance of social relationships, encryption and surveillance software tend to highlight the counterpoint, which is that such affordances are not themselves able to suspend existing power relations. File-sharing is an asymmetric technology. Surveillance technology and encryption technology are both, individually and together, symmetrical ones.

The tension between exposure and closure is irresolvable. The desire to widen the circulation of information, whether as a profit-oriented content industry or as a 'strength in numbers' file-sharing community (the bigger the group the more there is for everyone to share – as copying is non-rivalrous), stands at odds with the counter desire to limit access in either the protection of scarcity and hence prices, or in protecting identity in an attempt to avoid prosecution. All sides to disputes seek to 'manage the horror' of their inescapable vulnerability with myths of power and security, whether by technical or other means. When courtrooms and gadgets so often fail – even as persuasive fiction – it is no surprise that much effort has been directed at mass-media representation, in the attempt to persuade non-experts that they should not, cannot, better not try to file-share. Chapter 7 addresses these attempts to manage the mass media. Linking file-sharing with commercial counterfeiting, bootlegging and piracy – and then linking all these with terrorism, drugs, drug dealing, illegal immigrants, school and university student plagiarism, and identity theft – seeks to engender both a moral rejection of copyright infringing file-sharing and the belief that both the chance and the cost of getting caught are very high. These claims are tenuous at best and have proven highly counterproductive, being largely rejected, disbelieved and inverted by those targeted. In a classic case of deviance amplification, lumping file-sharers, counterfeiters and pirates together under the label of 'pirates' has led many who are not, legally speaking, pirates to embrace their new-found deviant identity. The label 'pirate' has become a badge of pride. Claims concerning new clampdowns and initiatives do more harm than good. Exaggerated and inaccurate accounts discredit their proponents.

Yet mass-media coverage is more than just failed propaganda. Study of such news coverage reveals the relative weakness of bodies such as the British Phonographic Industry (hereafter BPI), the Recording Industry Association of America (hereafter RIAA), the Motion Picture Association of America (MPAA) and the Federation Against Copyright Theft (FACT) in controlling and framing the stories they push. Frames have not tended to endorse the content providers' construction of reality. Media framing conflicts occur between organizations and institutions, and the voices of file-sharers never frame coverage, yet content industries face a range of other corporate bodies keen to contest their version of events. Large multimedia conglomerates, all of whom profit from the circulation of free content in one form or another, seem keen to carve up the empires of former dominant players. Record and film companies are often subsidiaries of the larger conglomerates that, in backing all the horses, appear willing to sacrifice some of their stable in the interest of winning on other bets. Many such companies have stakes in Internet service provision, mobile telephone networks, television, social networking sites, record companies, computer manufacture, software and gaming, as well as in film. The death of the major record label may see the rise of new grass-roots production and performance models of culture and business. It could be a stepping stone to a new age of ever more concentrated multinational and cross sector integrated corporate power. These alternative scenarios are explored in Chapters 8 and 9.

Chapter 8 questions the royalty based system of reward currently in operation in the recording industry. Based on a version of romanticism, the idea that artists are best rewarded by royalties, rather than being paid directly for their work or performance, is not borne out by past or present evidence. Study of the royalty system in the USA, France, the UK and elsewhere shows chronic failure to reward artists. Headline record deals and advances appear to make artists rich but are eaten up by a full spectrum of recoupable costs set against them. Most recording artists owe their record companies money, having failed to recoup. This is true even for most artists whose work is profitable for their labels. It is not surprising, therefore, that many artists resent their labels more than they do file-sharing fans. If record sales have almost no impact on most artists' incomes it is hardly their problem. Yet it is more than just a matter of indifference. Audiences saving money by downloading for free spend more money going to concerts. Ticket prices have increased in line with declining revenues from recorded music. Alongside performance-related merchandising, revenues from live performances are distributed much more in the artists' favour than are recording revenues. Artists benefit from free distribution. Why then would artists sign recording deals? This is explored in relation to the five purported functions of major record labels, each of which is being challenged by the advent of file-sharing. Where production, manufacture, distribution, and right management are becoming increasingly dislocated from major labels, the maintenance of relative monopoly power in promotion is the key battleground for their continued existence. Loss of this gatekeeper function would spell disaster – and this monopoly is being variously undermined.

Chapter 8 ends with a discussion of current shifts in representations of creativity and subsequent claims to a share of rewards. Creativity can be attributed to tradition, inner genius, interaction between performers, interaction between performers and audiences, or to the complex division of labour. Shifts in the balance of reward parallel shifts in relative aesthetic valuation of certain kinds of 'creative performance'. In the age of file-sharing we see the relative valuation of the creativity found in recordings decrease relative to the valuation (material and aesthetic) credited to the creativity (uniqueness) embodied in live performance. As challenges to the myth of the recording artist intensify, so both aesthetic and material valuations shift from rewarding music as capital to rewarding performance as creative labour.

Challenges to the established business model of recorded music and royalties brought about by file-sharing have created conditions for new business models. Artists can reach audiences without major record labels. In Chapter 9, six case studies highlight the possible. Two cases are of new artists finding an audience by means of free distribution of content. Two cases are of artists currently at the peak of celebrity, leaving their record labels and either releasing music directly or signing with a promoter rather than a record label, in both cases increasing their already considerable earnings. The third pair of cases concerns bands who are in the post-limelight stage of what were very successful careers and for whom self-distribution/ free-distribution online has increased revenues, either from recordings or from increased revenues from live events.

Alternatives abound. Such alternative futures are many, diverse and potentially at odds with one another. One such future is field colonization. In the absence of major labels, non-music based cross-media companies may occupy the commercial space vacated. This is prefigured in the practices of a number of such mega-players today. Such a scenario would intensify tendencies within the current business model of major labels, that of delegitimation (reliance upon law over trust in managing audiences) and deterritorialization (the reliance upon globally distributed recordings over unique and local performances). Alternatively, Madonna and U2's reliance upon law and mega-live shows combines ongoing delegitimation with reterritorialization. Relegitimation combined with deterritorialization can be seen in the practices of bands such as Radiohead and Simply Red, who have pioneered new trust relations with fans online even while emphasis upon live events declines. Relegitimation linked with reterritorialization strategies establish new trust relations between audience and artists. Audiences pay artists because they want to – even when the recorded music has been distributed freely with the artists' consent in advance. Live performance is the primary means of such payment. The Charlatans, Arctic Monkeys and Enter Shikari illustrate this possibility of making a living in a world of free content and a renewed willingness to pay.

Chapters 8 and 9 show the future is open to diverse possibilities, and current conditions are neither stable, equitable nor considered legitimate by most parties to the musical/cultural economic field. Chapters 5, 6 and 7 show that ownership and reproduction rights in the age of file-sharing cannot be secured by legal, technical and/or cultural guarantees. If Chapters 3 and 4 give the particular and general historical backgrounds to file-sharing and intellectual property rights, this takes us back to the fundamental character of the network society which was outlined in Chapter 2, and which this book seeks to elaborate upon.

Chapter 10 highlights the ongoing and open character of conflicts over file-sharing today, suggests the essential value of reflexive epistemological diversity in studying such conflicts, and suggests a parallel between the 'capitalist perestroika' of the last thirty years and that in the Soviet Union before its collapse. Where capitalism triumphed over statism in better harnessing the power of the informational mode of development, it now confronts 'informational perestroika and glasnost' from below.

The claim being made

This book extends the insights of cultural criminology (Presdee 2000) to an examination of the criminalization of culture. The study of file-sharing shows that while technology is not reducible to current dominant social relations of production and power neither is it an autonomous force. In making certain actions easier, technical affordances may alter the balance of social power, but only through their application within social networks of action. Such action occurs at various levels (in conversation and interpersonal interaction, within organizations, and across larger networks of production, trade, regulation and communication) and across a range of fields (law, research and development, production, trade and the mass and new media). To grasp such complexity requires research at the discursive, ethnographic and 'structural' levels of data-collection and analysis, even when such diverse research approaches challenge each other. We are compelled to accept the value of 'reflexive epistemological diversity' (David 2005) rather than retreating into singular theoretical and methodological camps. File-sharing is 'perestroika' and 'glasnost' from below: an economic restructuring and an informational opening up that challenge capitalist relations of intellectual property rather than merely updating productive forces to boost existing social relations, as was the initial application. Post-scarcity, afforded by new technology and its challenge to hierarchical and bureaucratic systems of control and allocation, has not been undone for all the legal, technical and cultural efforts to contain it. The future is not what it used to be. The future remains to be made, and made better. What has been happening in the musical field over the last decade is paradigmatic for the network society more generally. Currently, conflicts in the fields of computing, film, television, pharmaceuticals and agribusiness hinge upon disputes over intellectual property and the increased vulnerability of such property rights that are both virtual in nature and easily replicated across virtual networks. As virtual property becomes central to the profitability of global capitalism so its scope for global sharing becomes increasingly dangerous to a system based on scarcity. The intensified criminalization of sharing can be understood only in the context of this contradiction between profitability and the potential suspension of scarcity.

2

The Global Network Society: Territorialization and Deterritorialization

Introduction

File-sharing operates across the Internet. This chapter explores the character of this global network, in particular the structuring and enabling character of global computer networks. The chapter also examines Manuel Castells' work, that of his critics and that of others who have developed distinct and often divergent accounts of 'network society'. At issue is the question of how technical networks impact upon the social networks from which they emerge. Castells claims powerful effects, while critics dispute this. Castells does not claim that technology compels social change, rather that new technologies change the scope for action of individuals, organizations and groups. It is possible to accept insights from his work without rejecting those of his critics. Digital compression, peer-to-peer file-sharing software and the Internet itself emerged out of particular sets of social relationships, were reapplied and modified by different parties to such relationships, rendering certain courses of action more or less effective and affordable, and enabled various cultural, economic, legal and technical strategies and alliances. This chapter is organized around three key claims made by Castells regarding the character of the network society: that the informational mode of development is relatively autonomous from the capitalist mode of production; that the informational mode of development is driving the development of 'capitalist perestroika' in the form of globalization and the 'networked enterprise'; and that computer networks constitute a 'morphogenetic structure' conditioning the actions of individuals within it. All three suggestions require significant questioning and qualification, yet all three remain productive provocations in the exploration of the present. Each claim is discussed in relation to the counterclaims made by Castells' critics. The concept of 'affordances' is offered as a way to overcome unhelpful binary reductionisms, two examples of 'post-structuralist' approaches are discussed as illustrative of problems already identified in Castells' approach, while the chapter concludes with a discussion of the work of Gilles Deleuze and Felix Guattari as well as Michael Hardt and Antonio Negri, whose writing continues to draw attention to the possibility of radical social change within network societies, something that Castells and his critics are united in placing at the margins of their accounts of social reproduction in one form or another.

The relative autonomy of the informational mode of development?

Manuel Castells combines structural Marxist categories with elements drawn from Max Weber. His 'critical realism' focuses upon relations between the mode of production (otherwise called the social relations of production) and the forces of production (what he calls the 'mode of development'). In distinguishing between ongoing capitalist relations of production and what he calls the 'informational mode of development' he gives technological development a relative autonomy and causal efficacy that can appear 'technologically deterministic'.

Castells seeks to avoid the accusation of technological determinism or sociological determinism of technology, yet his account suggests developments in networked computing had significant implications for social development, even while the opposite is also true. He makes the analytical distinction between mode of production and mode of development (1996: 14). This parallels Marx's distinction between the relations of production (ownership and control over productive resources) and the forces of production (that which is available to be owned and controlled). Castells thus distinguishes capitalism and industrialism. While capitalist development promoted industrial production, industrialization was also achieved within statist modes of production. As industrial society can have different modes of production, so capitalism can have different modes of development. The move from industrialism to informationalism is such a shift. If the dominant logic of industrialism was the increase in physical production enabled by increased availability of cheap raw materials, in particular energy, the dominant logic of informationalism is the increase in informational production through the increased availability and integration of cheap information capacities. Castells suggests a five-dimensional account of the shift from industrialism to informationalism (1996: 61–2). First, there is the growth of technologies that act on information (computers); second, the increased pervasiveness of such technologies in every aspect of life; third, the increased capacity to integrate such technologies within networks; fourth, the increased capacity to foster flexibility within integrated production systems through coordinating information transfer and machine reprogramming. Finally, there is the increasing convergence of different technologies to generate integrated systems. For Castells these forces of production (i.e. the mode of development) are generating new conditions of possibility within the capitalist mode of production.

Castells recognizes role of the capitalist profit motive in developing information technologies and in applying them in particular ways. However, he is resistant to the view that capitalism determines the logic of technological development or its use. While the Internet may have been developed by the United States military, themselves driven by the desire of US capitalism to fend off the perceived threat of communism, the Internet is now used by radicals the world over to coordinate political protest (1996: 6–7). The combination of military and economic investment in developing information storage, processing and transmission capabilities is certainly central to the rise of the information age, yet neither determines development. Castells suggests that vast amounts of investment fuelled 'the autonomous dynamics of technological discovery and diffusion, including synergistic effects between various key technologies' (1996: 51).

> In other words, the first Informational Technology Revolution clustered in America, and to some extent in California, in the 1970s, building on developments of the two preceding decades, and under the influence of various institutional, economic and cultural factors. But it did not come out of any pre-established necessity: it was technologically induced rather than socially determined. However, once it came into existence as a system, on the basis of the clustering I have described, its development and applications, and ultimately its content, were decisively shaped by the historical context where it expanded. (Castells 1996: 52)

While the myth that Silicon Valley was the product of geeks in garages, rather than the massive investment of states and corporations in a period of military and economic globalization, is dismissed (1996: 60), Castells' account seeks to retain a relationship between technology and capitalism that is semi-autonomous. This 'critical realist' stance is questioned by critical theorists, who highlight the structuring of technology within 'hegemonic' relations of hierarchy, ideology and control.

Critical theoretical challenges

Early critical theory combined Marx with German interpretivism and its suspicion of modern techno-science (Kirkpatrick 2004, 2008). While defending the Enlightenment, Theodor Adorno and Max Horkheimer (1979[1944]) suggest: 'the deductive form of science reflects hierarchy and coercion' (cited in Kirkpatrick 2008: 51). Despite Adorno's (2002) critique of Heidegger's 'jargon of authenticity', the world revealing consciousness that precedes the 'enframing' of modern thought by instrumentalism, Adorno and Horkheimer (1979[1944]) and Marcuse (1986, 2002[1964]) retain a suspicion of instrumental reason. The 'original violence' by which nature is appropriated for purposes other than its own, a violence that – if unrestrained – forms the basis for instrumentalized relations between people, remains a concern for early critical theory.

Jurgen Habermas' reformulated critical theory abandons anxiety over instrumentalized nature. Instrumental/objective knowledge interests (1972) over nature are seen as unproblematic. Only misapplication of objectifying instrumentalism to purposive human actors violates Kant's categorical imperative. Where such instrumentalism is applied as social engineering and in the name of efficiency, Habermas calls this the 'scientization of politics' (1971[1970]), the post-ideological ideology of 'practical management' and 'modernization' typical of late capitalism. Habermas distinguishes instrumental system logic oriented towards control from communicative action oriented towards understanding. Political and economic systems seek to colonize the communicative realm, ordering people by rules of efficiency and control, but such systems remain parasitically dependent upon lifeworld communication, oriented towards understanding, as social rules require inter-subjectively achieved interpretations in practice (1984, 1987). Habermas shows the limits of technocratic governance and the foundations of resistance to it.

However, Graeme Kirkpatrick (2008: 56) suggests:

Habermas' concern is not with technology as a mode of human action per se, which he understands as quasi-natural, but with the inappropriate use of instrumental reasoning to solve problems that involve meaning and value. However, the system/lifeworld distinction abstracts technology from society … he acknowledges that in practice the two spheres interpenetrate. However, the separation of system and lifeworld conjoins technology, in its pragmatic function, so to speak, to a permanent association with coercive authority and makes it inherently opposed to reason and communication.

Elsewhere, Kirkpatrick suggests Habermas sees 'technology as innocent, perhaps even benign when seen in social evolutionary perspective' (2008: 74). Essentially Habermas equates particular technologies with neutral and efficient technology as such (rather as Castells does). Habermas neglects the politics embodied in tools, focusing only on misapplication. Following Andrew Feenberg (1991, 1999, 2002), Kirkpatrick suggests such 'process critique', addressing how technology is applied, misses 'product critique' of tools built for unethical purposes and 'design critique', attention to the social interests built into tools and passed off as simply efficient. In Feenberg's 'dual aspect theory' tools straddle the interface between physical and social functionality. They must 'work' on nature but must also 'work' in social contexts. Equating technical reason and 'hegemonic technological rationality' is to accept partial constructions of efficiency as natural and to limit technology to truncated ends.

Kirkpatrick's work focuses on 'design critique'. To bolster this shift he rather exaggerates Habermas' limits. Suggesting that with increased telecommunications Habermas' separation of instrumental and communicative action is outmoded (2008: 35) rather misses the point of Habermas' distinction between action oriented towards control and action orientated towards understanding, and overlooks the fact that Habermas' definitive study of the rise and fall of the Enlightenment public sphere was itself a study of mediated communication (1989[1962]). Contemporary conflicts over commercial and communicative action through new-media highlight the continuing relevance of Habermas' theorization of early European print media, though highlighting significant differences in the structure of new-media architecture, i.e. the absence of an editorial centre. In this way the architecture of the medium's design is significant, as Kirkpatrick's 'design critique' focus suggests, even if it is not the whole story. It is premature to dismiss Habermas' focus and insights just to make space for Kirkpatrick's, valuable as they are.

Kirkpatrick's 'design critique' applies Feenberg's dual aspect theory to search engines, PC interfaces, and computer games. '[C]reeping standardization' of Internet search engine algorithms, converging around Google's 'spider bot' method of locating and ranking websites according to the number of web-links to them (2008: 140–52) may at first appear merely the most efficient means of finding a site. However, this standardization reinforces what is already most visible and marginalizes non-corporate and alternative sites further. Standardization also enables those with the means to pay consultants to 'position' sites, constructing them in such a way as to move up search engines' ranking systems. Standardization increases the consequences of 'position', jumping all the generically structured queues. Challenging the suggestion that 'this works' equals 'neutrality' disrupts technocratic claims that one version of efficiency equals progress as such. Kirkpatrick highlights a range of alternative search engine designs.

The rise of the 'user friendly' interface appears to help the non-expert user, but inhibits their understanding and so keeps them under control (Kirkpatrick 2004: 22 and 26–68, and 2008: 73 and 122–5). Sherry Turkle's (1995) suggestion that the Windows interface seduces the user into a 'life on the screen', a postmodern freedom to explore multiple identities and positions, is rejected by Kirkpatrick as a manipulated illusion. He proposes a Brechtian modernist aesthetic critique of false and misleading interface designs, in favour of direct engagement with the machine through writing syntax commands. Learning and writing commands would give users greater control and freedom to configure the machine. 'User friendly' interfaces are said to configure the user to limited menu/icon options.

'The mechanical, austere and challenging interfaces on older operating systems were in a sense, consistent with a more realist aesthetic of technology design' (Kirkpatrick 2004: 23). At times Kirkpatrick's 'design critique' is realist, challenging designs which obscure real world power relations and domination – such as in the case of search engine algorithm standardization or where covert surveillance and adware are used to manipulate users. More often Kirkpatrick's critique is strictly modernist, rejecting artifice and metaphor in form in favour of explicit presentation of the medium's own workings. Modernist attention to the medium's truth in relation to the mechanics of its functionality gives less significance to true representation of the world beyond the medium. The primacy of 'design critique' in Kirkpatrick's critical theory lends itself to such attendance to the character of the medium over the practices of users as such. The primary agents are designers. Users are seen in large part as passive, having been configured by the designs said to contain them.

The power of 'hegemonic technological rationality', despite Kirkpatrick's questioning of it (2008: 152), is most definitely assumed in his account of potential resistance. Critical theory's account of technocracy's pacification of class struggle itself struggles with questions of change and/or resistance. Critical theory came to substitute itself for 'imminent critique', the self-contradiction and self-confrontation claimed in classical Marxist accounts of class-based societies. This can be seen in Kirkpatrick's 'design critique', itself seeking to effect 'progressive rationalization' in the face of dominant constructions of efficiency. But who would adopt such alternative and more challenging designs? Kirkpatrick finds some hope in computer gamers, who he sees poised on the knife-edge of seduction by the interface/screen and a desire to explore the algorithms that structure the game/system. Drawing on Sloterdijk (1984), Kirkpatrick (2004: 69–88) identifies a tension between the cynicism of suspended disbelief in the virtual game on the screen, and the cynical questioner who wants to probe beneath and perhaps question 'the rules'. Instilling knowledge of computers (to some extent), the dialectic of gaming is offered as a proto public sphere for a new modernity.

Kirkpatrick suggests computer simulated war games fostered a realization that the cold war was irrational, thereby encouraging its end. This is hard to verify and designers/gamers offer only modest hope for redeeming technology. However, when Kirkpatrick's focus on design is allied with product and process critiques imminent in the development and conduct of file-sharing, technologies of sharing may offer a greater hope for democratic and progressive rationalization. Having distanced his critical theory from earlier suspicions of technical reason per se and from accounts that render technology as neutral tools (2004 and 2008), as well as in his distancing from constructivist and positivist accounts of technology (2008), Kirkpatrick's 'minimal technical attitude' of critical engagement with technology and technical reason as a progressive force 'meshes better with a realist stance on the technical object' (2004: 7). This does not mean critical theory can be simply fused with Castells' critical realism, as Christopher May's empirical objections outlined in the next section attest. Nevertheless, the scope to draw insights from both traditions is increased, even while enabling a more subtle engagement over their still significant differences.

Feminist critiques

Feminist Internet research tends to parallel critical theory. While Sadie Plant (1998) suggests the Internet's network character has a particular elective affinity with feminine weaving over masculine hierarchy, this is more ironic subversion of masculine assumptions and designed to highlight the non-reducibility of social life and/or technology to existing relations of power. Alternatives exist, and can be fostered. Dale Spender (2003) similarly highlights the potential for network communication to disembody and eliminate gender distinctions online, even while she goes on to show how, in practice, men use sexist language and images to colonize cyberspace. Sherry Turkle (1995, 2005) suggests the disembodied character of computer 'geek' culture excludes women. Flis Henwood (1994) shows how the gendered assumptions of teachers and boys reproduce female exclusion and self-deselection from computing. Nevertheless, the rise of the computer and the revaluation of 'typing' over more 'physical' forms of engagement with 'technology' have shifted gendered relations. Masculine forms of dominance in framing skill and power remain (Wajcman 1991), but women's paid employment has been entrenched not weakened with the shift from manual to non-manual engagement with machines (Webster, J. 1996). Donna Haraway (1991, 1997), through her work on cyborgs, hybrids and the post-nature fusions of humans, machines and other organisms, touches on the Internet only tangentially. Technology is bound to patriarchy and capitalism, but for her there is no recourse to a natural order. It is technology itself that both undermines older repressive ideologies and fosters new ones. Like Habermas, Haraway suggests instrumental rationalizations in the interests of control can foster critical challenges.

Informationalism and 'capitalist perestroika'?

The central argument of Castells' *The Information Age* (1996, 1997 and 1998) is that we are becoming a global network capitalist society. In line with Marx, Castells argues that social development is driven by economic conflict. Capitalism has become global, over-running both pre-capitalist and statist alternatives. Network capitalism is characterized by increasingly distributed enterprises, trade systems and financial markets. Traditional forms of geographical and class-based community are fragmenting. The network society is, therefore, characterized by increasing individualization and increasingly global connectivity. The tension between self and net – in economic, political and cultural terms – is coming to form the dominant site of identity crisis and reformation (1996: 3) in economic production, political power and personal experience (1996: 14–15).

The context out of which the informational technology revolution emerged and into which it developed was that of the United States' rise to global dominance, economically and militarily. Castells' critical realism holds that technology develops by producing increasingly powerful objective tools for the control of nature; and such an objective yardstick, for all the potential for social manipulation and direction, gives technology a level of autonomy from simple social determinism, and technical artefacts impact upon social relations as though from outside. Increasingly powerful tools enable increased economic productivity. Increased productivity is one of the key drivers of social change, but it is not the only one. The other three, Castells suggests (1996: 103–5), are: gaining access to larger, more integrated and affluent markets; increasing the gap between cost and price (which may be achieved by a number of means other than efficiency); and effecting macroeconomic management at national and international levels. The network society emerges as technical shifts in the mode of development (the shift from industrialism to informationalism) enable shifts in the other three dimensions. These other shifts are within the mode of production (capitalism) and can be summarized as the shift towards global network capitalism, what Castells (1996: 18–22) calls 'capitalist perestroika'.

The rise of global corporations requires greater information storage, processing and communication capacity, and their provision has enabled the combination of greater centralization of ownership, more rapid flows of capital through stock markets, and the development of integrated and lean forms of production and distribution (flexible production and global trade). Network capitalism is founded upon what Castells (1996: 172) calls the network enterprise: 'the network enterprise makes material the culture of the informational/global economy: it transforms signals into commodities by processing knowledge.' The 'culture of the informational/global economy' is what Castells calls 'the spirit of informationalism'. '[t]he "spirit of informationalism" is the culture of "creative destruction" accelerated to the speed of the optoelectronic circuits that process its signals. Schumpeter meets Weber in the cyberspace of the network enterprise' (Castells 1996: 199).

The consequences of this creative destruction are multidimensional. In the realm of work the new network enterprise in the global market promotes flexibility, leading to new forms of economic insecurity for many and greater wealth for elites. According to Castells, we are now experiencing 'the individualization of work and the fragmentation of societies' (1996: 201). Established collective identities of class and nation are being undermined by the new global informational capitalism, a new world of experience characterized by what Castells (2000) calls 'real virtuality' (the increasingly significant amount of dis-embedded/mediated experience), 'the space of flows' (the increasing mediation of place by mobility – whether of things, people or information) and 'timeless time' (the abolition of distance and the increased scope for coordinated action at a distance). For Castells, the gap between haves and have nots lies in relative access to informational resources and can be mapped in terms of virtual, spatial and temporal integration within the net.

Volume II of *The Information Age* (1997) describes the fragmentation of national and class identities and the rise of new social movements (regionalism, environmentalism and feminism in particular), and the transformation of the state from nation state to network state (with its consequent dislocation between government and democratic accountability).

Critical theoretical challenges

From within the Marxist tradition Christopher May (2002) questions the radical nature of change in Castells' 'network society'. Identifying four dimensions of supposed radical change in Castells' work, May concludes that continuity in each is far greater than change. First, the idea that society has been fundamentally changed by information technology is questioned. For May, relations between owners of the means of production and waged workers is not fundamentally changed. Second, May suggests Castells' separation of the mode of production from the mode of development is unjustified. The nature of work and class relations is not radically altered and talk of individualization of work is much exaggerated. Trade unionism and workplace politics is certainly fluid, but the rise of flexible production – with core and periphery employment, increasing part-time/ temporary contracts – cannot be explained by a shift in technology. Additionally, it is still the case that the majority of employees in advanced economies work full-time. The rise of industrial production in developing countries and the increased paid employment of women across the world suggest the rise of industrialism, not its demise. The very separation of industrialism and informationalism is hard to justify. May suggests the same logic of increasing productivity and profitability underpins capitalism in physical and informational production. Third, May (2002: 81–113) questions whether new social movements are either the result of the network society or a sign of the death of class politics. Old and new movements use new technologies to achieve action and communication. Finally, the belief that the state is fundamentally transformed is questionable, both in terms of its demise in the face of global markets and in terms of its centrality in democratic political conflict. May is concerned by Castells' structuralist language, and his claims for the semi-autonomous and radical effects of new technologies.

> There is nothing natural, nothing inevitable about the information society: while we can only make our own history in the circumstances we find ourselves in, we should recognise that these circumstances are not as fixed or narrow as many commentators on the information society tell us. (May 2002: 161)

This view is not fundamentally at odds with Castells' own view, but May offers a valuable corrective to technological determinist readings of Castells.

The network as morphogenetic structure?

Volume III of *The Information Age* (1998) charts the relative position of different regions in the information age (the former Soviet Union, Africa and Latin America, Asia/Pacific and Europe). The United States is very much the epicentre of the new global transformation and the focus of attention in Volume I. Such a grand accounting exercise tends to present a process far above the heads of all those living through such changes. While networks are commonly used in sociology to emphasize human agency, this is not Castells' intention.

> Presence or absence in the network and the dynamics of each network vis-à-vis others are critical sources of domination and change in our society: a society that, therefore, we may properly call the network society, characterized by the predominance of social morphology over social action. (Castells 1996: 469)

Social morphology refers to structural characteristics in social systems (see Archer, 1995). Castells asserts that the network society is a social structure, something that is not reducible to or controlled by conscious actors. It is an environment in which humans act, and which constrains and enables such action. In this sense Castells is an anti-reductionist. Society cannot be reduced to the actions of individuals. Castells' structuralism is in diametric opposition to ethnographic research.

Ethnographic, ethnomethodological, conversation analytical and discourse analytical studies have addressed the design process, the interaction between design and use by 'non-experts', the discourses that surround computer surveillance and simulation models, as well as the relationships between networks in the formation of communities and technologies. Particular attention has been paid to the question of whether technology has effects. In addition, the question of how to conceptualize the social in relation to the computer will also be examined. This theme flows from the ethnographic and discursive focus upon action and language, largely in opposition to attention and belief in social 'structures'. If technology is not independent of the social and social structure does not mould technology, what is going on? Ethnographic and discursive researchers highlight the ways computers are imagined and used, challenging both technological and sociological reductionism.

Ethnographic alternatives

Christine Hine's (2000) ethnographic study of Internet use involved observation of, interaction with and interviewing users of both the World Wide Web and a range of Internet newsgroups. The focus of the research was Internet coverage and discussion of the English nanny Louise Woodward's court battle against charges of murdering the child she was looking after in the USA. Hine's interest lay in the anthropological themes of community and identity formation. Would interaction in non-physical and often non-temporal proximity lead to weaker normative expectations and regulations? Would the characteristics of the medium affect the way people interacted? Hine suggests the space created for interaction on the Internet is both performative and a performance (2000: 116). In one sense the Internet creates a new environment where people can interact without being co-present. In this sense the Internet has effects. Interactions that would not otherwise occur, do occur. Yet the medium itself does not determine how people will interact. The way that the Internet is used is itself a performance, the medium is interpreted and applied in ways determined by social negotiation between the parties to the interaction. This process of performance has two dimensions for Hine. The first sense of performance lies in creating contexts and rules of behaviour. Groups create routines and places on the net where they meet. Groups also establish patterns of expectation, inclusion and exclusion. These regulate anti-social behaviour (2000: 115). Hine rejects the idea that loss of face-to-face proximity will have necessary consequences. People using the Internet are not denuded of normative context. While the medium does not provide normative context, participants do. In the second sense of performance Hine (2000: 144) highlights that participants in online interactions often continue interactions from non-Internet life and interactions online always play upon materials drawn from outside the Internet to create cultural context. Of particular interest in the case of Louise Woodward were national identity and television coverage, two sets of cultural resources that enabled online participants to identify themselves as a 'community' – one that the Internet encouraged but did not create.

Daniel Miller and Don Slater researched Internet use in Trinidad and found: 'Trinidadians have a natural affinity for the Internet' (2000: 2). The expectation that the poor have less access and interest in information technology (hereafter IT) was confounded in this study. In what is by most indicators an economically poor island, the researchers found that one in three households had direct access to the Internet, and there was little negativity and technophobia even among those without. Miller and Slater conclude that far from being a detached and dis-embedding technology, the Internet is deeply embedded in Trinidadian life. As a mobile population, with high levels of migration across the world, the Internet fits. A libertarian ideal of free movement also resonates with a cultural emphasis upon freedom, born of a history of slavery and resistance. Structural accounts fail to capture the creativity by which communities engage and remake technologies. For Miller and Slater, the ethnographic approach avoids both the sociological determinism of Castells' 'network society' and its technological determinism.

David Mason et al. (2001, 2002a and 2002b) use ethnography to examine workplace surveillance. Fieldwork in diverse workplace situations examined use of 'surveillance-capable' (2002b: 558) technologies, technologies that collect data on the activities of employees, whether or not this is either intentional or applied. Use was studied in detail. Rather than assuming how or by whom capabilities would be used the research team observed what happened. It was not simply the case that capabilities were used by management to spy on staff, to increase work pressure, or to individualize work evaluation. This presumption is referred to as 'apriorism'. Mason et al. suggest the value of ethnography lies in its more inductive approach to finding out what is really going on. Capabilities were negotiated to a variety of ends and in a variety of ways. Technology requires active involvement of staff in its use and the data such systems generate is the result of negotiation, interaction and interpretation. Use that does not increase management control cannot automatically be assumed to be resistance. Using systems to monitor work in order to keep a record of your actions could be resistance against management pressure, or conformity. Sometimes staff felt monitoring impinged privacy; sometimes they did not. The meaning of the technology and what it meant for the technology to be working properly was negotiated in context rather than being a top-down imposition. Technologies afford possibilities, as do workplace situations, but neither determines outcomes.

From ethnography to discourse

Steve Woolgar (2002: 14–21) summarizes a range of 'virtual society' ethnographic and discursive research projects. He proposes 'five rules of virtuality'. First: 'The uptake and use of the new technologies depend crucially on local social context'. Information and communication technologies (ICTs) are embedded in social life, not vice versa, and they certainly do not abolish social context. Second: 'The fears and risks associated with new technologies are unevenly socially distributed', again reflecting local contexts. Third: 'Virtual technologies supplement rather than substitute for real activities'. Fourth, it is suggested: 'The more virtual, the more real'. New ICTs drive and extend existing mobility, communication and interaction. Finally: 'The more global, the more local'. ICTs do not abolish locality.

'To talk of the impact of technology, then, seems to require us artificially to separate the technology from some "social group" in the service of assessing "the effects" of one upon the other' (Grint and Woolgar, 1997: 93). Better to say: 'The "technology" is the machine's relations with its users', rather than to imagine the machine as something outside society. This seems strange. The machine still sits there when we leave. Grint and Woolgar (1997: 80–2) cleverly highlight the discursive construction of the computer as a freestanding thing in their account of the labelling placed on computer casings to discourage the user from lifting the lid and transgressing the boundary between thing and user. However, while the boundary is enforced by rhetoric the machine still has a physical reality, with limits and possibilities. Grint and Woolgar critique the view that information technology has its properties and capacities 'hard-wired' into it by its designers. They point out that in reaction to technological determinists, a generation of social researchers emphasized the social shaping of technology. This social shaping approach implied that technology was driven by macro social structures, with no intrinsic consequences of its own (MacKenzie and Wajcman 1985,1999). A reaction to this tradition was to emphasize the way that technological design built in certain features that had political consequences (see Winner 1985). Grint and Woolgar reject technological determinism, social determinism and technological neutrality, the latter because it seems to imply that the technology exists independently of its uses, waiting to be used one way or another. In abolishing the distinction between technology and its uses, they suggest that any artefact in use is a unique configuration. From their ethnomethodological perspective, using technology differently remakes the technology. Such rhetorical hair splitting makes a particular point and does not dispute the existence of physical objects with particular properties.

> We have no wish to insist that machines actually are texts. Rather the point is to play against this metaphor, to see how far we can go with it. What happens to the structure of our discourse when we introduce the notion of machine as text? What, if anything, is special about machines by comparison with other texts? What are the limits of talking in this bizarre way? (1997: 70)

Challenging discourse analysis from within

Ian Hutchby (2001) responds to the apparent abolition of artefacts in the language, if not the intention, of Grint and Woolgar, using conversation analysis of the way humans interact with and through computers, and the expectations displayed in interactions with computers – expectations drawn from human conversation. Conversation analytical attention to the orderly yet spontaneous character of human talk highlights difference between humans and machines. Computers are not oriented towards understanding, performing programmed responses not human 'conversation'. Humans interacting through the Internet generate their own normative contexts to regulate performance (Hine 2000). However, the videophone did not 'take off' because it fails to provide the kinds of 'taken for granted cues' available in face-to-face communication (Heath and Luff 1993). The conventional telephone does not afford such 'cues' either but, as the videophone was promoted precisely in order do so, its failure reduced its appeal. In reviewing Lucy Suchman's (1987) ethnography of work within a hi-tech company, Hutchby notes the way designers imported a range of metaphors and assumptions from the field of computing into their designs for human–computer interfaces. Assuming human thinking mirrors the computational character of a machine encouraged designers to provide interfaces based on incorrect assumptions. Human conversation displays intentionality and an orientation to understanding not present in machines. Hutchby concludes by saying (2001: 140): 'The difficulties experienced by users in both cases emerge from a lack of fit between the expectations associated with the normative structures of ordinary interaction and the artefacts practical communicative affordances.' Hutchby outlines a range of such affordances as well as the interactional work and communication breakdowns that ensue when humans interact with and through machines. Similar research explores libraries (Zeitlyn et al. 1999), medical expert systems (Collins 1990) and McDonald's (Kusch and Collins 1998).

Hutchby's 'affordances' avoid seeing computers as carrying in built logics of use, programmed either by technicians or society, or seeing machine as texts only meaningful in the way they are read by users. Affordances are the limits and possibilities of physical artefacts. While limits do not determine uses, to ignore limits is to ignore a fundamentally important difference between humans and machines. Recognition of this difference underpins ethnography, ethnomethodology, conversation analysis (CA), social interest theory, Marxism and most feminist scholarship (David 2005), even if each needs reminding for different reasons.

Affordances bridge Castells' suggestion of technological 'impact' and his critics' attention to the social shaping of technology at different levels. Affordances highlight that without use there is no technology, but also that usage has limits. Different objects offer different possibilities. Critical realists' and critical theorists' attention has been on the cutting edge organizations and designs within the network society, neglecting hidden users who clarify and illuminate their insights. Where May is correct to suggest that corporations remain corporate and in that sense hierarchical for all their distributed infrastructure, that networks now enable every computer to offer new affordances which challenge corporations does present scope for radical change. Where Hine, Miller and Slater show that technologies can only be understood in relation to the communities that use them, it is also true that the performative scope to act is changed (as is Castells' suggestion also). Hostilities towards the music industry for its pricing of recordings existed long before network technologies enabled relatively easy circumvention of payment. Piracy and home taping suggest that file-sharing is not just a technical possibility that created a cultural desire.

The 'post-structuralists' Alexander Galloway and Frederick Kittler – in radically different ways – highlight the value and limitations of attempts to study technical networks as relatively autonomous, socially determining, morphogenetic systems rather than as social practices.

Post-structuralist approaches

Alexander Galloway (2004) suggests early study of the 'information society' neglected the material reality of information technology, while later discussions of the 'network society' tend to treat the term 'network' as a metaphor for new forms of social interaction rather than as a physical infrastructure and a command language built to distribute (regulate the flow of) data across an electronic grid. Galloway suggests such 'vapour theory' of networks allows projection of polarized visions of social change onto technical systems, first wave liberation technologists (Zuboff 1988, Gates 1995, 1999 and Reingold 2000) and second wave dystopian theorists (Bogard 1996 and Lyon 2001) fail to understand the technical contradiction at the heart of the machines themselves. While Galloway overstates technical contradictions within the Internet, his detailed discussion of software and infrastructure are useful both in qualifying the theoretical projections he seeks to make and in challenging either/or constructions of network potential.

Though critical of Castells, Galloway replicates his focus upon the technical realities of networks even while coming to different conclusions. Critical theorists, such as May (2002), observe in Castells a reified technical infrastructure too close to a 'historical materialist' form of Marxism, where technical forces of production drive out 'dated' social relations of production and ferment social transformation. Critical theorists suggest technology is not an autonomous force for social change.

Like May, Galloway's 'political economy' sets itself against Castells' account of the Internet as a transformative social force, framing his discussion of Internet protocol within Deleuze's (1992) account of the 'control society' (discussed below). For Galloway, the architecture of the Internet, the management style embodied in its protocols, along with the concealment operating at every level of its interfacing, reproduce the society of which it is a part. However, unlike May, who sees the continuities within 'capitalist society' manifested online, Galloway suggests Internet protocol materially mirrors the reordering of the mode of regulation from a 'disciplinary' society (based on a Foucauldian decentralized power) to a 'control' society (based on Deleuze's conception of distributed power). Domain names are allocated by a hierarchical set of designated agents (once totally centralized but now partially decentralized), while distributed interaction requires a set of universal standards (protocols). The fact that peer-to-peer interaction via distributed networks requires such a universal set of agreed programming standards leads to what Galloway calls the 'protocological society'.

Increasingly individualized communication requires increasingly standardized media. Galloway exaggerates the difference between the centralised (thought increasingly de-centralised) power over domain name allocation and the distributed nature of data-transfer within the Internet. Removing China's domain name from the domain name system (DNS) would be more akin to removing the word China from the English dictionary than removing it from the English language. Galloway's observation that China's '.ch' domain name could be removed within 24 hours is correct at one level, but the actual numerical Internet address would remain. What would disappear would be the ability of search engines using the most updated versions of the protocols to locate Chinese Internet sites. As such, the relationship between the dictionary and the language has changed. We are more reliant on looking things up (through search engines) when using the Internet than we are in our everyday language. Internet users rely on the centralized 'adhocracy' of the Internet Engineering Task Force (IETF) to give them a system that links up. The extent to which such reliance has consequences needs to be investigated at the level of actual usage. Galloway seeks such power relations in the very material character of the Internet's language, its semantic naming system and its syntactic protocols. Galloway locates contradictory but substantial power relations within the material realm of the machine and the functional constraints and constitutions said to emerge from its command language. Attention to the protocols is largely separate from the discussion of his case studies of power and resistance, viruses, cyberfeminism and tactical media (2004) as well as of terrorist networks (2004, 2005).

These cases are only tenuously linked to his overarching 'protocological society' theory, and relatively marginal to his attempt to theorize the Internet as a language indifferent to the meaning communicated through it. Such a structuralist/post-structuralist attention to the semantics and syntax of the Internet as a material language discourages any serious attempt to theorize the substantive content – and thereby actual use of the Internet – because syntax is said to condition the parameters of semantic content in advance, rather than semantic content driving divergent uses of syntactic systems. This explains Galloway's strenuous, and at times contorted, attempts to explain protocol in its own terms (as a system, even if a self-contradictory – post-structuralism compliant – system). It also leaves his work open to the accusation of reification, despite his otherwise interesting observations about reification through concealment. While interesting, Galloway's theoretical framework inhibits research into much that is of interest about the Internet and its use. While 'vapour theory' allows for the projections of cyber-optimists and cyber-pessimists, this is no less true of the structuralist/post-structuralist 'materialist theories' of Castells and Galloway.

If much is gained from engagement with Galloway's work, perhaps as much can be gained through a critical distancing from the work of Friedrich Kittler. Kittler's account of three stages in the development of media – 1800 reformulation of storage media, 1900 developments in transmission, and more recently the development of computational media – correspond, as Kittler rightly shows, to popular and intellectual representations of the human subject. Influential constructions of the mind draw still upon the latest media technology. Romanticism, psychoanalysis and structuralism/ post-structuralism/systems theory pass off metaphors drawn from the machines of their day as analytical categories. Kittler suggests today's network fusion of 'partially integrated media systems', of storage, transmission and computation, will create (or has created) a fully integrated 'system' – a self-contained information loop, no longer 'media' as it would not need external points of reference to mediate between. This play on Foucault's (1974[1966]) 'Death of Man' through an inversion of McLuhan's (1964) 'Extensions of Man' portrays a symmetrical system as unsustainable, in reality, as the systems theoretical framework that seeks to conceptualize it. Systems theory is a 'performative contradiction' (David 2006a: 81–2). Paul Virilio's claim that 'the message is the velocity of the medium' (2000: 141), making human intelligence the extension of artificial intelligence, fails to explain the systematic failure of such high speed info-war to convince. Similarly (contra Kittler 1997), the German military's definition of radio *broad*casting as a technical weakness didn't stop it catching on, and Intel's imprinting of the PC's basic operating system onto the chip's silicon circuits does not programme the PC user as a 'subject or underling' of corporations. Kittler's fascinating histories and counterintuitive accounts of media technology's relationship with war, literature and the human sciences (1990, 1997, 1999) offer myriad insights and intellectual provocations. Nevertheless, his 'attempt to construct sociology from the chip's architecture' (1997: 162) reduces social relations of technology to the codes of media machines and metaphors for the human subject drawn from them. The failure to distinguish the command language of computer syntax and the inter-subjective characteristics of human language, interaction and meaning formation, continues to encourage misrepresentations of humans as computers (David 2002), and continues to ensure their inability to examine human–computer interactions without reifying the former in the mirror of the latter.

Contingency, contradiction and contestation

> Marx termed the twofold movement of the tendency to a falling rate of profit, and an increase in the absolute quantity of surplus value, the law of the counteracted tendency. As a corollary of this law, there is the twofold movement of decoding or deterritorializing flows on the one hand, and their violent and artificial reterritorialization on the other. The more the capitalist machine deterritorializes, decoding and axiomatizing flows in order to extract surplus value from them, the more its ancillary apparatuses, such as government bureaucracies and the forces of law and order, do their utmost to reterritorialize, absorbing in the process a larger and larger share of surplus value. (Deleuze and Guattari 1984: 34–5)

The above quotation captures both contradiction and contingency. Two contradictory processes are paralleled and the contingent nature of both is highlighted. What Marx (1995) refers to as the law of the counteracted tendency is the tendency for the rate of profit to fall within competitive market conditions. Goods being sold above their cost attract increased supply. When this exceeds demand prices will be depressed, as is the rate of profit. Various countermeasures can be enacted to reduce cost, expand markets, and integrate horizontally or vertically to reduce competition or to reduce price elasticity (by customer loyalty). One such countermeasure is to prohibit entry with trade barriers, charters, professional or commercial licences and other mechanisms that criminalize market entry by others. Capitalism increases productivity to reduce cost. Rising output raises the prospect of reducing scarcity to the point where supply exceeds demand, thus threatening prices and profitability. As such, market inhibiting mechanisms are as much favoured in restricting competition as are technical and productive innovations designed to reduce cost. The rise of intellectual property monopolies designed to protect profitability are only contemporary manifestations of longstanding counteractions to the tendency for the rate of profit to fall.

As such, for Marx, while crisis tendencies afflict capitalism by its very competitive and profit-oriented nature, such tendencies must be set against equally significant counter-tendencies towards the protection of existing dominant positions by anti-competitive regulations. There are no necessary outcomes in such dynamics and the way groups and individuals seek strategically to ally and compete cannot be predicted fully in advance. Actors must make choices as to how their best interests might be served, even as their interpretations of what such interests might be are also subject to competing claims and demands.

For Deleuze and Guattari a similar contradiction lies in the pressure within capitalism both to exceed state and regulatory boundaries (to evade restrictions), and yet to seek regulation and protection from attempts to challenge regulations that protect them (to re-restrict at a higher level). While information technologies for storage, processing and transmitting data have emerged as part of existing economic, political and military strategies, these strategies are themselves open to many alternative possibilities. It is useful to explore how such new affordances may make certain things more or less possible. Where once bootleg tapes and home taping tweaked the margins of the record industry's monopoly over recorded music, digital compression and network distribution (both technologies developed by the entertainment industry in the first instance) significantly alter the relative costs and benefits of such appropriations.

The way artefacts act to stabilize and/or destabilize the relative position and composition of social groups is something highlighted by the now defunct Actor Network Theory. Latour's (2005) attempt to fend off any over-rapid movement towards sociological determinism, wherein established social categories are wheeled in to explain the use of artefacts, is legitimate – even if he rather labours the point. Like Castells, Latour can be questioned for placing too much emphasis upon the potential for artefacts to reconfigure the balance of power and composition within and between social groups, yet the point remains true that negotiations over the formation and application of artefacts always involves some renegotiation over the composition and relative dominance of humans. Such renegotiations will not always be significant; however, they will not always be insignificant.

File-sharing offers an interesting case study. Expanding market reach and reducing cost by deterritorializing production of informational goods, in particular by means of digitalization of storage (digital compression) and transmission (file-sharing protocols), evaded local regulations, but the same artefacts were appropriated by competitors and non-market actors circulating freely by the same mechanisms to an even wider global network. Those that once sought to escape regulation demand re-regulation at a higher level. Whether this will be successful is an open question.

While Deleuze and Guattari (1984) highlight the open and contingent nature of ongoing developments in struggles over power, culture and profit in global information flows, Deleuze's (1992) diagnosis of the shift from territorialized discipline (in the form of Foucauldian institutional spaces and disciplinary fields) towards deterritorialized control through networks of information and money (surveillance and debt) is more concerned to outline the 'coils of the serpent' within 'societies of control'. Deleuze's final suggestion to the next generation that 'it's up to them to discover what they're being made to serve' (1992: 7) gives no answers, only the insight to keep looking. This book takes the hint.

Michael Hardt and Antonio Negri (2000) refer to the deterritorializing action of networked multitudes within and yet beyond the control of global empire. The actions of hundreds of millions of peer-to-peer file-sharers, in taking information technologies and using them in ways that challenge dominant logics of application and development represents just such a networked multitude – an illustration of deterritorializing leapfrogging beyond control by its own tools, and just such a challenge to existing social relations by means of the affordances made by artefacts that could well have been used otherwise. Yet, while such deterritorialization 'from below' may challenge dominant practices, it can also be linked to new forms of reterritorialization, either through legal enforcement or new forms of trust. The discussion of alternative business models in Chapter 9 highlights how diverse configurations of proximity and trust play out the possibilities of de/reterritorialization and de/relegitimation.

Conclusions

Where Castells grants relative autonomy to technology only to suggest such new forces of production are driving the emergence of a new capitalism, his critics tend to suggest established social relations continue to call the shots. Similarly, while his critics suggest Castells is a technological determinist, these critics are themselves more often than not guilty of reductionisms to their own preferred levels of causal explanation (language, interaction, hegemonic regime or mode of production). This chapter has sought to highlight these symmetrical counter-reductionisms and to resist them. Valuable insights have been highlighted at many levels. It is valuable to take insights from researchers working at all levels of analysis precisely as in so doing it is possible to identify the failure of any one level of explanation to effect closure. Social change is neither determined nor discounted in advance. This chapter draws upon the concept of 'affordances' as a bridging term that allows for analysis across levels of explanation, from language and interaction, to institutional and systemic social relationships and practices, without recourse to reductionism of various kinds. Castells' critics suggest he goes too far in claiming technical affordances transform social relationships. In some senses they are correct. In others Castells does not go far enough. File-sharing technologies afford perestroika from below not simply the reinvention of capitalism through new tools, though this is an alternative affordance.

3

File-sharing: A Brief History

- The hacker ethic – and U2's manager
- Media – compression and transmission
- Early Napster
- The closure
- The rise of peer-to-peer
- The development of a common media and platform
- From peer-to-peer to peers-to-peer (torrents)
- Commercial development – MP3 players, iPod and iTunes
- File-sharing and social networking (decommodification and democratization)
- Mass/new media history
- Web 2.0 and 3.0 – recommercialization or not?
- From consumer revolts to revolts amongst artists

The hacker ethic – and U2's manager

Under the headline 'Silicon Valley's hippy values "killing music industry"' Owen Gibson (*The Guardian*, 29 January 2008) writes:

> U2' s manager yesterday called on artists to join him in forcing the 'hippy' technology and Internet executives he blames for the collapse of the music industry to help save it. Paul McGuinness, who has plotted the rise of the Irish group over 30 years, said technology gurus in Silicon Valley such as Apple's Steve Jobs and Microsoft's Bill Gates had profited from rampant online piracy without doing anything to stop it. 'I suggest we shift the focus of moral pressure away from the individual P2P [peer-to-peer] thief and on to the multibillion dollar industries that benefit from these tiny crimes,' he said.

McGuinness's attempt to blame the computing industry for declining revenues in recorded music may in part stem from a desire to blame someone large enough to successfully target for compensation, and a target so wealthy and powerful as to make the claims of the recording industry – that they are the impoverished victims of the current shift in music listening – seem credible. Given failures to win sympathy for their case when prosecuting teenagers for sharing music, what better strategy to pursue than to turn attention to Bill Gates, someone who has garnered even less sympathy than the recording industry's executives in the course of his monumental commercial success? In short, McGuinness's claims may be easily discounted as merely special pleading and self-interest, unlikely to persuade anyone not in some way expecting to get paid by the successful prosecution of such suggestions.

Yet McGuinness has half a point. We may not be persuaded by the moral claims. Right or wrong, new technologies make it easier today to access recorded music without paying the holder of its legal monopoly. McGuinness can also be challenged in suggesting that Gates and Jobs are the legal beneficiaries of crimes undertaken using technologies purchased from them. No specific Apple or Microsoft products were developed for the purpose of copyright violating peer-to-peer file-sharing. That such practices can be undertaken using their products, makes them no more the legal beneficiary than a car manufacturer whose cars are involved in speeding offences or bank robberies.

McGuinness is correct to suggest the 'hippy values' of Silicon Valley, and what Pekka Himanen (2001) calls the 'hacker ethic' (after Levi 1984), pose a partial if not intentional threat to the taken for granted practices of established information distribution and control. While Jobs and Gates are not the best examples, the desire to explore the potential of any given technology does challenge reliance upon the status quo. What Castells and Himanen call 'the spirit of informationalism' (the passion to explore the potential of today's cutting edge technologies) is not a determining and independent force, any more than was Weber's (1930 [1905]) 'Protestant ethic', yet its 'elective affinity' with new networked conditions of work and creativity incentivizes 'hacking', breaking down informational constraints to set information free. Without a conscious and politically motivated desire to 'rebel' (though some have such a desire) the status accorded to anyone who can 'go beyond', who can 'hack' today's limitations, spreads through globally distributed networks of peer recognition. It is not technological determinism, but rather 'informationalism' and the hacker ethic that challenge present arrangements. Extending the possibilities of information technology in the face of current legal and economic barriers becomes a vocation of serious play.

Some innovations are taken up. Others are not. What is taken up may be taken up in ways other than were intended by their developers. Change is not simply the expression of technical 'evolution'. It is merely the case that exploration of informational potential opens up new forms of distribution that could bypass traditional suppliers of informational goods. Himanen (2001: 85–110) notes the 'spirit of informationalism', the hippy ethic that McGuinness is so concerned about, is about setting information free. However, this is understood as much in terms of freedom of speech as it is about free access to information. The struggle against censorship has much in common with the free circulation of ideas, but protection of free expression also motivated developments to protect anonymity via strong encryption. As Himanen documents, hackers were as concerned to provide new technologies that kept communication private as to provide others that opened communication up. If anyone represents McGuinness's hippy hacker it is John Perry Barlow, former songwriter for The Grateful Dead and co-founder of the Electronic Freedom Foundation. For Barlow (1994, 1996), it was the attempt to infringe privacy online that motivated his declaration of independence for what came to be known (largely thanks to him) as 'cyberspace'. Privacy and strong encryption are as important to McGuinness's plans to profit from the sale of informational goods in an age of digital file-sharing, as peer-to-peer file-sharing systems are a threat. It is only half-correct to blame machines and the techies who love to find the next big thing.

Himanen (2001: 188) cites another co-founder of the Electronic Freedom Foundation, Steve Wozniak (also co-founder of Apple Computing):

> I came from a group that was what you might call beatniks or hippies – a lot of technicians who talked radical about a revolution in information and how we were going to totally change the world and put computers in homes.

The revolution has certainly shaken the ground beneath the feet of traditional recorded music intermediaries. Yet the way things have and will work themselves out requires more than an attention only to technologies and techies, hippy or otherwise.

Media – compression and transmission

File-sharing combines commercially motivated innovations in information storage and processing, as well as more hacker induced innovations in transmission. File-sharing requires its two parts, the files and the sharing, to fit together. The recording and storage of music in a digital computer format has a relatively long history, with its origins in recording studios. These techniques filtered out in time into the modes of storage by which recorded music was packaged for sale. Digital recording enabled greater flexibility in the production and mixing of sound, and in the circulation of musical material between studios and from studios to physical pressing/production factories. The development of the compact disc, as well as the now defunct laser disc and mini-disc, followed on from these production side developments. In line with their production-based antecedents these new digital retail copy formats combined the benefits of ease of transmission, reduced production costs and a range of more contested benefits relating to sound quality and durability. They also warranted the wholesale resale of back catalogues to those shifting format from vinyl (and tape) to compact disc. Reduced cost, increased prices and higher sales due to reformatting saw a huge growth in profitability in the 1980s and 1990s.

While some prefer the sound of vinyl records, digital recording is better able to reproduce itself without corruption. Something may or may not be lost in the recording of live performance on a digital recording device. Those who prefer the 'warmth' of valve amplifiers and speakers can record into a microphone positioned next to such a stack, rather than directly into a digital mixing desk. Nevertheless, subsequent reproduction from digital format to digital format is less prone to loss of fidelity than were analogue techniques. While the rise of the compact disc from 1982 did not immediately throw open the floodgates, the availability to consumers of cheap re-writable discs a decade later led to ripples of anxiety over the possibility of higher levels of piracy. As Lee Marshall (2005) points out, the practice of bootlegging, whether commercial or home taping, never represented a substantial threat. Studio out-takes, live show recordings and private taping from radio or records, encouraged legal sales. Release of 'extra commercial' material (out-takes and live performance) simply bolstered the identity of the committed fan, who would also buy all the commercial releases, even as it boosted the 'rebel' mythology of artists working under contract for royalties. Home taping fostered a culture of music listening in those who would then go on to purchase music they liked when they could afford to do so. Digital releases were, however, more problematic. The record company executive Maurice Oberstein observed at the time 'Do you realise we are giving away our master tapes here?' (in Sandall 2007: 30).

The development of digital compression techniques to enable ease of storage and transmission once again originated within the entertainment industries (music and film in particular) as a tool for enabling producers, mixers, directors and editors to work on material recorded in different locations, and to facilitate other internal needs to distribute work in progress and production. The Moving Picture Expert Group (MPEG) coordinated the development of standards for video conferencing in the late 1980s (MPEG 1989). MPEG1 (MP1) reduced the bit rate for moving pictures to that of an audio CD, at considerable cost in image quality. The Video-CD was superseded by the DVD which used higher MP2 compression standards. MP2 also incorporated 'scalable and multilevel resolution standards' (Watkinson 2001: 4) that were the reason for the development of MP3. As such, there are no additional coding standards in MP3 but it became the basic format for storing and transmitting music files digitally, where MP2 is now the industry standard for digitally transmitted television. MP4 integrates with computer graphics as well as giving better image quality and is used in iPods.

As such, compression technology was developed for and by the entertainment industry, rather as digital recording was. The development of the Internet, the World Wide Web and of user friendly web browsers in the 1960s/70s, 1980s and the 1990s respectively occurred in parallel with the above developments in digital recording, but in non-commercial domains. They were developed by a curious array of scientists, government agencies and computer hackers (Moody 2002, Jordan and Taylor 2004, Terranova 2004). The fusion of digital recording, compression and transmission in the late 1990s came about with the advent of a user friendly interface that allowed Internet users with digitally recorded music on their computers to send files to each other. That user friendly interface was Napster.

Early Napster

The late 1990s were, it can be seen in hindsight, the golden age for the recording industry. The transfer from vinyl to digital CDs saw increased prices and sales. Collection re-formatting could not last forever and, therefore, some tail off in CD sales was inevitable. Falling sales cannot be solely blamed on file-sharing. While digital recording and MP3 compression developed within the recording industry, their significance was transformed with their reapplication within file-sharing systems, the first of which was Napster.

Born in 1980, Shaun Fanning started a computer science degree at Boston's Northeastsssern University in the late 1990s (Merriden 2001). MP3 formatted music files on the Internet meant a wealth of material was 'out there' for those who knew how to look. Downloading was not complex for 'techies', but trawling existing search engines for particular tracks, artists and albums was time consuming. Fanning did not set out to invent file-sharing, downloading, digital compression or even what is now understood as 'peer-to-peer' (P2P) exchange. Rather, the programme he wrote allowed people to display their music collections and facilitated requests to 'uploaders' from those wishing to 'download' items displayed. This programme took Fanning's childhood nickname 'Napster' (Murphy 2002). It relied on a range of existing developments and, unlike subsequent incarnations of peer-to-peer, exchanges were routed through a central server. Napster was only indirect peer-to-peer, facilitating sharing but also physically mediating it.

Launched in June 1999, Napster's original user base was made up of the very computer science students who were best placed to search the Internet and download music for themselves. Views divide as to how Napster spread, and how quickly. Anthony Murphy (2002: 10) of the UK Patent Office, without clarifying his sources, claims Napster grew from a small core to thirty-eight million users in its first six months prior to legal action being taken against it. This law suit came from the RIAA in December 1999 and was the first salvo in a wave of legal actions that would in the end see Napster, in its initial form at least, cease to exist. Others suggest Napster's use peaked in 2001 with twenty-six million users (Comscore 2001). Another source suggests a peak of eighty million registered users and almost three billion files traded in February 2001 (UK Parliamentary Office for Science and Technology 2002: 1). Depending on which numbers are believed, legal action coincided with increased or decreased use.

Napster was forced to close because it could not enact requirements by US courts to monitor and regulate traffic through its server. Given the inability of Napster to do this it is questionable whether figures on use are more than expressions of belief by those with particular investments. Copyright defenders are persuaded that the law reduces infringement, while Napster celebrants tend to believe initial attempts to shut it down increased use (Goldstein 2003).

The closure

Legal actions against Napster – initially by the RIAA, then by a number of artists (including Metallica, Dr Dre and Madonna), and finally by A&M Records – were all brought under US law, and specifically under the newly enacted Digital Millennium Copyright Act (hereafter DMCA). Drafted to enforce two 1996 treaties signed under the auspices of the World Intellectual Property Organization (WIPO) within US law, the DMCA was passed by the US Senate and enacted by the then US president Bill Clinton in October 1998. Similar legislation was enacted in European Union law in 2000 in the form of the EU Copyright Directive. Other Organization of Economic Cooperation and Development (OECD) countries followed suit. Countries that have not explicitly enacted laws to this effect are required by membership of the World Trade Organization to uphold the claims of copyright holders against digital forms of infringement as defined within the DMCA. Napster were charged specifically by A&M Records with facilitating copyright infringement by its users, direct contribution to infringement through directly trafficking file-sharing through its server, and therefore liability for 'vicarious infringement'. Brought initially across the span of 2000, the case was initially heard in a California district court. Napster lost on all three counts and was required to prevent users conducting digital infringement. It was also required to pay damages. Napster appealed on the grounds that it did not determine what was trafficked through its service any more than did a telephone or an Internet Service Provider. However, the DMCA, being designed directly to target technologies liable to promote and enable digital infringement of copyright, was interpreted by the Ninth Circuit Court in Los Angeles as requiring service providers to take responsibility for what users use their service to do. The court rejected Napster's defence and, unable to enforce the conditions set by the court or to monitor the traffic through its server, Fanning's company went offline in July 2001. Unable to generate income, which it had done through advertising on its website, Napster was unable to meet the fine and court costs of twenty-six million US dollars and the company filed for bankruptcy in 2002 (Menn 2003).

The rise of peer-to-peer

The DMCA, and the cases brought under it against Napster, seemed at first to have scored a decisive victory on behalf of copyright holders. Making companies liable for the actions of their product's users suggested a tighter grip could be exercised in the regulation of digitally facilitated infringement. Napster's 'contributory infringement', the fact that users had to go through the company's server to 'share' files, was what allowed the action of users to be defined as the service provider's responsibility. This led to a new generation of programmes that, while learning the lessons of the Ninth

Circuit Court's decision, drew very different conclusions to the ones hoped for by the recording industry's more commercially successful artists. However, Metallica's later decision to headline the first Download Festival, Dr Dre's involvement in subsequent high profile court cases involving rap music, copyright and liability for the content of its lyrics as well as Madonna's later reversal on the question suggests that even these artists learnt something new in time.

To the extent that users of the Napster service were able to upload and download files between themselves the system was peer-to-peer, but as the users trafficked their sharing through the central server of the Napster system, the company played a direct mediating role in each individual interaction. The next generation file-sharing software was more fully peer-to-peer file-sharing with a fully distributed programme enabling users to exchange directly with each other, using the software independently of the site from which it was downloaded. Napster's design combined technical capacities with commercial attractiveness. While Napster's initial design sought to solve a particular problem, that of easily locating MP3 files on the Internet, having a central hub through which traffic passed was attractive to advertisers. However, the legal decision to criminalize such a central hub for trafficking copyright infringing file-sharing challenged this. What it also did was make it very attractive for someone else to develop an alternative 'technical' solution to the problem of finding MP3 files on the Internet that did not require such a legal Achilles heel. Such systems were not long in coming. If the legal solution in attacking file-sharing was to drive the cork back into the bottle at the narrowest point, the technical solution for those wishing to file-share was a totally distributed system (David and Kirkhope 2004).

The development of a common media and platform

Fully peer-to-peer systems had come into existence for sharing music and other material online from 2000, but these systems became far more popular with the closure of Napster's service in 2001. The move from a client/server relationship to a more fully peer-to-peer structuring of relations, where each user's computer acts as both client and server, circumvented the 2001 ruling. New law suits soon followed (see Chapter 5). Kazaa was originally developed in 2000 by the Dutch company Consumer Empowerment, using the file-sharing protocol FastTrack. FastTrack enabled users to share files between themselves without the need for a central client–server relationship. FastTrack was licensed to Morpheus, but then withdrawn in a dispute over payment and conditions. Kazaa fought various legal battles in the Netherlands and in the USA, was forced to more offshore, and was eventually closed down in 2005. Kazaa retained an element of centrality within its FastTrack file-sharing protocols. Users still had to connect to the centre to locate other users, even while actual file-sharing can be carried out directly. Kazaa was, therefore, more open to legal attack than what came next, Gnutella. Based upon an open source protocol, Gnutella uses a network structure for both file exchange and user location, so further distancing the software provider from the interactions of users (Vincents 2007).

The open source character of Gnutella is distinct from FastTrack's commercial character. Unlicenced versions of Kazaa (Kazaa Lite and Kazaa ++) have removed a number of the parent company's adwares. Adwares are additional software (sub-programmes) that collect information about the user and which can be sent back to the parent company. Kazaa was forced to cease trading from its, by then, Australian headquarters in 2005 because it could not regulate or monitor traffic fully by such forms of surveillance. In part this was because suspicions over FastTrack's capacity to embed adware led many to adopt modified versions, either by personally cleaning up versions of the software provided by the company or getting pirated copies such as Kazaa Lite of which the ++ version was the most popular. Kazaa was taking legal action against those it felt were violating its copyright even as they were being sued by others for the same thing. It was the success of those suing Kazaa that promoted the development of Gnutella, and the unregulated 'pirate' versions of Kazaa. Companies like Grokster, which retained Kazaa's FastTrack protocol structure, have been declared illegal and shut down along with Kazaa itself. Services like Morpheus, which has undergone many modifications over the years, and a revised version of Napster now seek to uphold a legal downloading policy. Chapters 5, 6 and 7 document the technical, legal and cultural dynamics that have since unfolded.

From peer-to-peer to peers-to-peer (torrents)

With distributed system providers – at least for a time – not being liable for the actions of users, attention in the US, EU and other courts turned to the prosecution of uploaders. As will be discussed in Chapter 5. The focus of legal attention on uploaders led to the development of further modifications of the peer-to-peer concept. Where one set of legal challenges led from partial to full peer-to-peer file-sharing, new legal challenges encouraged removal of the single 'peer' from the proxy position of server in the peer-to-peer replication of the client–server relationship. If files were not taken from any particular peer, then no one individual could be held liable for supplying copyright infringing files. Just as software providers were able to evade liability on the grounds that they were not directly supplying 'stolen goods', so individual users could evade liability if they only supplied one fragment of any overall file. BitTorrent (and torrent based systems) alongside FreeNet systems make it impossible to identify a single source, either by supplying fragments from multiple sources or by distributing content across the network of users so as to remove the single locatable 'origin' (Thompson 2005). By the time the law caught up with programmes that had adapted to the 2001 rulings, these had been partially superseded by systems that protected users rather than the companies whose software they used.

Commercial development – MP3 players, iPods and iTunes

Just as the law encouraged ever more elaborate technical developments in the provision of user autonomy and anonymity, so copyright infringing file-sharing had a dynamic impact on the provision of commercial and legal downloading sites. While many of the technical requirements for the supply of music files via the Internet existed before Napster, competition between record companies and their desire to protect their position as monopoly suppliers and distributors of their artists' work stifled provision of a common platform for commercial downloading. The emergence of a market for MP3 players came about because of copyright infringing peer-to-peer file-sharing. The development of the iPod, and of iTunes, highlights the competing pressures within the commercial recording industry to seek both maximum audience share and maximum control over the product – two pressures pulling in opposite directions and yet balanced precariously in the technical, legal, cultural and commercial character of Apple's formerly (until 2008) digitally rights managed (hereafter DRM) iTunes downloading service, and its DRM free MP3 and MP4 playing iPods. DRM refers to electronic encryption to prevent (hard DRM) – and surveillance to identify (soft DRM) – unauthorised use of computer-based intellectual property. A more full discussion of DRM is given in Chapter 6. Songs downloaded from iTunes could only be played on an iPod, yet iPods played songs from other commercial and non-commercial MP3 downloading sites. As we saw at the beginning of this chapter, some in the music industry believe Apple is thereby profiting (in the sale of its players) from the circulation of copyright infringing files. Apple maintains that DRM free players have legitimate uses and that it is not commercially viable to tie iPods only to iTunes, especially given that many users want to transfer music from their own CDs (which is legal in the USA at least). While uncomfortable with these arguments, each major record company signed up to allow iTunes to digitally distribute their music. The alternative was to have their competitors receiving some share of the legal download market, while MP3 player users would have no choice but to download illegally the music of those companies outside this legal channel. While each company could sell its own product via its own website the fact that Napster had pioneered single platform downloading threatened to marginalize companies that wanted to go it alone. Just as the legal actions taken against file-sharers shaped development, so peer-to-peer file-sharing drove the development of commercial downloading. The removal of DRM restriction from iTunes was seen in 2008 – under pressure from free sharing services and hackers (see Chapter 6).

File-sharing and social networking (decommodification and democratization)

Napster's birth coincided in June 1999 with the launch of another peer-to-peer phenomenon, MySpace: if not the first, then by far the most successful social networking site. MySpace enables users to host their own profiles within its formatting protocols. The user can post a variety of materials displaying their interests, and which can then be accessed and viewed by other users of the network. MySpace, along with most of its larger rivals, derived its income from advertising links. Like intermediate generations of peer-to-peer file-sharing services, MySpace, Facebook and Bebo require users to log on to its website in order to access their own and others' profiles, even while users decide who to include and exclude from their personal networks within the overall community. This allows such services to stream advertising within the pages that users see. This potential to stream advertising led Rupert Murdoch's News Corporation to buy MySpace, through NewsCorp's subsidiary Fox Interactive Media, in July 2005 (Reiss 2006). A number of other sites were also bought by advertising based media companies looking to move beyond established mass media.

Social networking combines technical and social networks and promotes the idea of democratic media (Buckley 2006). Just as peer-to-peer networks replace, in their fuller form, the distinction between client and server with all nodes (users) taking both parts, so within social networking systems each person 'broadcasts' and receives. Each member of the community can upload and download. As social networking sites still require logging on through the network's website they are only peer-to-peer in the primitive sense of the original Napster. Commercial drivers restrain the movement to full peer-to-peer network connectivity.

Where peer-to-peer file-sharing encourages a de-commodification of informational goods, social networking sites promote the democratisation of information. This distinction between de-commodification and democratization requires that we do not equate the two network phenomena. Artists distributing work for money via their own online sites highlights the distinction, even as such attempts to take more control over the sale of their work parallels consumer rebellions against corporate control. Of course there are tensions between file-sharing networks that 'make music free' and social networking sites where artists make available their work for money. The boundaries are not clear-cut so the relationship between P2P file-sharing networks and social networks is worthy of further examination.

Mass/new media history

Where Castells' critical realism emphasizes the Internet's 'morphogenic structure', the network's conditioning of the scope for possible action by those operating within and as part of it, critical theory draw attentions to the social, economic and political relations in operation through such technical networks. It is easy to parallel, for example, Jurgen Habermas' (1989 [1962]) study of media development in Europe during the eighteenth and nineteenth centuries with developments in new-media today. The initial radicalism of the early newspapers, representing the voice of a new and rising bourgeois class, was central in the development of a 'public sphere', a space between private interest and state power, but which questioned both. With the transition from challenger to dominant class the bourgeoisie became more cautious. The media became dominated by commercial interest rather than political communication. Leon Mayhew's (1997) critique of late twentieth century mass media professional manipulation, spin and hype leaves little scope for doubt as to the depth of mass media incorporation by instrumental interests over principles of undistorted communication. The same tendencies exist within new-media. The emergence of new means of interaction offers new opportunities for commercial exploitation. But, as Habermas' later work (1979, 1984, 1987, 1990) suggests, this linear history of instrumental corruption of value rational networks of communication is only ever one side of the story. Communication oriented towards control, such as command languages in computing (see David 2002), become problematic in relation to instrumental interactions between people as it is reliant upon yet resisted by communication oriented towards understanding. System-oriented action, the attempt to apply instrumental rationality in relations between humans, is therefore doubly limited. Unlike computer command languages, which are based upon mathematical rules, human language, culture and interaction rely upon rules that have meaning only in their interpretation and which, therefore, require an orientation towards understanding or intersubjectively achieved meanings not reducible to formal regulations or algorithms. Second, as human meaning cannot be reduced to rules, human beings resist their reduction from ends in themselves (that which it would be like to be) to means to an end. System or instrumental rational action may seek to colonize lifeworld interactions oriented towards understanding, but in so doing routinely provokes both a defence of value oriented actions and reflection upon the values which are being defended. Instrumental knowledge interests (the desire to control) threaten knowledge interests in understanding, but may at the same time provoke its defence and even encourage emancipatory knowledge interests in fostering alternatives to simply the division between instrumental 'modernisation' and traditional 'community' (Habermas 1972). Just as Robert Michels (1962), after four hundred pages outlining the iron law of oligarchy, offers only a passing remark as to its being offset by an 'iron law of democracy', so it is all too easy to observe the 'iron cage of instrumental rationality' without noting the resistances to it. For both Castells and Habermas instrumental systems – whether technical, bureaucratic or financial – condition the scope for action of those whose actions sustain them, but do not determine outcomes. It is, therefore, necessary to study the way events unfold. As we have seen, a range of technical developments emerged driven by different interests. As we shall see below, the fusion of digital recording, storage and transmission within file-sharing systems is unstable and destabilizing.

Neither Castells nor Habermas accept McLuhan's understanding of media, where the printing press generated linearity, instrumental rationality and cool detachment (1962), while the electronic multi-sensory media returns us to the warm humanity of a now global village (1964). However, Castells' descriptions of the transformative potential of new media production for existing social relations comes close at times to repeating McLuhan's suggestion that the medium is the message. McLuhan pushed the force of his counter-intuition into caricature. Castells also seems willing to overstate his position regarding how digital networks condition the social content flowing through them. While Brian Winston (1998) usefully catalogues the history of suppressions and reinventions by which dominant social interests contain technological development and take-up, this counter to Castells' type of claims regarding 'technological revolutions' rather obscures what might be fundamentally new beneath a vast array of historical 'debris'. It may not be the novelty of the particulars (which Winston correctly challenges) but the novelty of their networked integration that Winston misses, even while Castells may exaggerate. What Winston's account of electronic media history would have looked like had it been written after the advent of file-sharing and not before it, remains an interesting point of conjecture.

Web 2.0 and 3.0 – recommercialization or not?

Reference to Web 2.0 and even 3.0 are technical reifications. Such product update coding is used rather as a person might refer to their new partner as 'girlfriend 4.0', or perhaps after a conflict and resolution as 'boyfriend 3.2'. The numbers and decimal places don't refer to technical upgrades, rather to increasing exploitation made of flat distributed network capabilities over hierarchical forms of action and storage. Web 2.0 etc. talk is made almost exclusively in relation to commercial applications of flat storage, connectivity and scrolling formats (Jones 2008). As we have seen, the rise of social networking has been viewed as highly attractive to advertisers because such networks still retain elements of the client–server relationship. Two issues emerge from this. First, there is the degree to which such centralized control (through which advertising is streamed into people's profiles) exercises influence over distributed content. Where editorial control over content is centralized, advertising can impact on content, but where editorial control is distributed, can centralized advertising any longer affect content? This question of editorial control is returned to in more detail at the end of Chapter 7. Second, does such advertising cause users to move away from such sites? If peer-to-peer file-sharing has fostered and been driven by a desire for de-commodification, will advertising put people off or are users concerned only with not having to pay? This is a theme that will be returned to in Chapter 9. These two questions go to the heart of whether so called Web 2.0, network commodification, has a future. Early attempts to mimic free downloading peer-to-peer file-sharing by QTrax, a free music download site where music files were embedded with advertising, and where users had to agree to pass their personal details to the service provider – who could then sell this information on to other advertisers – died before it was ever up and running. The story of QTrax (as with that of Kazaa before it) suggests rejection of adware (embedded spyware), while MySpace and Facebook suggest relative indifference to upfront advertising. Provisionally it appears that re-commodification requires the user's trust, not any legal right or technical ability or constraint. This brings us to the recent actions of a number of high profile artists.

From consumer revolts to revolts among artists

Peer-to-peer file-sharing has been paralleled with the free distribution of unsigned artists' work by artists themselves using social networking sites. A more recent development has been the rise in established artists placing their music online, either for free or for money. For various reasons (see Chapter 8) the belief that exclusive distribution through established record companies is the only, best or even viable way to make money from making music is increasingly questioned. This questioning of the archetypal career path is growing among artists yet to sign a deal as well as among those that already have. As such, record companies are being challenged from both sides. Whether the network characteristics of peer-to-peer file-sharing and/or social networking are developed through forms of de-commodification and/or democratization, and with the myriad permutations of these distinct but potentially complementary potentials, traditional forms of commodification through hierarchical and monopolistic structures face a serious challenge. We might witness the reinvention of the market, in overcoming monopoly, or we may yet see a shift in markets from the sale of recording to recording as advertising for something else. If recorded music becomes the menu, what then is the meal? For the artist it may be live performance, personally sold music or a sponsorship deal.

Chapter 9 develops a typology of such potential alternative business models, based on axes of high and low legitimacy (trust) and proximity – the former based on the degree to which new foundations (of trust) underpinning exchange between artists and audiences are established in the absence of either technical or legal monopoly protections, while the latter relates to shifts in the primary location of such exchange, from the physical record to either the live event or the digital download (or both). The case studies discussed in that chapter show how all four scenarios set out within the two by two high and low legitimacy and proximity matrix are currently in play as alternative futures relative to the established business model of selling music.

4

Markets and Monopolies in Informational Goods: Intellectual Property Rights and Protectionism

- Introduction
- Intellectual property: an essential contradiction
- The pre-history of patents and copyrights
- Non-rivalousness
- Natural rights discourses versus utilitarian balance of interest constructions
- American, British and French traditions: freedom, control and Enlightenment
- Towards an international system, but slowly
- Hollywood pirates, Mark Twain and Mickey Mouse
- The fall and resurgence of international IP regulation
- Fee culture or free culture?
- The young versus the old
- Conclusions: competition versus closure

Introduction

The social nature of property rights is readily apparent through historical and geographical comparison (Marshall 2005, May and Sell 2005), but natural justice arguments for property rights remain (Vaidhyanathan 2003, Lessig 2004). Scarcity and the physical limits of material objects provide a metaphor for claims regarding 'natural' monopoly. 'You can't have your cake and eat it!' 'The tragedy of the commons' extends this metaphor. Post-scarcity in informational goods renders such arguments redundant, yet the history of intellectual property law shows the emergence of parallel arguments about scarcity in creativity and effort that can be offset by copyright, trade mark, trade secret and/or patent. These developments exemplify the sociological concepts of 'closure' (Weber 1991), the countertendency against 'the tendency for the rate of profit to fall' (Marx 1995). While file-sharing manifests in extreme form the tendency for the rate of profit to fall within conditions of 'free' competition (as technology reduces to nothing the labour necessary to 'make' each additional unit of production), intellectual property rights are designed to suspend free markets by means of monopoly protection ('closure'). For Weber (1978, 1991), controlling access to ideal and material resources and life chances defines power, just as power conditions the scope for maintaining such 'closure'. Where for Marx exploitation underpins social relations of power, for Weber social relations of exclusion and inclusion condition the possibility of such 'closure' over surplus value, i.e. the claim to own the fruits of the productive process. Raymond Murphy (1988: 1; see also 1985) summarizes Weber's conception of closure as: 'formal and informal, overt and covert rules governing the practices of monopolization and exclusion'. Contested constructions of creativity as either performance or capital play out such a dispute over the fruits of artistic work and works of art.

The conflict over AIDS inhibiting drugs, between Western patent holding drugs companies and the governments of developing countries who wish to use cheaper patent infringing derivative drugs, focused the world's attention on the relative rights of monopoly patent holders and public interests. Donald Light and Rebecca Warburton (2005) note claims over development costs in the pharmaceutical industry are often widely exaggerated. Richard Lewontin (2000) points out that two of the three key AIDS inhibiting drugs were not developed in the private sector, despite subsequent private patents. Having taken the South African government to court over its use of derivatives in March 2001, the 39 pharmaceutical companies taking the action dropped the case on hearing the defence were to call witnesses to testify as to the gulf between the cost of development and the profit margins being made on the sale of patented AIDS inhibiting drugs (May and Halbert 2005, May and Sell 2005). While avoiding this high profile confrontation, a global intellectual property framework has developed over the last decade, even while gains in formal legislation have not ensured major corporations – whether in patent protected biomedicine or copyright protected creative and media industries – have got things all their own way.

This chapter charts the emergence of intellectual property rights law in various countries and in various fields over many years, towards today's global regime. This chapter also identifies an 'ageing effect' across four dimensions of the creative process. The young require a creative commons, where the old call for 'closure'. This can be seen as societies develop, as individuals move through their careers as authors and/or inventors, as new creative media emerge from older forms, and as tastes, styles and genres emerge within artistic fields. The most jealous protectors of intellectual property today – whether these be states, individuals, corporations and their representatives, and/or established field representatives – only emerged as a result of their previous success in profiting from yesterday's creative commons, often in the face of accusations of piracy or in conditions where intellectual property (hereafter IP) law did not exist or was evaded. Where IP law protects today's winners it closes the door to new forms of innovative 'hacking', while shoring up the very monopoly rents that will motivate innovators to 'hack' them.

Intellectual property: an essential contradiction

This book is about file-sharing, the practice of which often violates copyright. Copyright is one form of intellectual property right (hereafter IPR), the others being patents, trademarks and trade-secrets. All contain an essential contradiction, between their construction as property rights and the recognition that knowledge should not be owned in perpetuity. Copyright is a legal monopoly over copying a particular creative expression (Vaidhyanathan 2003). The copyright holder may or may not be the original author (or their employer) and the holder may be individual or corporate. Not all countries maintain author rights after sale. Defining where ideas end and expression begins varies.

Copyright covers artistic expression and form; patent covers technical designs for functional objects and processes. This is, however, not clear-cut, with computer software now covered under the 1996 WIPO Copyright Treaty. Patents require a demonstration of originality, non-obviousness, utility and the means by which an object or process works. Copyright does not require a demonstration of these four things and no longer even requires formal registration, which patents do. Trademarks are an offshoot of copyright relating to symbolic forms that are identified with particular organizations, and whose free use might mislead the public, while trade secrets are an offshoot of patents, relating to distinctive ingredients within particular products.

The contradiction in IPRs lies in assigning private ownership over cultural products when origin can never be so readily fragmented. Every form of IPR law, in all countries and at all times, has recognized that ideas in principle cannot and should not be privately owned. Laws have granted a time-limited state regulated monopoly on use, rather than full ownership rights. Such time limitation has a dual purpose in relation to creativity and price. Time limitations balance incentives for the rights holder and the creative potential to innovate further once such private rights are revoked. Second, the profits of the rights holder are set against the rights of the public not to be forced indefinitely to pay monopoly rents. Time-limited control represents a social contract, somewhere between social rights such as pension and health protection, and full property rights, which are also simply legal conventions and as such are social contracts. Property rights are social constructions, not natural, physical or logical properties such as might be said to be the properties of oranges, oxygen and/or triangles.

The pre-history of patents and copyrights

Christopher May and Susan Sell (2005) provide a valuable pre-history to the notion of IPRs. Branding of animals and skins, and maker's marks on pottery, metalwork and jewellery show a desire to identify ownership and origin (2005: 44), but what they protected was a mix of physical things and craft skills. The tension between craft guild control and individual IP holder emerged much later. While the Greeks saw the rise of autonomous and commercial poets, notions of individual genius, ownership and origin in ideas remained limited. Similarly, though Rome regulated counterfeiting of coins and craft goods, it remained only a crime to take the emperor or another's name falsely, while there was no specific protection for designs, innovations and other creative works (2005: 47). The absence of printing technology limited the copying of written works and there was little money in 'writing' as such.

In medieval Europe church claims over theological work and transcription, while generating claims of plagiarism, suppressed notions of authorial origin. The non-private ownership of ideas by individuals was passed on from the church to the universities, and as such it was plagiarism – not property rights – that governed academic behaviour. Guilds regulated trade in crafts and began to seek protection over design and technique in the late Middle Ages. May and Sell (2005: 51–2) note Genoese silk merchants in 1432 and Florentine woollen guilds in 1472 gaining protection for figures and patterns, while the English court offered Royal Grants, protections and 'letters patent' in the 1440s to attract craftsmen and merchants to the realm. France promoted authorized guilds with stiff penalties for non-members who practiced protected crafts. The periods of such grants, protections and patents were typically fourteen years – the span of two apprenticeships. This allowed new techniques to pass into the labour force when the monopoly relapsed. Fourteen years became the common unit of balance between private interest in monopoly and the public benefits of abolition.

While the term 'patent' existed before 1474, the first formal 'patent office' came into being in Venice in that year, creating a rule-governed system of rights to replace arbitrary royal favours. The rise of the Ottomans and the discovery of the Americas saw the decline of Venice as the centre of trade and innovation in Europe in the fifteenth century, but the dispersal of its many foreign patent holders back across Europe (along with other migrations of talent from Constantinople and Spain) spread a great many ideas, one of which being the formal registration of innovations in exchange for protection. This talent flow fuelled the wider Renaissance and the Reformation, all encouraging notions of the individual, creative genius and the positive value of innovation.

Non-rivalousness

Unlike physical objects, information is neither used up by being used, or unavailable to one if being used by another. Information is not consumed. Christopher May (2004) refers to information's non-rivalousness. If one person is using a hammer and a bunch of nails, this hammer cannot be used by someone else at that time and the nails cannot be used by someone else for the duration of their application. However, the idea of using a hammer to drive in nails and the idea that nails can hold things together are not limited to only being used when someone else isn't. Use can be infinite and simultaneous. May (2004, 2007b) notes that informational asymmetries are the foundation for markets in informational goods. Such goods are not diminished through copying and circulation, and their utility is not automatically diminished if shared. However, the capacity to profit from information depends upon retaining some asymmetry based on scarcity. In certain situations (such as in the sale of cars, houses, electrical goods, etc.) the law requires suspension of information asymmetries relevant to the goods' value. However, the basis of intellectual property rights is that informational asymmetries are retained in relation to certain other goods, such that the information itself becomes a commodity rather than simply a factor affecting the value of other goods. This construction of scarcity allows informational goods to gain the quality of rivalousness found in physical goods.

Intellectual property rights create scarcity. They do not 'manage' a condition of scarcity that preceded their assignment. The argument for property rights emerges from issues in allocating scarce resources. As long as two people cannot use the same hammer at the same time, some system of allocation is required. Ownership is only one such possible system. Such arrangements have no logical extension to post-scarcity conditions. Garrett Hardin's (1968) 'The Tragedy of the Commons' adds another dimension to the idea of scarcity often cited in defence of property rights. Not only do property rights constitute a method of allocating use and consumption of scarce resources, they also inhibit further increases in scarcity by avoiding overuse. Grazing their sheep on the common each individual maximizes personal utility by grazing more sheep. In the absence of regulation this encourages over-grazing. No control over each other individual means limits to over-grazing cannot be enforced. The sum of individual actions undermines the common good if the common remains common. If everyone keeps using the same hammer, in the end it will break. A defence of intellectual property rights suggests creativity is scarce and in need of protection from over exploitation. As this chapter will highlight, authors such as Lessig (2004), Vaidhyanathan (2003), May (2007a and b) and May and Sell (2005) reject this view of scarce creativity being nurtured by private property rights, or at least the 'thick' forms of protection currently being rolled out by WIPO and the WTO. These authors highlight that creativity requires free access to a rich cultural commons, what Lessig calls the creative commons, not just incentives set in place by the closing down of such a public realm. Economic development, personal creative development, media development and genre development require a strong creative commons and are inhibited by thick forms of protectionism. Hardin's concern that infinite incentives and finite resources would result in physical tragedy does not warrant the fear that access to a non-finite cultural resource would lead to a limiting of incentives. Parallels between ideas and objects cut both ways. You don't pay the garden centre for loss of earnings when you take cuttings (Rojek 2006: 142–3, 2007: 91).

Natural rights discourses versus utilitarian balance of interest constructions

The history of intellectual property rights displays a tension between natural rights arguments and policy oriented conceptions of law serving to balance the interests of 'originators' and 'users'. May and Sell (2005: 108) distinguish between, on the one hand, a romantic conception of the creative genius and their natural and inalienable rights over the 'fruits' of such genius and, on the other hand, a policy-oriented pragmatism, which they call the utilitarian view: 'utilitarian notions are designed to reward creation and diffusion, whereas natural rights or romantic notions privilege the goal of stewardship or the right to "manage" one's property after it is created.' They go on to suggest, following Mark Lamley, that 'ex ante' justifications for IPRs flow from utilitarianism while 'ex post' justifications come from romantic models. Ex ante arguments refer to before the event issues, i.e. motivations, while ex post arguments refer to rights to do as one pleases with what is yours after the fact of their creation. For utilitarians private property is an institution the rationale for which is that it serves the greatest possible good. If the institution of private property motivates wealth creation and good stewardship of resources, it remains justified. Whether this is in fact the case remains in dispute, but the utilitarian logic is based in utility – whether something works – rather than in notions of intrinsic values. What are labelled 'romantic' constructions of property draw upon natural or inalienable notions of 'rights'. May and Sell rather brush over differences within the two dominant traditions of natural and inalienable rights. Where for John Locke (1988) life, liberty and property are fundamental characteristics of human nature, for Hegel (1991) property rights represent the social foundation for formal equality of recognition between historically emergent individuals. For Hegel, the idea of natural rights was oxymoronic and what it refers us to is rather a collective construction of the 'modern' individual as expression of a long historical progression, something that is then projected backwards as natural and universal. In this regard, Hegel's approval of property rights is on grounds closer to utilitarianism than to Locke. Yet Hegel is commonly associated with Locke in the emphasis upon individual property rights in ideas, and in opposition to utilitarian constructions. Why should this be so? The answer lies in the twisted history of 'romanticism'. Most commentators associate romanticism with the defence of the author as creative genius. Hegel's challenge to the rationalist and empiricist traditions in philosophy, with his claim that all knowledge is historically specific, conditioned by the spirit of the age, aligned him with the romantic movement; similarly his attention to the struggle for recognition in history also chimed with the romantic attention to particular experience over universal truth, justice and beauty. But, Hegel's romanticism highlights something about this tradition which is largely overlooked in contemporary accounts, that being the sense in which the romantic artist expressed the spirit of the age – not simply individual genius. Contemporary constructions of the romantic artist accept two hundred years in which law, commercial interest and artistic tradition have sidelined this (David 2006b). Early romanticism attempted to give a voice to nature and to community. The English lakeside romantic poets sought to express beauty and sublime nature to get beyond individual identity. They often published anonymously, or collectively, again in rejection of rationalist constructions of creative individualism and genius. The Brothers Grimm were folk anthologists who sought to save the oral traditions of their German homeland and to express the culture of which they were a part. In rejecting formal conventions of artistic composition as criteria for judging work, romanticism's emphasis upon expression and experience was not simply a turning inward to the artist's own inner world, but rather to the relationship between that world and the world around them. Later constructions of romanticism replaced this complexity with the lone genius, the self-generating source of creativity.

The younger Hegel celebrated the radicalism of revolutionary romanticism while in old age felt the established order best realized the struggle for formal recognition. So early romantics challenged the authority of rationalist individualism and private property only to become fierce conservatives in old age, not least in arguing for authorial property rights in the creativity they would once have believed expressed higher, natural or cultural forces. Romanticism's complex and contradictory nature was only later shorn to serve particular interests.

Locke's construction of natural rights in property contains a tension, between an idea of property as just desert for labour and as a quality intrinsic to human nature. This is outlined in the fifth chapter of his *Two Treatises of Government* (1988). If natural rights can exist in life, liberty and possessions (Locke refers to all three as human properties), is it to be assumed that a right to self-possession (in life and liberty) needs to be earned or is it a right that remains inalienable? For Locke life and liberty are intrinsic rights, while possession of objects (property rights) requires the mixing of life and liberty with them. In other words, humans gain rights in things only to the extent that they expend labour in remaking nature. Does a property right in things remain only as long as the owner continues adding to it through labour, or do rights remain in perpetuity after initial investment? Might property rights logically be redefined as labour rights? To the extent that Locke believes property rights should remain, it is because they are seen to be suitable incentive to continued investment. In this, Locke accords with utilitarian thinkers. While philosophers distinguish deontological constructions of ethics (universal and inalienable conceptions of appropriate action) from consequentialist ones (where the ends justify the means) (Williams and May 1996), the history and philosophy of property and IP rights muddy these distinctions to their core. The law is not founded on logic. Rather law articulates conflicts of interest, disputes over the construction of interests, and alliances of such contested and constructed interests.

American, British and French traditions: freedom, control and Enlightenment

The first century of the United States of America was built upon a disregard for foreign intellectual property rights and significant reservations about their domestic application (Lessig 2004). In part this was the expedience of a new nation seeking to catch up with its more developed rivals. It was also a rejection of the role copyright had played in the upholding of Crown censorship restrictions in the American colonies prior to independence. There were also principled objections to artificial monopolies. Thomas Jefferson (Lessig 2004: 84) states: 'He who receives an idea from me, receives information himself without lessoning mine; as he who lights his taper off mine receives light without darkening mine'. The US Constitution frames intellectual property rights as private but state-regulated monopolies, justified only if they promote innovation and the general enhancement of wellbeing rather than simply personal gain (Vaidhyanathan 2003: 20). Jefferson, James Madison and George Washington each saw such rights as policy devices, not intrinsic property rights, even while each took a slightly different angle on what might or might not be classed an inalienable possession.

In England, prior to 1710, publishers held to a common law assumption that works bought from authors belonged outright to the buyer. Rights to publish were regulated by the state and publishers also operated a cartel (the Conger) among themselves – a gentlemen's agreement not to publish works being produced by other members of the club (Lessig 2004: 85–6). Similar arrangements had been enforced across Europe in the seventeenth century but this had been disrupted by the Thirty Years War, after which Dutch pirate publishers in particular flourished making cheap copies of what had previously been restricted (May and Sell 2005: 78). English unification with Scotland saw attempts by Scottish publishers to undercut English publishers' monopoly prices. In response, the 1710 Statute of Anne established the principle of authors' rights and of their right to assign limited duration copyrights to a lawful publisher. The law gave an initial 14 year copyright term for new works, that could be extended by a further 14 years if the author remained alive, while existing works received a blanket 21 year period of protection (Vaidhyanathan 2003). Once these terms expired there was a rush to bring out cheap unprotected editions. Publishers with profitable titles that were falling out of copy protection sought to fall back upon the older common law assumption that once bought a work belonged to its purchaser in perpetuity. Initially this view prevailed, but over the course of the mid-eighteenth century the law came down fully on the side of limited period protection and the rejection of perpetual intellectual property rights. May and Sell (2005: 93) suggest: 'the Act of Anne was primarily concerned with regulating the printing trade and only as a secondary concern established a potentially common law copyright for authors'.

Revolutionary France initially suspended intellectual property rights and performed a number of reverses on the issue. The Enlightenment impulse toward the progressive dissemination of knowledge tempered bourgeois self-interest in knowledge as capital (David 2006b: 426). Patent rights were extended through Europe by Napoleon, but the system established struck down three-quarters of applications on the grounds of insufficient original-ity or public benefit to grant restriction (May and Sell 2005). Copyright was brief and ended with death.

While distinct in their framing of IPRs, Britain, France and the United States all came to draw a strong distinction between intellectual and mate-rial property. While economically developed states concerned themselves with such things internally, internationally states tended to ignore the claims of foreigners. As with publishers so with states. Protection was demanded except when deregulation was advantageous.

Lee Marshall (2005) provides a detailed account of the role played by William Wordsworth in the strengthening of British copyright. Wordsworth became the figurehead in a campaign in the 1830s for perpetual copyright extension. As an old man Wordsworth sought to safeguard an inheritance for his daughters. He drew upon a construction of the romantic artist as cre-ative originator and, therefore, rightful owner of the products of their creativity. In 1842 the law extended copyright protection to life plus seven years or 42 years, whichever was longer. As has been noted above, Wordsworth's construction of romanticism late in life, a construction of the romantic artist as 'self-made-man', is a far cry from the earlier 'A Defence of Poetry' in which Shelley argues that the artist expresses 'less their spirit than the spirit of the age' (cited in David 2006b: 427). Wordsworth's own earlier suggestion that the best memorial to Robert Burns would be the immortality of his words is a far cry from his later concerns for financial inheritance. Wordsworth's deployment of a romantic conception of the struggling artist, as source of originality, has been central to subsequent defences of intellectual property rights and their extension. However, it is wrong to suggest that 'the "logic" of Romanticism is towards perpetual copyright' (Marshall 2005: 79–80). This takes the older man's version of his youth for the whole.

Towards an international system, but slowly

Emerging states resist the ownership of ideas claimed by dominant states, so established printers and publishers were challenged by new entrants.

Established authors seek to enclose the creative commons from which they themselves emerged. We should recall these transformations when today's dominant states, fields, innovators and genres proclaim as universal a set of rules which their own histories refute.

While the law was being strengthened in Britain, elsewhere the Dutch and the Swiss moved to suspend or at least not enforce intellectual property law from the middle of the nineteenth century up until the early years of the twentieth century. The second half of the nineteenth century saw two parallel developments. First, for large and complex industrial corporations powered by developments in physical and chemical engineering, research and development became a key driver of economic advantage, and companies sought means by which they could control such innovation. In 1871 the United States passed legislation allowing corporate authorship. This gave companies ownership over innovations developed by their employees. Six years later Germany passed similar legislation (May and Sell 2005: 127). The German legislation changed the term 'innovator' to 'applicant' in patent forms. It would not be until 1909 in the United States, and later elsewhere, that similar changes would be enacted in relation to copyright through the legal convention of 'work for hire', wherein the artist is paid for their time while what they create belongs to their employer (in part a return to the situation prior to the Statute of Anne). Corporate authorship and work for hire stands in contrast to the construction of romantic authorship put forward by those who equate Romanticism with individual creative genius.

The second development in the later years of the nineteenth century was the emergence of international treaties covering IPRs. In the mid-century debate raged between free-trade abolitionists, who saw copyright and patents as artificial monopolies restricting competition, and intellectual property protectionists who defended what they felt to be the foundations of a property-owning social order. *The Economist* campaigned for abolition. John Stuart Mill equated abolition with 'free stealing under the prostitute name of free trade' (in May and Sell 2005: 116). Abolitionists felt protection only aided 'cheating foreigners' who violated the fair play of 'civilised peoples'. Both sides argued the case in terms of business advantage. In the end business elites compromised between national protection and international trade by means of international treaties. The two key treaties were the Paris Treaty for the Protection of Industrial Property (1883) and the Berne Treaty for the Protection of Literary and Artistic Works (1886) (May 2007a). These two treaties, governing international standards in patent and copyright respectively, continue to this day as the foundation for the current global intellectual property rights regime. The agency established to coordinate the membership and enforcement of these treaties has changed name and address over time and is today the World Intellectual Property Organization, based in Geneva.

Hollywood pirates, Mark Twain and Mickey Mouse

The United States remained outside the Berne Treaty until the 1990s as it continued to refuse recognition of copyright to works not physically made in America. Within the USA emerging industries saw parallel disputes between old and young. 'The film industry of Hollywood was built by fleeing pirates' (Lessig 2004: 53). Thomas Edison learnt the power of 'patent thickets' from his early work in railways and then in electric light. He deployed hundreds of loosely defined patents, which acted as a minefield enabling him to control emerging areas. He took possession of the ideas of his employees and rivals by patenting their innovations. Just as he had patented the incandescent filament light bulb, despite not being the first to develop it, so he patented longstanding spooling techniques in cinematic projection and set about ruthlessly exploiting his monopoly rights. He compelled his rivals to licence through him the technologies they already used to make film via his Motion Picture Patent Company. The MPPC subsidiary, the General Film Company, set about regulating the licensing of cinema projectors, often through the physical destruction of unlicensed, or hacked, projectors that Edison claimed were copies of his patented technology. Edison drove out foreign completion from Pathe, while successfully incorporating his domestic rivals Biograph and Vitograph. However, a group of independent film making companies, led by William Fox, fled to Southern California to escape Edison's domination of the East Coast film world (Cook and Bernink 1999).

Hollywood was not just founded on patent infringement. It was also founded upon a general disregard for the authorship rights on the literary works it adapted for the screen. The US film industry moved from early disregard for copyright, when it was doing the poaching, to latter concern to control such things when it owned them (Vaidhyanathan 2003: 83–105). When D.W. Griffith made a film adaptation of Mark Twain's 'The Death Disk' – itself adapted from Thomas Carlyle's *Oliver Cromwell's Letters and Papes* – in the early years of the twentieth century, Twain made no objection, and even the US Copyright Act of 1909 did not include film. However, in creating the notion of work for hire in relation to artistic works, this Act did make film-making companies focus upon how to secure ownership over the work of their adaptors.

Vaidhyanathan shows how the gap between idea and expression applied at the start of the twentieth century, a gap that viewed the distinction between visual and literary representation of the same ideas as sufficient not to extend copyright over the former to cover the latter, diminished systematically during the twentieth century. At the beginning of the century a film was seen as a distinct expression from the textual expression it may have been based upon. By the end of the century (2003: 114) 'total concept and feel' or 'mood' became sufficient to claim that one expression infringes upon the copyright of another work.

Just as Wordsworth 'matured', so did the United State's champion of literary authorship, Mark Twain. Borrowing from Southern oral traditions and European literature, Twain only later championed strong copyright enforcement duration. 'For Twain, piracy was theft, plagiarism was bad manners' (Vaidhyanathan 2003: 67). An early self-confessed borrower/plagiarist, Twain's success led him to seek stronger protection against the very poaching that had aided his development. While the US public and publishers had benefited from cheap copies of British books, by the late nineteenth century, successful US authors and the larger publishing houses began to find themselves undercut by cheap, unregulated copies of both foreign and US authors' work. Tighter copyright regulation for foreign authors' work would increase prices and so benefit both established authors and publishing houses with the best links to Europe. The 1909 Act increased protection terms to 28 years, plus a further 28 if the author was still alive at the end of the first period. The Chase Act of 1891 had granted protection to foreign authors but only for books printed in the USA. These two laws benefited established US publishing interests, even if they excluded the US from the Berne Treaty for another century. Twain began as a celebrator and defender of the creative commons: 'Only near the end of life and career did self-interest win out and trump his concern for future authors and artists. Mark Twain's shifting thoughts on copyright parallel the disturbing trend in American copyright policy in the twentieth century' (Vaidhyanathan 2003: 80). That trend has been towards tighter control and longer duration. The trend was not linear and uninterrupted (May and Sell 2005), but for all the subsequent ups and downs of twentieth century IPR enforcement, the overall situation by the end of the century was one of far greater regulation.

The same progression from pirate to protectionist characterized the history of both radio and television in the United States (Lessig 2004: 58–61). Cartoons also moved from parody within the creative commons to the site of intense copyright protection and extension. Mickey Mouse's 1928 appearance in *Steamboat Willie* was a parody of Buster Keaton's 1927 film *Steamboat Bill Jr*, itself based on an earlier popular song. Parody is lawful as 'fair use' in the US (Goldstein 2003) and as 'free speech' elsewhere. For all this, Lessig notes, the Disney Corporation today lobbies tirelessly to uphold copyright in its fictional figure head. The terms of such copyright are routinely extended; that Mickey Mouse began life as a 'hack' is glossed over.

The fall and resurgence of international IP regulation

The period from the rise of film to the rise of the personal computer and the Internet saw IPR law placed on the defensive before itself rising again. It was the United States that led the way in both moves. In the 1930s, New Deal Democrats challenged the monopolies put in place by patent thickets. After the Second World War such policies were extended both at home, with the break up of cartels in various economic sectors, and abroad, in breaking up the German and Japanese corporate networks whose vertical and horizontal integration (by purchase and patent), it was felt, had fostered aggressive expansionism, anti-democratic control, militarism and war (May and Sell 2005: 139). Communist regimes developed rapidly until the 1970s by ignoring Western intellectual property rights. The US accepted patent infringement as it helped the rapid development of Japan, South Korea and Taiwan – states held up as examples of capitalist success. Domestically, development seemed best fostered by open circulation of new ideas. Relatively weak patent enforcement encouraged dynamism in Silicon Valley relative to tighter control and slower growth around the Boston technology hub (Light 2004).

Resurgence of IPRs begins with the Reagan/Thatcher era, at least domestically in the US/UK, and these two countries led the global resurgence in the years after the collapse of the Soviet Union and the rise of global trade in informational goods. The collapse of the Soviet 'alternative' and China's marketization left developed countries free to push a global trading and property rights framework. The absence of challengers and the presence of increasingly powerful informational industry lobbies, around computing, music, film, biotechnology, pharmaceuticals and agribusiness, allowed just such a framework in the form of the World Trade Organization and its TRIPS agreement. WTO was born in 1995 to replace the General Agreement on Tariffs and Trade (GATT). Where GATT fostered negotiations to reduce trade barriers, WTO set out legal requirements that each member state must pass into domestic legislation. GATT dissolved and previous members were required to sign up to the new, more aggressive organization on pain of being frozen out of world trade. Linking IPR with trade rules TRIPS, as a part of WTO, enforces copyright and patent with violation tied to immediate trade sanctions. Where the World Intellectual Property Organization managed treaties and registered claims, it lacked the teeth to punish non-compliance. WTO/TRIPS were designed to overcome this limitation. TRIPS requires all states wishing to participate in world trade to pass and uphold IPR legislation designed by and for the current conditions of development of the most advanced states, whether or not this best meets the needs of all societies. That more developed states themselves actively evaded such laws when they were at a lesser stage of development is forgotten. The WTO's detachment from the United Nations allows it to push a 'maximalist' IPR agenda, irrespective of the counter case for limits and exemptions for the world's less developed societies.

WTO and WIPO have, since 1996, operated a dual approach, with the former enforcing a legal baseline, while the later continues to push for new and more stringent constructions of intellectual property (May 2007a). Presenting itself as merely a technical advisory body, WIPO claims it is neither partisan nor political but, as May demonstrates, this is not true. On the rare occasions where developing societies have tabled challenges to the interests of dominant IP rich states within the WIPO general assembly, such discussions have been either diffused or suspended under intense pressure from wealthy governments and corporations.

Despite UN technical advisory status requiring a priority on development rights, WIPO's financial and staffing structure, drawing both money and expertise from the states and corporations whose patents and copyright claims it was established to uphold, lead WIPO to upholding IPR first and foremost. It remains an article of faith that the best interests of developing societies lie in doing what more advanced states say they should do, rather than what such advanced states themselves once did.

Fee culture or free culture?

Led Zeppelin settled out of court in 1985 when sued by Willie Dixon over a song Dixon wrote for Muddy Waters in 1962, and which Led Zeppelin was said to have infringed in their 1969 song 'Whole Lotta Love' (Vaidhyanathan 2003: 117). Shortly afterwards Led Zeppelin sued the Rap artist Schooly D for sampling their track 'Kashmir' without permission (Vaidhyanathan 2003: 132). All these songs draw from the blues tradition, so who can truly claim the 'buck' should stop with them? Vaidhyanathan discusses John Fogerty, sued by his previous management for allegedly infringing his own previous work. Fogerty successfully displayed in court how his music shared common and deeper roots than could be pinned down to any one original artist. However, the law has tended to go the other way. A string of cases found in favour of those claiming to have been sampled without permission. What Greg Tate (cited in Vaidhyanathan 2003: 130) calls 'ancestor worship', the recording industry and its lawyers call theft. For them the only 'true' ancestor worship is ancestor payment. The extent to which today's new generation are constrained by the monopoly power of older generations may be the measure of where we sit on the spectrum between a feudal 'permission culture' and a democratic 'free culture' (Lessig 2004).

The young versus the old

The history of intellectual property exhibits a number of tendencies. Developed states promote increased duration, spread and application of intellectual property rights, and decreasing the distinction between property rights in objects and in ideas. The public good and intellectual commons (culture as such) have been diminished relative to private interests and culture as capital. This tendency has seen reversals, but has in recent decades undergone considerable intensification. Just as developed states seek to protect intellectual advantages over less developed ones, so developed players in publishing, film, radio and music – while born out of piracy – became increasingly protectionist as they acquired more to protect. The

Table 4.1   *'Growing old disgracefully'*

Level of action	Historical 'ageing effect'	Paradigm cases of 'old hypocrisy'	Resistance from the 'young'
States	From development to intellectual property protectionism	Britain, France and the United States of America	Developing countries manufacturing their own derivative HIV inhibiting drugs
Industries	From market adaptation to patent/copyright thickets	Chemistry, pharmaceuticals, agribusiness, film and music	New technology companies for whom giving access to free content promotes media innovation
Genres	From innovative avant-garde to conservative defence of tradition	Within and between literature, film, sport, music, science and academia	Rap sampling rock, sampling blues, sampling …
Individuals	From learning from others to earning from others	Wordsworth, Twain, Disney, Lennon and McCartney	File-sharers, new musicians, open source and other computer programmers and hackers

same is true when we look at the lives of 'great' literary figures and artists in other fields. The creative commons that nourished the young artist became a threat to the established artist seeking to capitalize on their success. Finally, in the music industry, blues artists and composers prosecute rock and pop artists, who have sought to sue rap artists for the supposed violation of their original creativity. What is claimed in one case to be the original being copied is itself, in other instances, said to have been copied from an earlier work.

In all four senses of becoming established ('getting old'), at the level of states, media sectors/companies, artists/authors, and field/genres, established positions lay claim to the past while the young lay claim to the right to develop, i.e. claim a right over the future. This struggle is presented in a language of property rights versus rights to develop (economically, culturally and/or in terms of expression). This language remains contested. Such disputes are not resolved at the level of legal semantics, but, rather at the level of competing constructions and contestations of interest.

Table 4.1 presents an outline of the four levels of action at which the transition from novice to established authority tends to involve attempts to effect closure around the creative process. At each level, in different ways the principle of sharing as a source of creativity is replaced by the principle of protection as a reward for creativity. At each level paradigm cases are highlighted of those whose early success was gained by the creative commons but whose later success saw them promoting intellectual protectionism. Yet each new generation witnesses resistance, whether this be developing countries setting the right to develop against the right to own ideas, new companies and industrial sectors whose innovations challenge old patterns of profit and protection, new genres that both poach and challenge the substance and form of previous works and conventions, or at the level of individual appropriations within genres, industries or states.

Conclusions: competition versus closure

For Marx the crisis tendency in capitalism lies in an economic dynamic that drives out the source of profit in the very act of pursuing it. Ever greater efficiency and competition drives down prices and if sales cannot be sustained this squeezes profits. File-sharing reduces marginal cost to next to nothing and makes every consumer a producer, thus increasing competition. Marx's fundamental weakness was in not taking his own advice. While pointing out the tendency for the rate of profit to fall in conditions of innovation and competition, he also pointed out the existence of counter tendencies. However, in thinking such counter tendencies were weaker than the main drive of capitalist competition, Marx underestimated the array of social closure mechanisms that would be set in place. These mechanisms are synonymous with the sociological critiques of Marx, and in essence represent the cultural, political and legal 'closures' imposed upon and required for the existence of 'free-markets' (so called). Closure is one sociological description of non-economically reductive devices used to regulate and integrate social life, and other sociologists have used other terms to capture the irreducibility of social life to unfettered economic competition. In this context I am less interested in the differences than in the fundamental sociological observation that cultural, political and legal 'closure' devices limit while also sustaining the possibility of capitalism. The history of intellectual property rights is the history of a particular set of closure mechanisms, set in place to enable and to regulate markets in ideas and their expression. Trades unions fight to effect closure around certain forms of work. Professional associations do the same for 'middle-class' work. Welfare states seek closure around constructed national communities. Property rights, and intellectual property rights as a related field, should also be understood in these terms. They are not natural, but constructions of interest. They express particular alliances and conflicts. They can only be understood through the history of their fabrication, not by recourse to universal discourses of rights or necessity.

5

Legal Genealogies

Introduction

The global framework for intellectual property rights highlights that globalization is as much about regulation as deregulation (Holmes 2003), but limitations also highlight contradictions. Diverse legal frameworks and the wide variation by which the same laws are interpreted in different jurisdictions are explored. Geographical variation and changing legal interpretations of property rights and infringement have significantly shaped the development of file-sharing technologies. Initially Napster offered a sharing service that required transfer through a central server and its legal demise was premised on its supposed 'active collusion'. This attack on active collusion promoted the development of new generations of software enabling direct exchange between users. Rulings in 2003 and 2004 upheld the Sony Ruling whereby technology providers were not liable for illegal use of systems with legitimate applications. This led prosecutors to focus on software users, which encouraged new programmes which sample from multiple sources to avoid individual liability. Just as legal threats led to new technology developments, so these technical developments and their uses encouraged new legal challenges to the Sony Ruling, now partially overturned in the United States. Since 2005 technology providers, in particular circumstances, can be held liable for users' actions. This provoked new softwares of evasion and exemption. Cat and mouse dynamics of law, technology and use condition the development of each in relation to the others.

Within Anglo-Saxon case law or in statute-based legal systems, lawyers seek to 'clarify' whether actions break the law. This of course assumes that the law is clear and consistent, such that acts are either lawful or not. This clarity and consistency may or may not exist. Laws change, laws differ between jurisdictions and laws are open to interpretation. Attempts to create a global legal framework for intellectual property rights protection run up against all three of these challenges. The practice of genealogy involves tracing backwards through time divergent and ever subdividing lines of ancestry, and very often involves selecting some lines and not tracing back others. In the context of mapping the emergence of a global IPR framework, the concept of genealogy is useful as it flags up both the diverse lines of ancestry that flow into the present as well as the tendency for such histories to be recounted selectively. Naming systems selectively record ancestry and, as such, slant genealogical trees, tending to highlight particular components that contribute to the present over others. The power to select which ancestors to highlight is the power to write history backwards. In the case of legal genealogies the current dominance of the United States is significant but the diversity of other legal histories and structures needs attention as this, in part, helps to explain the failure of attempts to enforce the US model across the world.

Michel Foucault (1977), drawing upon Nietzsche, used the concept of genealogy to highlight the way historical accounts always plot a path backwards from the present. This path is always a selective one focusing on the issues and events most relevant to present concerns and in accordance with current beliefs about the direction of history (usually a narrative of why 'we' are the logical outcome of developmental tendencies). Such histories render the present a quasi natural outcome of past events by ignoring the paths that started in the direction of alternatives. For Foucault, genealogy was a method for highlighting the contradictory histories of those elements of human life that are often seen to have no history at all (natural justice, sexuality, madness and family, for example). For him, genealogy sought to explain specific moments in time (the present or past periods) without reference to teleological outcomes or foundational origins. This chapter, following on from Chapter 4, seeks to maintain attention on the divergences and alternatives even while showing the processes and strategies at work to produce an integrated global intellectual property rights protection regime.

Technology and legality

Himanen's (2001) 'hacker ethic', a vocation-like orientation to tinker with technology to see how things can be modified and 'improved', is incorrectly equated in traditional media with 'cracking', breaking into computers or otherwise tampering in ways presented as malicious or inconsiderate (Jordan and Taylor 2004, Yar 2006, Wall 2007). Just as the word cyberspace shifted from the fiction of William Gibson (1984) in the 1980s to become a synonym for the Internet and web only in the 1990s, something Bruce Sterling (1993) attributes to the activism of John Perry Barlow, so the word hacker shifted its meaning. It is, therefore, worthwhile remembering that digital-compression and file-transfer protocols were developed in the commercial sector in the first instance. These technologies were not intrinsically anti-commercial or produced for criminal purposes. The original Napster service was closed not because of the intrinsic criminal character of the technology, rather the software's providers were directly party to users' exchange of copyrighted material yet unable to prevent it. It was legal to exchange un-copyrighted materials via Napster, or copyrighted material with the copyright holder's consent. Subsequent developments emerged to avoid legal liability for users' unlawful actions.

Chapter 3's history of Napster's demise, the rise of Kazaa and Morpheus whose software allowed users to exchange files independently of the software provider, then Gnutella which enabled users to exchange files and locate other users independently of the software provider, and more recently of Torrent services that enable downloading from a stream of uploaders such that no one contributor can be said to have provided the whole item, highlights the intimate relationship between technical change and law. Technology adapted to law, while the law sought to adapt to each new technology. Do providers develop software 'within' the law or does each new generation of software only seek to get around the law? Does this mean that such technologies are lawful, or the opposite – knowing attempts to enable and encourage infringement through the construction of a 'blind eye' to user infringement? Legislation such as the US Digital Millennium Copyright Act (1998) define as unlawful digital technologies that enable copyright violation but, as Chapter 3 noted, the courts in the USA have waxed and waned over technology providers' liability. This chapter will seek further to explore, across time and across the world, the tension between intention and consequence as it is played out in legal frameworks seeking to deal with technological innovation.

The US legal genealogy

The 2001 court decision to close Napster succeeded only in promoting new file-sharing software unburdened by the need to route exchanges through a central server. RIAA attempts to close down Grokster and Morpheus (and their protocol/programme provider StreamCast Networks) in 2003 through a case brought before the Ninth Circuit Court in Los Angeles failed on the grounds that, unlike Napster, these two systems did not involve the provider in the specific interactions between sharing peers. When presented with the claim from the RIAA lawyers that ninety per cent of files shared through these softwares were infringing copyright, judge Stephen Wilson observed that this still meant that such services had legal uses, and the question for him was whether the provider of a service with lawful uses could be held liable for the actions of its users. He concluded (as cited online in Delahunty 2005):

> Defendants distribute and support software, the users of which can and do choose to employ it for both lawful and unlawful ends … Grokster and StreamCast are not significantly different from companies that sell home video recorders or copy machines, both of which can be and are used to infringe copyrights.

Wilson upheld the 1984 decision of the US Supreme Court that the Sony Corporation was not liable for what users did with its Betamax video recorders, as legal uses did exist for a machine capable of copying television programmes (such as 'time switching' recording of programmes to watch at a later point) and, second, that Sony were not directly engaging or encouraging illegal uses of the machines they were selling (Savage and Healey 2004).

After the judgment on 25 April 2003, the recording industry alongside representatives of the US film industry sought to have the judgment overturned in the California Appeals Court in Pasadena. The Court agreed to hear the appeal at the start of 2004. The plaintiffs argued that file-sharing software providers were, through advertising revenues, profiting from the promotion of illegal activities even where they were not directly party to specific infringing actions. The defence claimed that to prohibit innovation on the grounds that a new technology could be used for illegal purposes would create a 'permission culture' (Lessig 2004) in which an act would have to gain legal status before being allowed, rather than being presumed innocent until proven guilty of any particular crime. The Appeal Court's judgment, announced on 19 August 2004, again found in favour of the defendants, upholding the Sony Ruling, and rejecting the claim that the providers of software that enables distributed peer-to-peer file-sharing can be held responsible for the actions of their users.

Again thwarted, the case was taken by the content industry's representatives to the Supreme Court in Washington DC in December 2004. The case began in March of 2005. On 27 June 2005 the Supreme Court found partially in favour of Metro-Goldwyn-Mayer in its action against Grokster and Morpheus. Initial concerns not to stifle innovation in the service of vested interests were in large measure overturned to the benefit of copyright holders, but with significant caveats.

> We hold that one who distributes a device with the object of promoting its use to infringe copyright, as shown by clear expression or other affirmative steps taken to foster infringement, is liable for the resulting acts of infringement by third parties. (Justice David Souter cited online in Delahunty 2005)

Does providing a file-sharing service when users know most of what will be exchanged through it infringes copyright constitute 'promoting infringement'? In Grokster's case, as with Kazaa (who's FastTrack software Grokster used – see Chapter 3), the 2005 judgment led to closure. Both retained an element of centrality in the way users located each other, even while sharing takes place independently. In Morpheus' case, having shifted from FastTrack to Gnutella, it was able to claim no knowledge of who was sharing what with whom, adding provisos requiring users to declare that they would act lawfully, and as such avoid closure. This is not to say users do accord with such declarations.

The 2005 Supreme Court ruling did not help content providers as it only encouraged entirely decentralized systems such as Gnutella and BitTorrent, the latter further fragmenting the process by uploading from multiple sources. The former Gnutella-distributed architecture is now the basis for the most popular file-sharing systems (such as LimeWire, Wildfire and Zeropaid). In consequence, the more significant judgments were the two earlier ones which upheld the Sony Ruling. As technical developments overtook the 2005 ruling the legal moves that flowed from the 2003 and 2004 decisions carried on apace, these being actions against individual file-sharers, in particular for uploading material for others to download. In the last four months of 2003, the RIAA began legal proceedings against 382 uploaders, with this figure rising to 914 by the end of February 2004 (David and Kirkhope 2004: 441). By July 2006 this figure had risen to 20,000 (Electronic Frontier Foundation 2006). In the year to January 2008 the RIAA had issued over four and a half thousand 'pre-litigation settlement letters' against students in over one hundred and fifty US universities and colleges (Bangeman 2008). Threats of legal action against universities and students in the US are an attempt to pursue targets that can be readily identified and pressured.

The first US jury trial against someone accused of uploading music turned into a hollow victory. The RIAA's successful prosecution of Jammie Thomas in October 2007 found the unemployed Native American single parent guilty of 24 counts of infringing copyright and – at over nine thousand dollars a time – liable for around a two hundred and twenty thousand dollars fine, which she appealed against. In May 2008, the presiding judge in the original case admitted incorrectly accepting RIAA claims that making these music files available via the Kazaa file-sharing system constituted dissemination when, in law, it only constitutes making them available. District Court Judge Michael Davis admitted that technically dissemination occurred only when these files were actually transferred and copied to another person's computer. The basis of the prosecution lay in this being done by MediaSentry, a company working for the RIAA. MediaSentry made copies of files Thomas had made available. Such a 'sting' tactic is not lawful, and this formed the basis of a retrial which concluded on 24 September 2008. 'Making available' was not 'dissemination' (Kravets 2008). On 18 June 2009 a federal jury found Thomas guilty of deception, raising the fine to $1.95m. Unable to pay Thomas may pay a $5000 settlement, appeal the decision, declare bankruptcy, challenge the fine on eighth amendment grounds of excessive and cruel punishment, or await changes in the law on punitive damages. Failure to make up-loaders pay, or to target software providers and

Internet Service Providers leaves copyright defenders targeting individual down-loaders, their worst case-scenario (Williams 2008). Pre-litigation threats have worked in thousands of cases. However, almost all such cases brought by the RIAA, including Jammie Thomas', have been against people using Kazaa or other systems reliant on older forms of sharing software, where it has been easy to trace who shared what with whom. Even if the RIAA does win the Thomas case, it would already have been too late, as most file-sharers have moved on to Gnutella or BitTorrent systems. Gnutella makes tracing interactions harder especially for pre-litigation demands issued on the basis of 'suspicious levels of use' not actual knowledge of what has been exchanged (see Chapter 7). BitTorrent 'tracker' sites have been heavily attacked legally for their directing of users to other user's files, such that these sites act as a central server, at least in locating sharers. This is similar to what Kazaa, Grokster and the original Morpheus were prosecuted for. While a myriad of such tracker sites have been closed, this has led to other sites gaining strength and to relocation to jurisdictions that do not deem such tracker services as unlawful. Tracker sites are only proxies, not actual central servers, so attacking them is rather like breaking up rhizomes only to propagate them further (Deleuze and Guattari 1987).

A curious case of international and inter-media comparison

What started in the USA has been applied across other jurisdictions with varying success for copyright defenders. The first example drawn on here follows the issue of defining the act of 'making available' and 'disseminating', but in a slightly different domain. Who is the importer in cases of parallel importing of informational goods? If I lend you a CD and you copy it, I make the material available but you are the one making the copy. If I make a copy of that CD and put it onto a computer such that others can choose to listen to it, the question remains open, legally, whether I am responsible for another person's copying. The Jammie Thomas case suggests not, but conflict continues. A comparable example is 'parallel importing' and the different interpretations of the practice within the European Union. The Hong Kong based company CD-Wow! was successfully prosecuted by the BPI in 2004 for 'anti-competitiveness' in selling CDs online at prices set in markets other than those where buyers lived. BPI members have the legal right to set differential prices in different markets, and parallel importing – the practice of selling goods in one market at prices set in another location – is illegal. How undercutting regional pricing monopolies can be called 'anti-competitiveness' remains unclear, but the BPI was successful in claiming that CD-Wow! acted as an importer in physically posting CDs to online ordering UK residents. Germany and France define the importer as the person making the request, and not the person posting the material – or, for that matter, the postal service that transported the goods (Mitchell 2004: 12).

As payment is sent electronically the goods become the property of the purchaser before sending. Importation is then the responsibility of the purchaser. While UK law views a person downloading child pornography, 'terrorist documents' or other unlawful material in the UK from abroad as 'importing'/'disseminating', the BPI found it easier to prosecute one supplier than many thousands of customers, and because it was able to win its case in court, CD-Wow! was required to pay the import duty on all its UK sales. Customers in other EU countries continue to benefit from CD-Wow!'s supposed 'anti-competitiveness' (David and Kirkhope 2004). In March 2007 the BPI again took CD-Wow! to the UK High Court, this time for breach of its earlier agreement not to send CDs to the UK without paying import duty (West 2007). At the end of May 2007 the BPI won its claim for £41 million in losses and costs; CD-Wow! went into receivership in August.

Legal interpretation of liability, whether in relation to importing or in making available and disseminating, is not built on consistency. Across jurisdictions and from issue to issue interpretations vary. The sociological determinants and consequences of such variations require attention. It is the sociological temptation to reduce such variations too quickly to predetermined socially structured interests. Latour's (2005) counterpoint, that such constructed conventions and their playing out in terms of what and where, and by how much profits can be generated, is crucial to the establishment, maintenance and modification of interests and the alliance of parties that come to believe that their interests are being best served in one way rather than another. How three EU countries interpreted the practice of CD-Wow! highlights this. Nevertheless, as Latour concedes (2005: 14), attention to the contingent construction of alliances should not lead us to ignore longstanding stabilities of interest. That sociologists might tend to lazy reliance on structural categories says something about the robustness of such categories. Otherwise, why would they make life so easy? The BPI's victory in this case highlights the power of vested interests, even if the bankruptcy of CD-Wow! only encouraged less targetable sources of music.

In parallel to this is the case of Jon Johansen, who was prosecuted for revealing the source code for DVD digital rights management and, thereby, offered the world a key to accessing otherwise protected material. Johansen was prosecuted in his native Norway three times, and acquitted each time on the basis that writing a programme capable of unlocking DVD encryption amounted to a mathematical solution to a puzzle rather than any actual theft. The DVDs he personally unlocked were his own, and under Norwegian and US law it is lawful to make copies of DVDs for personal use. Others who use the software Johansen helped to develop may also do so for legitimate reasons (BBC News 2003 – web source). Providing a technical solution is not a conscious incitement to criminality. Johansen's case will be discussed in greater detail in Chapter 6.

Comparative legal frameworks and interpretations

No rule contains within itself the rules of its own application (Wittgenstein 1953). While the WTO and WIPO have persuaded signatory states to harmonize domestic copyright law with their principles (see Chapter 3), this has not prevented a myriad of divergent practices and interpretations springing up when such laws are set against existing state legislation and parallel international laws regarding human rights, privacy and freedom of expression. Different states have reacted differently, leaving a confused patchwork in the implementation of what Holmes (2003) calls 'immaterial imperialism', the globalization of US led IP enforcement. A number of examples are set out below. The first concerns the relationship between the UK's Copyright, Designs and Patents Act (1988) (hereafter CDPA) and the more recent European Convention on Human Rights (adopted into UK law in 1998 as the Human Rights Act) (Danay 2005) (hereafter ECHR and HRA respectively). Freedom of expression under the ECHR clashes with the rights under the CDPA of copyright holders to prohibit the circulation of protected material. While P2P file-sharing does constitute 'infringement' under the CDPA, at the same time the restrictions placed upon individuals by the CDPA preventing them from expressing and communicating their preferences to others (through non-commercial sharing) is not a restriction 'necessary in a democratic society' and hence a violation of free expression prohibited under the ECHR.

> As a result, should this statutory restriction [on the communicating of copyrighted material] be impugned in a UK courtroom in the context of P2P music file-sharing, such a court may be under an obligation to exculpate infringing parties under the 'public interest' defence or to make a declaration of incompatibility under the HRA. (Daney 2005: 60)

Much effort has been made to smooth over these differences in the years since 2005. Clive Thompson (2005) reported on the use of BitTorrent by the Swedish site The Pirate Bay. He cited the comment of one of its 'pseudonymous owners, Anakata', who wrote to one US film company:

> As you may or may not be aware, Sweden is not a state in the United States of America. Sweden is a country in Northern Europe [and] US law does not apply here … It is the opinion of us and our lawyers that you are fucking morons. (Thompson 2005)

In 2005 Swedish file-sharers could claim protection from prosecution on the grounds that under then Swedish law attempts to identify their file-sharing activities violated personal privacy. The more recent history of The Pirate Bay (discussed below), and the subsequent implementation of new European Union directives on Copyright and Personal Data into various EU state laws, including Sweden's, highlights ongoing conflict. Comparison with parallel developments in the United States also verifies, but only to a point, Anakata's assertion that Sweden is not a state in the United States. Within months of Thompson's article Sweden had passed into domestic law the European Union Copyright Directive. This contained a strengthened definition of infringement which included making available and not just distribution. As such, the EU was in advance of the United States in expanding the definition of infringement, even while the filtering down to national laws has blunted this edge.

Okechukwu Benjamin Vincents (2007) compares the US and EU legal balance between copyright protection and data protection. While the United States had a more aggressive legal attitude to overriding personal privacy in identifying copyright infringement, recent EU legislation has sought to match and even surpass this. However, where first amendment rights to privacy have been used to limit aggressive intrusion in the United States, the EU Personal Data Directive has been more powerfully deployed limiting the rights of copyright holders to demand from Internet Service Providers (hereafter ISPs) the real world identities of those account holders suspected of copyright infringing file-sharing. US copyright holders and their representatives have issued subpoenas on ISPs to gain account holders' personal details for the purpose of pre-litigation demands, even while such actions are now more heavily regulated than at the start of the millennium. In the EU similar attempts have been undertaken, but with far more limited success. Refusal to hand over such information has been more common in Europe. In Sweden, and a number of other EU states, the law requires that copyright holders who suspect an Internet account of being used to traffic copyright violating material hand over what information they have to the police, who then need to investigate and, if a case can be made, take out a criminal prosecution. While the EU Personal Data Directive, and its state specific manifestations, do allow for privacy to be overruled without consent where such information relates to the upholding of other aspects of the law, the more limited freedom for non-law enforcement agencies to demand such data in the EU has led to far fewer prosecutions, even while not protecting The Pirate Bay from legal assault by the proxies of US corporations. For all the differences between US and EU law in letter and interpretation, the obligations of all these states to introduce into domestic law stronger electronic copyright enforcement, as set out by the WTO's 1996 TRIPS treaty and the WIPO's 1996 Copyright Treaty (WCT), provides a strong note of continuity. Whether the differences are more significant than the similarities is in part determined by the interpreters' location and commitments.

Prasad and Agarwala (2008) make the interesting point that in 'Cyburbia' the notion of the nation-state as regulative frame has fallen into 'legislative obsolescence', not at the level of individual prosecutions, but in the minds of hundreds of millions of P2P file-sharers. Prasad and Agarwala premise their argument on Alan Greenspan's 1983 suggestions that economic incentive is premised upon property rights, and that intellectual property rights are property rights like any other. They seek 'solutions' to what copyright holders consider to be the problem. They observe that legal action against individual users is costly and ineffective.

> The P2P network provider is generally sued, under the doctrine of secondary infringement, for it is difficult to sue individual infringers as it is not worth the 'time' and 'money' to pursue a multitude of individual infringers, who download copyrighted content without any sense of obligation to pay. (Prasad and Agarwala 2008: 3)

They seek legal justification for the more expedient targeting of software providers, driving the cork in at the narrowest point. They refer to programmers as network providers. This is misleading as users constitute the network. The software used enables social networks on existing physical infrastructure. Prasad and Agarwala reject the conventional interpretation of the Sony Ruling, the defence of dual use, and the US Supreme Court judgment in 2005 that secondary infringement requires active knowledge and incitement. They cite 'the staple article of commerce doctrine'. This holds that liability cannot be assigned to a provider if a product's 'common use' is lawful. As file-sharing networks carry more infringing traffic than compliant material the doctrine cannot apply and providers should be held liable. This interpretation of law actively seeks to find a solution on behalf of copyright holders and to stop 'the evil designs of pirates' (2008: 11). The authors call for a 'positive "copyright policy"' (2008: 11), permanently updating the laws in all countries to contain each new technical innovation and thereby uphold copyright. This is in effect what WIPO seeks to provide. The authors, rather like WIPO, claim to offer impartial technical advice. Starting from the premise that intellectual property is property like any other, and that property rights are the fundamental foundation of economic life is not impartiality at all. The next three state-specific cases show that assumptions about property rights, copyright and 'piracy' cannot be generalized, even when all three states are signatories to the same international treaties on intellectual property.

National specifics from three cases: Canada, UK and Hong Kong

Isabella Alexander (2007) parallels the UK *Gowers' Review of Intellectual Property* (2006) with the 1906 Copyright Act, itself the result of a decade of campaigning against unlicensed sheet music. Alexander parallels today's The Pirate Bay and James Frederick Willets, who at his trial for distributing unlicensed sheet music in 1904, described himself as 'King of the Pirates'. Using 'Piracy' to describe file-sharing is misleading. UK law distinguishes bootlegs (unauthorized releases of material not available in authorized form), counterfeits (replicas of authorized releases) and pirated material (reproductions under different labels and packaging). All three are commercial crimes. File-sharing would only constitute piracy if it was commercially motivated or caused direct financial loss. Early twentieth century campaigns portrayed hawkers of unlicensed sheet music as mainly of the criminal classes and alien Jews, matching today's FACT campaigning to associate counterfeit DVD sales with illegal immigrants (Alexander 2007: 649). Today such counterfeiting is routinely equated with piracy and with file-sharing. The street hawkers of 1900 were in business. Today's file-sharers are not. Where sheet music had been produced illegally by lithography by criminal gangs for profit, the file-sharer today who downloads a copyrighted file is not committing a criminal offence. It is rather a civil infringement of copyright, and the person making the file available is not the one making the copy. It would be necessary in UK law to show how making that file available actually caused one less legal sale. Where the BPI, FACT and other copyright defenders have sought to label file-sharing as piracy, pure and simple, it is not enough to show that a person has been uploading material, i.e. making it available. Rather, it is necessary to show either commercial gain and/or specific damage to claim 'piracy'.

The Canadian Supreme Court in 2004 decided that to determine whether or not a copyright infringement had been committed in Canada it was insufficient to show simply that the material had been uploaded in Canada, or that the material was hosted by an ISP based in Canada. Rather, with one dissenting judge, the Supreme Court ruled that the appropriate basis for making a judgment was what it called the 'real and substantial connection test'. While the WIPO Copyright Treaty (1996) covers both distribution and making available, the interpretation of this into Canadian law distinguishes the former as sufficient to constitute a crime, while the latter, as in the UK and the USA, is at worst civil infringement, if that. As such, to bring a criminal prosecution in the Canadian courts it was deemed necessary to demonstrate that a real and substantial proportion of the uploading, storage and downloading took place in Canada. This is not to say that prosecutions could not be brought across multiple jurisdictions, only that a criminal prosecution could not be brought in Canada simply for any one of these three actions alone (Leong and Saw 2007).

Given that the RIAA has been most successful in pre-litigation demands for compensation – demands that require identification of personal data from ISPs – and that such data is much harder to gain outside the United States, this path is a limited one. The limited success in having single parts of the process designated as sufficient for criminal prosecution has also limited the non-civil route of calling in the police.

Chan Nai-Ming was the first person in Hong Kong to go to prison for enabling others to download copyrighted material. While many others have been convicted for commercial scale counterfeiting, Chan Nai-Ming was sentenced to three months imprisonment for uploading films onto the Internet and encouraging others to download them (Weinstein and Wild 2007). The court's judgment was based on the defendant's active invitation to others to download films from his website. Both the original trial magistrate and subsequent appeals court judge agreed the defendant had actively promoted the downloading of specific copyrighted material. As such, it was decided that the defendant was not merely making available but also guilty of distribution. Weinstein and Wild conclude that many have been prosecuted successfully worldwide, but a small number of convictions have not significantly reduced file-sharing. They suggest that content industries invest more in the development of digital rights management technologies. As will be shown in Chapter 6, DRM encryption and surveillance technologies present as many obstacles as have the legal avenues described here.

The emperor's new sword

Using the law to prevent file-sharing, and to have the law strengthened and harmonized for this purpose, has had at best mixed results. In the United States lobby groups, and in particular the RIAA and the MPAA, have fought a number of high profile cases after the closure of Napster in 2001. From District Court, to Appeal Court and finally to the Supreme Court these bodies eventually succeeded in rendering software providers liable for the uses made of such systems, but only where providers are actively and knowingly promoting infringement. This conclusion, in 2005, was a rather toothless victory, and legal actions against users, initiated in 2003 have remained the main legal line of assault. Whilst tens of thousands of pre-litigation demands for compensation have been successfully pursued, when the issue has come to court it has failed and created very bad publicity. Such a strategy has also been limited within the European Union, where data-protection legislation has made it hard to access user details for civil prosecutions. Where European Union directives have undermined the distinction between making available and distribution, in practice the distinction is maintained in national courts. The distinction also continues to present an obstacle to those undertaking civil prosecutions in North America. Other jurisdictions have witnessed related obstacles. The lobbying of content industry representatives has produced significant developments in legal harmonisation, at the level of overarching directives and treaties, but at the level of individual state law making and enforcement, putting such words into copyright enforcement practice has been more divergent.

Brian Holmes (2003) refers to the 'immaterial imperialism' of WIPO's programme of copyright harmonization and extension. Holmes is scathing in relation to the double standards applied by a body forceful in upholding payment to copyright holders but so very lax in ensuring money is reasonably distributed to the artists copyright holders claim to represent. Holmes (like May (2007a)- see chapter three) highlights the influence wielded by WIPO in framing national legislation. However, even where states have undertaken to conform to WIPO managed treaty obligations as well as to WTO TRIPS obligations, and have framed national legislation in line with WIPO 'technical' guidance, how such laws are then interpreted in nationally specific courts, and how citizens then understand and behave in relation to file-sharing, cannot be simply read off the pages of such global guidance notes.

As Weinstein and Wild (2007) suggest, a handful of convictions for file-sharing (as distinct from commercial counterfeiting), and even fewer custodial sentences, has made no significant difference to the ongoing practice, except to encourage more covert forms of sharing. Even the tens of thousands of pre-litigation demands for compensation have done little to diminish the practice of file-sharing, whether in the United States where most of these demands have been made or elsewhere. While Chan Nai-Ming's conviction for wilfully promoting infringement will put people off making such manifest, active invitations, his use of BitTorrent in itself meant anyone downloading the files he made available, would have in fact gained packets of data from a large number of uploaders and not solely from Chan Nai-Ming. New services make it harder to suggest that someone making files available was actively promoting their distribution. Given the active promotion of anonymity softwares and networks by the United States in relation to dissenting voices in China, and especially Hong Kong, it would be hard to suggest that the providers of such technologies were not protected by the principle of dual use.

While the next chapter will show such anonymity is no more secure in principle than the encryption on offer to protect copyright holders, in practice the sheer volume of traffic combined with legal limits to access and the added time required to decode encrypted material will make prevention no more likely by technical means than by legal ones. Holmes (2003) refers to WIPO and its harmonization programme as the 'Emperor's new sword', but this sword is more like a fishing net used to catch plankton. Holmes is right to point to the failure of the copyright system in rewarding artists. He gives the example of the composers' rights organization in France, where he lives. Of its 100,000 members, only 2,500 can vote, as eligibility to vote requires that a member earn more than 5,000 euros per year from royalties. Only 300 members actually make a living wage from royalties. Similar figures have been suggested for other territories (see Albini 1994 and Love 2000). This chapter points to a symmetry. For all the rhetoric about enforcement in the new 'immaterial imperialism' the groups claiming to represent media industries, who themselves claim to represent artists, are about as ineffectual in preventing infringement as they are in passing on the benefits of paying customers to the companies and artists they claim to defend.

More on the Sony Ruling

The ongoing conflict between US-led film and recording companies and the Swedish file-sharing 'tracker' The Pirate Bay continues to highlight competing interpretations of liability in relation to technology. While a US Supreme Court Ruling in 2005 did find technology providers potentially liable for criminal use, if such provision was actively and knowingly encouraging criminal usage, this ruling has remained open to significant interpretation. Interpretation polarized in Sweden where The Pirate Bay's 'tracker' service, pointing users to the routes to accessing material in BitTorrent format, is said by its critics to be actively and knowingly encouraging and enabling infringement. Defenders say that Swedish law does not prohibit tracker services and that The Pirate Bay is a file-sharing community service enabling the sharing of various material, much of which is open source and uncopyrighted. The organizers of The Pirate Bay are actively opposed to copyright protection and proclaim this, but they deny directly distributing or making available copyrighted material. Rather the service allows users to identify what others have on their computers and to share them. Again, the BitTorrent format means that downloaders are given a composite copy made up of elements from all those offering that file. The separation of the tracker service from the individual users, and the distributed character of the upload make it difficult for prosecutors successfully to identify who is breaking what laws. The Pirate Bay operates using open-source software. It is not possible to prosecute the software provider in the way one would prosecute a commercial company with a legal personality. Liability is again distributed in a new way. Prosecutions generated publicity and usage surged. The service became a symbol of Swedish independence and non-subordination either to the European Union or to the United States. A police raid in 2006 saw large protests. After a three-day suspension The Pirate Bay doubled its user base. Claims made that the raid was a government response to threats of trade sanctions via the WTO circulated and further politicized what came to call itself a 'movement'. Prior to 2006 and afterwards, The Pirate Bay has participated in and adopted open source technical innovations to increase the distributed character of its practice and that of the community of users it is a part of.

BitTorrent based services developed and continue to develop in direct relation to the legal frames put in place to regulate them. In June 2008 Sweden passed into law a new security measure enabling the police to monitor all Internet traffic in the name of national security. The response has been the development and application of new forms of encryption to slow down and hamper such 'wire-tapping'. Legal action against The Pirate Bay was brought under this new law by the RIAA and the MPAA almost immediately and this trial concluded on 17 April 2009 (see page 72). Rather, as with Napster, success in closing The Pirate Bay would be likely to be highly counterproductive as numerous alternatives based in less regulated locations are waiting in the wings. However, failure to close down this powerful symbol of file-sharing culture would also be damaging for those bringing the actions.

Conclusions

The legal genealogy of file-sharing has seen keen conflict over the definition of law, crime and evasion/compliance. At what point does the evasion of criminal liability become law abiding behaviour as opposed to a deliberate avoidance or wilful neglect? The meanings of such terms as direct involvement, encouragement and knowledge have been points of legal dispute between parties for whom differences in the interpretation of such terms are the difference between legal protection and criminal liability. Such interpretations have no natural or correct foundations. The doctrine of 'dual use' advantages sharers, while the doctrine of 'common use' would benefit protectionists. The law becomes a space in which sides fight it out, even if such battles in part influence the formation of the sides.

At another level of legal dispute the question of liability circulates around the concept of the legal actor said to be knowing and active. From centralized systems have emerged decentralized systems, and from these have emerged distributed ones. At each stage technologies have moved to alter the conditions of action and knowledge on the part of the supplier. Now, with the development of fragmented Torrent forms of sharing the person uploading is not aware of what elements of a file they are contributing, while Torrent trackers are turning to encryption to hamper wire-tapping. This also decreases their awareness of what is being shared, just as postal workers can't read letters in envelopes. At the same time the development of open-source programmes for Torrent sharing, and with the circulation of open source versions of now bankrupt former commercial sharing programmes (such as Kazaa ++) the attempt to crack down on identifiable legal actors is encouraging the emergence of distributed network or virtual actors that cannot be easily pinned down. The closure of CD-Wow! only made space for less locatable network actors, and the closure of Torrent tracker sites has served only to encourage their emergence in more open network spaces.

On 17 April 2009, a Swedish court sentenced four founders of The Pirate Bay, Fredirk Neij, Gotfrid Svartholm Varg, Peter Sunde Kolmisoppi and Carl Lundstroem to one year each in prison. They were ordered to pay the equivalent of over two million UK pounds in damages. They were convicted of 'breaching copyright law' in encouraging file-sharing and making available copyrighted material, though the more severe charge of 'assisting copyright infringement' (distribution) was dropped. The four immediately appealed the verdict, and still evade actual imprisonment. Ironically, the conviction and sentence was leaked onto the internet before it was read out to the accused, no doubt an infringement of data-protection though not copyright as such. The Pirate Bay did not cease operations, having long since distributed its hosting activities to a range of other jurisdictions. The conviction did increase the profile of the geek pirate heroes, and does not appear to have diminished the practices they advocated. Writing on his Twitter Kolmisoppi suggested at the time of the verdict: 'Even if I had the money, I would have burnt it rather than pay'. Later, in an online press conference he reiterated his point: 'Even if I had the money I would rather burn everything I owned, and I wouldn't even give them the ashes.' If the four do ever end up in jail it will be interesting to see whether the Swedish authorities try to deny them access to the Internet. However unlikely such a custodial sentence is it is hard to image that the recording and film industry lobby groups who brought the action look forward to the prospect of such an online martyrdom with any relish, though failure in securing the conviction would have been no less problematic for them.

The concept of 'piracy' is ambiguous. The recording industry lobby routinely uses the term to label file-sharers, but the category in law typically requires a demonstration of commercial intent and/or commercial consequences (i.e. a direct loss). While it is often proposed that recent declines in recorded music revenues are the result of file-sharing, this is a speculative claim which cannot be demonstrated and it can just as easily be shown that those who file-share also buy more recorded music than those people who don't. The argument over causation can run and run. Interpretive flexibility in this area (David and Kirkhope 2004) leaves the question open, even if all sides are happy to jump to their preferred conclusions. The term piracy then is problematic, both as long as there is no commercial gain, and as long as the assertion of loss remains speculative. One might conclude that attempts to paint file-sharers as pirates are endeavouring to lump sharers with professional criminals and thereby damage their reputations. The Pirate Bay's appropriation of such a lawless buccaneer status accorded to file-sharers by their critics illustrates how such a strategy may not have the effect it may have been designed to achieve. A T-Shirt reads 'Internet Piracy is Killing the Recording Industry', and then below an image of a cassette with crossed bones is written 'And It's Fun'! As Chapter 7 will show, such cultural subversions are no less problematic for copyright defenders as have been the legal and technical inversions and resistances outlined in this chapter and in Chapter 6.

The distinction between making something available and distributing or dissemination is as ambiguous in the virtual domain as is that between importing and exporting. The way such disputes have been conducted is based on the strength or otherwise of lobbies rather than upon coherent arguments. The same has been true in interpretations of the relative balance of human rights, freedom of expression, data protection, personal privacy and copyright protections. Where an act takes place, such that it would be covered by the laws of one country rather than another, and even when most countries have signed up to harmonization of their respective laws, remains an issue: in terms of whether a prosecution is brought, whether it is a civil or a criminal case, which parties are brought to account, and how the law is then enacted.

All sides claim their actions and their interpretation of law are based on an idea of fairness that others should be able to agree with. Yet different constructions of what is fair highlight the problematic notion of natural justice (as discussed in Chapter 4). The forceful attempt to push forward a strong copyright agenda through the courts appears to have had little impact on the incidence of file-sharing, and at the same time has undermined the legitimacy of the recording industry in the eyes of their primary target audience. Whether such a loss of legitimacy can be seen to serve the interests of the record companies whose representatives pursue such actions is an interesting question, one they no doubt ask themselves on a regular basis. That such a strategy gives prominence and power, not to mention large amounts of money to pursue this legal pathway, to these representatives may explain their emphasis upon its maintenance. Given the relative failure of this line of action, a fruitful line of future research would be to study the relationship between the record industry and their legal representatives. The loss of legitimacy that has arisen from current strategies may make it hard for such companies to win back their target audience, and hence force further reliance upon legal and technical enforcement. Alternatively, new business models may emerge that bypass such additional layers of mediation and protection and utilize new-media in different ways which combine effective communication with legitimized forms of payment that audiences are, therefore, willing to pay for.

6

Technical Mythologies and Security Risks

- Introduction
- The surveillance society?
- From Foucault to Deleuze: from discipline towards control
- The panoptic sort?
- Cybercrime
- Surveillance – a limited hope for the recording industry
- Attempts at anonymity
- Counter surveillance
- The birth of digital rights management
- Hard and soft DRM today
- The problem with format capture: closure versus exposure
- Managing the horror
- The dialectic of technology
- Conclusions

Introduction

Given the legal limitations described in Chapter 5, and the role played by digital recording, compression and transmission technologies in the practice of peer-to-peer file-sharing, much attention has been given by the recording industry in recent years to technical barriers to copyright infringement. At the same time, technical solutions continue to be developed to address the problem of getting caught, getting prosecuted or getting stopped. Previous chapters have given much attention to the legal liability of technology providers. This chapter will focus on surveillance and encryption capabilities, identification and protection in the digital realm. Classic, contemporary and cyber-specific accounts of surveillance will be examined. The tendency to provide theoretical closure on such constructions will be challenged. The attempt to develop and apply surveillance on the Internet will be taken as illustrative of the limitations of such 'Big Brother' 'Social Science Fiction' (Bogard 1996). Even the choice of who to 'spy' on creates unintended consequences that can cancel out intended outcomes. Just as surveillance has limits, so too have attempts to create technical barriers to such infringement of privacy.

Claiming the ability to know and the ability not to be known goes to the heart of power in the information (informed/informer) society, but remains always partial and contested. Perfect information and perfect privacy are myths that serve social ends but, as ends contradict, so these ends tend to suspend the capacity of technology to resolve conflict one way or the other. This is highlighted in the case of counter surveillance. If surveillance can catch file-sharers, then it can also be used to catch those lurking in cyberspace looking to catch file-sharers. The application and adaptation of technologies serves diverse ends so it does not determine outcomes. Surveillance and encryption cut both ways. If record companies could successfully encrypt digital recordings, so too could file-sharers encrypt their shared files and hence prevent detection. The question would then be whether one side or the other could access non-encrypted versions of this data by non-Internet means, whether in the form of playing encrypted music into a separate recording device or seizing suspected file-sharers' personal computers, hard discs and access codes. However, such perfect digital encryption does not exist. All attempts by the recording industry to produce secure digital rights management systems have failed. Digital broadcasting, DRM free digital players and the proliferation of open-source de-encryption and sharing software have rendered the dream of a technical prohibition on copyright infringing file-sharing, merely that – a dream. Nevertheless, in managing the horror of such a realization, the myth of technical solutions offers some hope for the continuation of business as usual. If enough people can be persuaded that they can't file-share, or that if they do they will be caught, then a market can be maintained – if only by deception and the threat of coercion. The main problem with this approach is that the record industry's core target audience, or at least what was once that core, is the group least likely to be taken in by such mythologies. This theme is developed in Chapter 7.

The surveillance society?

Anxieties about a supposed surveillance society precede the network society. Yet what has been for some an increasingly regulated and monitored society, has for others been one of increased anonymity and deregulation. Classical sociological accounts of modern urban, industrial and capitalist society were divided over this question. While for Durkheim (1984a[1893], 1984b[1898]) increased organic integration within an industrial society created greater interdependency and a potentially greater regard for the differences that were necessary for the efficient operation of the social whole, so it also allowed for a loss of social integration and regulation. The restraining force of community observation declined in mobile, urban conditions. This sense of moral deregulation and anonymity is echoed in Tönnies's (1988) account of transition from small-scale community to large-scale society. Eighteenth and nineteenth century fiction, from Trollope (1994[1875]), Austen (1990[1813]),

Rousseau (1987[1761]) and Mary Shelley (1998[1818]) to Goethe (1989[1774], 2005[1808]), Dickens (2007[1854]), Hugo (1998[1862]), Dostoyevsky (2003[1866]), Eliot (2008[1871–2]), Zola (2008[1885]) and Hardy (2007[1895]) echo this perceived breakdown of moral communities of small-scale prying eyes with the development of large-scale, rapidly changing modern living. It is precisely this respectable fear of moral decline in the absence of traditional oversight – of family, church and neighbours – that led to the development of distinctively modern forms of regulation and surveillance by increasingly ambitious states. While traditional fears about moral dislocation and the dangerous classes continued in both mass society models of sociology (Robert Michels 1962, Vilfredo Pareto 1991, Alexis de Tocqueville 2008[1856], Jose Ortega Y Gasset 1930) and in literature (Canetti 2005[1935], Bulgakov 2007), this mythology was joined by another anxiety: that of the increasingly powerful state using ever more powerful means of manipulation and control in the interest of totalitarian governance. While social scientists, including Weber (1991: 196–239), Lukács (1972), Michels and Pareto, as well as the early Frankfurt scholars (Adorno and Horkheimer 1979[1944], Adorno et al. 1964[1950]) focused upon the material and ideological dominance of the modern state relative to its fragmented populations, the fiction of Zimiatin (1987), Huxley (1932) and Orwell (1949) paid greater attention to the power of surveillance in the management of modern regimes.

Of all the literature, academic or fictional, on the topic of surveillance, it is Orwell's *Nineteen Eighty-Four*, and its totalitarian leader, Big Brother, that has come to dominate both intellectual and popular visions of state information gathering on its population. While highlighting the potential of a totalitarian regime to maintain total knowledge and, therefore, power over its citizens, such a vision can also create the very thing it seeks to condemn – a population which believes that it is permanently being watched and hence controlled. Sociologists have taken the bad news from Robert Michels' iron law of oligarchy while ignoring what Michels called the iron law of democracy (1962: 406). Similarly, the temptation to embrace the shock value of totalizing accounts of surveillance, those that suggest an all embracing net of information about each of us, in literature and in academic accounts, is all too often succumbed to. This chapter provides a more balanced account of surveillance and encryption, counter surveillance and anonymity within digital domains.

From Foucault to Deleuze: from discipline towards control

Attendance to the surveillance at the heart of modern societies has been most forcefully established in the work of Michel Foucault. His studies of both the character of modern disciplinary regimes of knowledge (1971[1961], 1976[1963], 1980[1976], 1991[1975]) and of the historical breaks that characterized the move from earlier forms of power/knowledge to modern forms (1974[1966], 2002[1969]) challenged conventional accounts of progress, narratives of historical liberation from a repressive past to contemporary freedom. Modern forms of disciplinary power constitute and administer social order and social subjects in new, modern and 'scientific' ways. The very notion of being set free in modern societies is based upon expert claims to know both who 'you' really are, and what is really 'good for you'. Such claims to knowledge require and justify expertise and the authority to deploy techniques that will bring about the desired freedom from ignorance, madness, pathology or perversion. For Foucault, modern societies are governed by experts, and expertise is governed by disciplines. Core disciplines in such societies are medicine, psychiatry/psychology, penology/criminology, the state science of statistics, as well as pedagogy. Other social sciences take up a range of auxiliary positions. Core disciplines succeed in disciplining a field of practice, and such fields command spaces of practice. The rise of the modern hospital, asylum, prison and school are bound up with the rise to power of scientific disciplines claiming the authority to govern such spaces in the interests of those within them and for the rest of society. Each discipline claims a knowledge that warrants their authority to practice, a science to found their engineering. Modern 'epistemic regimes' (knowledge-based systems of order) found their authority claims in 'scientific method', a combination of observation, control and analysis. Each field became a laboratory where such scientifically controlled observation and analysis can be carried out. Abbeys, leper colonies and dungeons, with their particular epistemic frameworks, were replaced with spaces of empirical examination – of surveillance. For Foucault, the need to show that such regimes were scientific in their gaining systematic empirical observation came first, and whether or not this actually benefited the inmate was always secondary. Early hospitals allowed medical training but killed far more patients than were cured, and the health-based rationale for placing lots of sick people in one place remains dubious. Modern asylums and prisons contained and allowed for greater observation, but also showed very limited success.

Each discipline regulated an institution and each institutional space regulated a field of human deviance. Systematic surveillance enabled knowledge, and knowledge supposedly enabled each discipline to know best how to deal with such deviance. The medical gaze (1976), the new psychiatric confessional (1971) and the panoptic prison design (1991[1975]) fused science with technologies of containment and 'correction'. Social science, at the heart of modern society, represented a key method of social control. Far from setting people free, modern societies produced new methods of managing and manipulating those that deviate from its conventions. Moving beyond the regulated spaces of disciplinary institutions, surveillance operates across the wider society by means of what Foucault calls bio-power/biopolitics (2003), the attempt by states to regulate and constitute whole populations by means of disciplines such as public health, civic design, social policy and elements of the biosciences.

The rise of new forms of personal expertise – around diet, exercise, life-coaching, home improvement, relationship management, career development, etc. (Giddens 1992) – is in part a continuation of Foucault's account of modern society. Many such experts claim scientific status. However, such experts (with the exception of some nutritionists) have not gained state recognition as professions and rarely manage to affect the kinds of closure gained by medicine and psychiatry. Neither do they have the right to enforce actions such as is the case in prisons and schools. These forms of counter expertise are market governed rather than state sanctioned. Also, such fields often reject science and rather claim charismatic and/or traditional forms of authority (Weber 1958). In these senses, they manifest the decline of modern forms of surveillance, at least in Foucault's sense. Since the 1960s social and biomedical sciences have lost much authority relative to notions of personal choice and market decision making. Foucault's own work, as part of the so-called anti-psychiatry movement, helped in challenging the role of closed institutional fields, and encouraged more market-based, community-centred strategies at least in relation to social and psychiatric services. In relation to hospitals and prisons things have been far more mixed, with resources often increasing even as belief in their beneficial effects has declined. Hospitals and schools have witnessed intense conflict between professionals and managers over who should govern such spaces. The claim to authority by means of professional knowledge, gained from scientific surveillance and justified by the reformation of deviant individuals and groups, has come under increasing challenge.

Gilles Deleuze (1992) suggests we are moving away from what Foucault called a disciplinary society of scientific epistemic power, towards a 'society of control'. Here, access and denial are based exclusively on financial criteria and, therefore, surveillance shifts to the monitoring and management of monetary storage and circulation. Accounts and accounting become the key epistemic frames for the surveillance of individuals and organizations. Auditing the past and actuarially calculating the future become the key instruments of expert judgement. Exchanges, valuations and the ability to pay require constant, moment-by-moment global surveillance, as does the protection of accounts, assets and intellectual property. Credit reference agencies become the gatekeepers regulating access to housing, transport, travel, health and education. Such agencies have access to personal data that is prohibited under data protection legislation to almost anybody else, including scientific and social scientific researchers. Others compile and integrate data on purchases, earnings and benefits. When credit can determine health, education and housing allocation more readily than can the judgements of medics, teachers and/or civic planners, Foucault's experts are not the gatekeepers they might have once thought themselves to be. For Deleuze, the surveillance society has moved from the professional gaze to the profit margin, the ongoing colonization by capitalism of new and emerging domains of social life that would not have sustained commodification in the past.

The panoptic sort?

If the network society has been characterized, by Castells (1996), as the increasingly pervasive integration of information technologies of storage, transmission and analysis, the issue of what information is collected in the first place determines whether such a network society is best described as an informed society or as an informer society. Much debate has hinged upon the positive and negative implications of such a pervasive networking of information, and over who does and should have access to such data. David Lyon analyses 'social sorting' (2001). Using Foucault's account of the modern Benthamite prison model, designed to enable all prisoners to be viewed at all times or at least to maintain the impression of such observation, and applying it beyond Foucault's account of closed disciplinary institutions, Lyon examines the ways in which information is gathered on a minute by minute basis every time we use a swipe card, credit/debit/loyalty card, library card, pin number, username and/or password. In addition, personal data about earnings, benefits, tax payments, residence, electoral details, criminal convictions, credit checks, applications for employment, memberships of clubs, gyms and other groups, subscriptions for charities, trades unions, entertainments, mobile phone and computer usage are all stored. Health records along with records of sensitive health checks such as for HIV and genetic screenings that might effect insurance and other entitlements, are all held on systems that cannot be relied upon never to disclose information. Social sorting refers to the increasing integration of such information, providing greater scope for organizations to profile individuals virtually for financial, legal, health, promotional, employment, insurance or entitlement purposes. Lyon presents a picture of an increasingly powerful surveillance society in which the all-seeing panoptic gaze is ever extended and under which the individual is increasingly known and controlled. Acknowledging scope for resistance (2002), Lyon highlights the potential for power.

Lyon's work and the framework from which it operates, have been doubly criticized: first for overstating the downward direction by which such information travels, and second for being unclear as to who is coordinating all this information, if anyone. David Mason et al.'s studies (2001, 2002a, 2002b – see Chapter 2) of 'surveillance capable' information gathering computer systems in workplace settings problematized 'apriorism' by which it is assumed that technologies with surveillance capability will always be used to serve the interests of dominant groups. They argue that technologies create opportunities for all actively engaged parties within a situation, and to assume one side will always be the recipient of the strategies of another is to assume such a group is totally passive. They also argue that the assumption of dispute needs to be challenged, as to assume prior sides within any situation is to ignore the way new technical possibilities can be deployed and used in ways that change the 'rules of the game'. While this ethnomethodological emphasis upon the construction of interests by actors in the course of interactions parallels the actor network approach of Latour (2005), Mason et al. do not specifically ally themselves to this approach, rather emphasizing the results of their empirical ethnography. Ethnography is best placed to identify such fluidity, and less well able to identify longer lasting patterns that are often called structures.

Roy Coleman's (2004) structural account of surveillance technologies in Liverpool, however, also highlights the difficulty of identifying a priori structural groups and interests at work in disputes over CCTV cameras and urban governance strategies. While Coleman seeks to show how city centre regeneration in Liverpool has been driven by capitalist interests, the construction of such an interest in his account highlights how various factions and clusters of actors move in and out of alliance as different techniques and strategies are tried out. Coleman refers to 'the ruling class', 'the dominant class fraction', 'local and corporate elites', 'the power elite', etc. in the attempt to pin down a moving target – one in which the interests of local residents, street traders, retail and related workers, consumers, local shop owners, local elected representatives, representatives of large chains, and developers move in and out of alignment in relation to the use of CCTV cameras to 'reclaim the streets'. Where Mason et al. emphasize the fluidity of constructed interests, Coleman retains structural categories in his attempt to explain strategies in terms of prior interests, even while their fluidity highlights the difficulty of so doing. Each approach highlights the scope and limits of the other. Surveillance technologies are not all-powerful systems of one-directional control, as is suggested by Lyon's conception of the panoptic sort. However, neither are they the passive reflection of the play of prior interests or, third, a field of action in which such interests and identities are created from scratch.

Cybercrime

The full range, scope and debate around cybercrime is beyond the parameters of this book. Others (Yar 2006 and Wall 2007) provide insightful outlines of a field that covers both traditional crimes now aided by electronic means and new forms of crime specifically centred on the appropriation or disruption of computer content. The issue of interest here is the relationship between cyberspace, crime, surveillance and anonymity. Just as Foucault detailed the rise of new forms of surveillance alongside the rise of new forms of anonymous urban living, so new forms of cyber surveillance emerge in relation to the greater potential for anonymous interactions in that realm. If electronic surveillance worked it could be used to detect file-sharers or detection agencies looking for them. If electronic encryption worked it could be used by record companies or file-sharers seeking to prevent record companies identifying files being shared. Just as digitalization and file compression were developed for commercial purposes and then used to decommodify, so surveillance and encryption technologies developed for the purpose of upholding copyright can be used for the opposite purpose. This contradiction is less significant to the extent that strong surveillance and strong encryption have not been successfully developed. However, the rhetoric of both surveillance and digital rights management are routinely deployed in disputes.

If a system of encryption for the protection of digital files that could not be broken into electronically were to exist, this would prevent direct copying of music, such as from a CD onto a computer file. However, all existing music currently in circulation beyond such protection could then be encrypted by file-sharers for sharing among themselves without the risk of detection. This scenario assumes both record companies and file-sharers could maintain the distribution of the 'keys' required to de-encrypt such data (whether from CDs or from computer files) only to those they could trust not to 'leak' them. Such leakage would enable either copying or prosecution. The likelihood of maintaining such real world security, even if virtual security was maintained, is remote. With file-sharing networks and commercial sales the aim is to make material available to a wide audience, whether for community sharing or for making profits. The impact of passing information only to people one could rely upon not to leak keys would be the collapse of either market or community. As yet not achieved, and in practice highly damaging, the prospect of technical encryption serves only a rhetorical purpose, as Chapter 7 will investigate further.

Surveillance – a limited hope for the recording industry

The use of Internet surveillance to identify file-sharers has produced many thousands of pre-litigation demands and a few trials. The majority of the former have taken place in the United States. Initial file-sharing software made it fairly easy to locate users as they had to interact through the software provider. However, the very thing that made it easy to locate users made finding them unnecessary. If record companies could show what file-sharers were sharing by looking at the software provider's archives, then this was sufficient grounds for claiming the provider was actively participating in the actions taking place. Such providers could be shut down. The original Napster was doubly surveillance friendly, as users had to both locate others and exchange files through its central server. Closing Napster for these reasons meant actually tracing its users was superfluous once the system they used was stopped. In the case of Kazaa and Morpheus, exchanges were distributed but primarily locating other users still required going through the software provider. Initially both providers evaded prosecution on the grounds that they did not directly participate in exchanges, and a wave of pre-litigation actions took place based on data gathered by using the software to locate uploaders, then to download from them. In 2005, US courts found partially in favour of the entertainment industry and declared systems such as Kazaa and the original Morpheus liable when users located each other via their servers. Most US pre-litigation demands and prosecutions had been against people using Kazaa, as it was relatively easy to locate them. When Kazaa declared bankruptcy at the end of 2005, this victory made the business of surveillance much harder as users switched to fully distributed systems.

Having created an environment that encouraged the use of less detectable systems of identification and exchange, surveillance turned to the monitoring of Internet Service Providers. If file-sharers were being encouraged to use systems that were ever more distributed in nature, and which tended to be available from sites outside jurisdictions keen to enforce strong IP protection, far easier to use the Internet traffic logs of their ISPs.

UK government consultation papers have put forward the suggestion that Internet Service Providers monitor Internet use for copyright infringing file-sharing activities, with the prospect of then prohibiting access to those found guilty of infringement (BBC News 2008a). Darren Waters (the BBCs technology editor) pointed out: 'If the law were enacted it would turn ISPs, like BT, Tiscali and Virgin, into a proactive net police force'. BBC News (2008b) quoted a spokesman for the UK Internet Service Providers Association (ISPA) who pointed to the 'technical' limitations of making ISPs responsible for monitoring file-sharing activities. While traffic through ISPs is recorded and stored, and while file-sharing activity typically uses large amounts of transmission bandwidth and so might be distinguished from other traffic, a large amount of perfectly legal downloading occurs. Simply going on fishing expeditions whenever a user appears to be taking up higher than average bandwidth is not something ISPs are keen to do as it would damage their market share. It would also represent a huge financial burden. If such a law were introduced it would certainly further increase the use of encryption and a likely switch of ISPs. The unintended consequence of closing down more visible systems of monitoring has been to make the business of surveillance far harder. If, instead of requiring ISPs to do the actual searching, the law required ISPs to hand over usage details of users that record companies suspect of infringement, this would infringe data protection and human rights legislation. The police are not keen to take on the task for logistical reasons.

Attempts at anonymity

The term 'Darknet' gained popularity when a group of Microsoft engineers used the concept to describe sharing networks on the Internet that were not generally accessible to those not already within that community of sharers (Biddle et al. 2002). The term had previously been used to refer to secure networks unattached to the early Internet, but now refers to 'friend to friend' (F2F) networks operating through the Internet. Typically, such networks remain small but FreeNet has the capacity to manage millions of 'friends', each connected by means of intermediate 'friends' or 'hosts'. Various versions have been developed and the 2008 version increases the scope for large numbers of users to distribute storage space between them, and to route exchanges through large numbers of hosts to evade easy detection. Requests for files are fed through an array of proxy servers (David and Kirkhope 2004). This extension of distribution has also been adopted by the latest versions of file-sharing software, such as Torrent systems and Gnutella based systems like Morpheus. Such systems claim to defend anonymity but the larger the networks become, the greater the scope for intrusion by surveillance agencies working for copyright holders; however, the distributed nature of uploading and downloading makes it very much more difficult to trace individual acts of infringement, to locate these in specific jurisdictions to enable prosecution, or to target the software provider (which is open source and constantly evolving). Darknets are not entirely blacked out, and while small F2F networks reduce scope for intrusion by false 'friends', they increase the scope for identification of individuals once a community is infiltrated. Larger F2F networks reverse this situation, with greater scope for infiltration but less chance of identification when such breaches take place.

Another popular approach to achieving anonymity is through the encryption of files within peer-to-peer networks. Many popular file-sharing softwares, such as LimeWire and uTorrent currently offer forms of encryption. In response to Swedish legislation in 2008, to enable the police to access all electronic traffic 'for national security', the BitTorrent tracker service The Pirate Bay has sought to promote more generic forms of encryption for all Internet traffic. At present encrypted files attract attention but their generic rolling out would reduce this. While encryption software makes such examination difficult, all forms of encryption are vulnerable either in the codes used to construct them or in the transmission of keys. Encryption does not offer a watertight solution, but increased use would increase the difficulty of knowing what to try and break into. The claim by The Pirate Bay to be on the brink of rolling out a new and powerful form of encryption is similar to repeated claims by the recording industry that they are about to do the same. While such claims all turned out to be exaggerated their 'rhetorical' effect can be significant. Harry Collins and Trevor Pinch (1998) discuss how Patriot missiles 'succeeded' in the 1991 Gulf War over Kuwait. It was unlikely that these missiles hit incoming enemy missiles. Rather, in enabling the Israeli military and government to persuade its population that they were being protected, at a time when Saddam Hussein was seeking to goad Israel into the conflict, the Israelis were able not to retaliate. Had the Israelis launched air strikes against Iraq, this may well have forced Saudi Arabia to withhold support for the US-led war being launched from their country against another predominantly Muslim state. While the Patriots may not have shot down any 'Scuds', their rhetorical value helped win the military conflict.

Other strategies for maintaining anonymity are less sophisticated and simply rely on revealing less about yourself. Options include accessing the Internet using a laptop computer in an Internet café, using an unsecured Internet connection, or a Wi-Fi network such as are being increasingly rolled out across whole university campuses and cities. Such points of access make it almost impossible to be traced. Another strategy is to split your computer's hard disk, or to have replacement hard disks, or to upload material to remote locations other than your own computer, and in jurisdictions not accessible to copyright holders. Numerous other forms of evasion exist. None is absolutely secure (Wang 2004, Electronic Freedom Foundation 2006).

Counter surveillance

The possibility of surveillance by record companies and their proxy agents may deter. On the other hand, file-sharers can counter monitor the infiltration of file-sharing networks by such proxies. Banerjee et al. (2006) researched the effect of 'blocklists', software ad-on files that identify and block connection to IP addresses on file-sharing networks that are identified as collecting information from other network members. Banerjee et al. note that ninety-nine and a half per cent of addresses listed on the blocklists they tested had no direct link with the content industry and that the vast majority were relatively passive. The research team ran a number of Internet accounts and searched for music using a range of file-sharing networks. Blocklists are long, and over ninety days in 2006 the incidence of connecting with such a site if one did not use the blocklist filter rose to one hundred per cent. It appears inevitable that over time an unprotected file-sharer will connect with a site identified as problematic and potentially engaged in anti-P2P surveillance.

Banerjee et al. then blocked the five most prevalent blocklisted 'ranges' (a set of IP addressed stacked together as part of the same organization's overall address). These five ranges represented ninety-four per cent of the active surveillance and blocking them reduced the chance of connecting to a blocklisted site to one per cent. Further filtering beyond this top five radically reduced the likelihood of connection. With only half of one per cent of blocklisted addresses linked directly to content industries, it is likely that many anonymous addresses (BOGON IPs) are hidden proxies. However, the ability of file-sharers to enact counter surveillance, and the possibility of combining this with greater distribution of content, Darknet features and encryption, means surveillance is a two-way street – as much part of one side's ability to attack as it is of the other side's ability to defend itself.

Finally, Banerjee et al. note that surveillance is five times more intense on the US west coast than it is on the US east coast, and that US levels of surveillance are far more intense than those in Europe, which are, in turn, far higher than in Asia. Awareness of the intensity of such actions, by means of counter surveillance, enables file-sharers to route accordingly. Of course, this cat and mouse game moves back and forth, and anti-P2P actors will seek to take note of the counter surveillance in conducting their business. The use of BOGON IPs for example, where identities are rendered anonymous (at least superficially) is one way to evade counter surveillance. Such invisibility is only partial. It just makes identification slower, hindering systematic attempts to 'manage the horror' one way or the other.

The birth of digital rights management

Knowledge underpins human action. Culture and capital are the two key constructions of knowledge today (Gouldner 1976). Gouldner suggested culture is knowledge generalized, while capital is knowledge privatized. The paradox of the network society is that the very means by which knowledge can be 'universalized' today are also the means by which such knowledge can be further restricted. In computing the development of the personal computer and the floppy disk made software increasingly open to free circulation. The advent of the Internet increased this insecurity. The history of musical recording follows the same path, from relative difficulty to extreme ease of copying and circulating. As access became easier, so greater attention has been placed upon control, otherwise known as digital rights management.

Zeitlyn et al. (1999) highlighted the paradox in relation to academic libraries in London. The mid 1990s saw the widespread introduction of online public access catalogues (OPACs). The result, in London, was that students and staff at over one hundred institutions were able, at the touch of a button, to see what each others' libraries held. Online visibility and geographical proximity saw an increased foot flow in the libraries of the better resourced institutions, leading to an expressed anxiety that the exchange of catalogue information was being used asymmetrically, with those from poorer institutions making more use of wealthier institutions' resources. This led to the introduction of electronic swipe cards on the doors of the more prestigious institutions' libraries. The advent of greater surveillance (knowing what was out there) led to new forms of closure (knowing who wants to get in and out, and only allowing some to do so).

David (1996) notes that the provision of online journal services to academic libraries on a subscription basis meant that newer institutions, with limited back catalogues of journals, were able, with current subscriptions, to gain access to both the back catalogue of such journals as well as an array of journals also published by the publisher they have a subscription with. Consortia of such publishers now make full content access to their material available where, only ten years ago, general access to electronic abstracts and indexing services was considered revolutionary. The downside of such services for end-users is, of course, that content remains in the hands of the copyright holder, whereas in the past, paper copies would have been located in each institution and would remain there irrespective of whether or not a journal's subscription was maintained. Today, if an institution cancels a subscription, what then happens to its access rights to the materials that were visible due to previous payments? Access rights in such institutionally based subscription services usually require institutional usernames and passwords. While anxieties have been expressed about the leaky character of such security measures, collection from large institutions such as universities is relatively unproblematic. Single download, format and/or machine specific, and time limited forms of electronic control are used to regulate the circulation of electronic material (such as music files and software) to individual users, but this is more problematic.

Whether in the form of a swipe card on the door, regulating who gets in to see the books on the shelves, a user name and password that enables access to online services, a unique registration code for downloading a copy of a programme or data-file from a network or disk onto a computer, or in gaining time-limited (pay per view) access to a service, all these forms of regulation of open access are commonly referred to as digital rights management (DRM).

Hard and soft DRM today

Christopher May (2007b: 67) distinguishes two ideal typical forms of digital rights management. The first (as described above) restricts access and prevents copying. The second embeds monitoring software into products to allow users' computers to be scanned. May refers to these as 'hard' and 'soft' DRM respectively. The former seeks technically to prevent what may or may not constitute infringement/fair-use, and thereby closes down the knowledge commons. The latter can damage users' computers and also represents a major infringement of privacy. May points out that for all the technical fanfare regarding hard DRM, they can all be overridden, and have required legal back up to ban programmes that override them, via the WIPO Copyright Treaty, the DMCA in the US and the EU and UK Copyright Acts. That all 'hard' DRM strategies have failed renders them merely as variants of 'soft' DRM, not preventing, but rather monitoring. 'Thus, norms of consumption will remain a key element for any rights-oriented content or software business' (May 2007b: 88). Legal threats, knowledge, technical competence, resources and attitude determine behaviour, not technical impossibility. May argues that technical know how remains a key limiting factor, as does access to software and a fear of legal action. Despite weak cultural inhibitions to file-sharing, May suggests: 'However, peer-to-peer file transfer is not only slow and time-consuming, for many it is beyond their technical capabilities and therefore the threat remains more potential than actual' (2007b: 103). While this may be true for older segments of the population, in advanced countries at least, for the music industry's core demographic age groups, this is not the case. May believes ease of access and poor technical ability explain the rise of legal download services, but by his own figures (one billion downloads in the three years to 2006) iTunes sold approximately the same number of files as were available on file-sharing networks on any typical day in that year.

By the end of the same year, according to Steve Jobs (2007), the number of downloads from iTunes had reached two billion. However, Jobs notes that with the sale of over ninety million iPods by the same date, the two billion would work out at around twenty-two iTunes for every iPod. The most popular iPod could carry around one thousand music files. Research at Apple indicated that most iPods were almost full most of the time. Jobs concluded that, as iPods would not play DRM protected files made available by other commercial suppliers such as Sony and Virgin, the vast majority of files held on iPods are non-DRM protected files – the vast majority of these coming from peer-to-peer networks. In April 2008 *Wired Magazine* reported that iTunes downloads had reached three billion, with one hundred and ten million iPods and iPhones sold. This meant that the average device by then contained legal downloads equivalent to three per cent of its capacity (Kravets 2008a). Kravets also notes that iTunes controls eighty per cent of the market in legal downloads. Eighty per cent of all legal downloads make up three per cent of the total capacity of the Apple devices sold. Given that there are hundreds of millions of non-Apple MP3 players and computers able to play non-DRM protected files, and with these players being unable (until 2008) to play iTunes' downloads, it is unlikely that commercial downloading represented more than one per cent of digital music files in 2008.

May's suggestion that as DRM breaching software violates the law it is generally unavailable is questionable. His own evidence suggests otherwise. He cites the case of Dmitry Sklyarov (2007b: 85) who was arrested on a visit to the US for developing DRM bypassing software to override Adobe eBook restrictions. Sklyarov was released without charge when Adobe asked that the case be set aside due to the bad publicity it was generating. The case of Jon Johansen also highlights the limited ability to enforce draconian interpretations of legal restrictions on the development and circulation of encryption breaking codes. Johansen's defence was that he developed the software code to override the copy inhibiting encryption on DVDs simply to make copies of his own discs for personal use (which is legal). Placing a mathematical code on the Internet was not unlawful either, he claimed. Both claims were eventually upheld by the courts in Norway. As such, the hard line interpretation of the WIPO Copyright Treaty, the DMCA and the 2005 judgments of the US Supreme Court were not complied with. The cases of Sklyarov and Johansen suggest the law still cleaves closer to the 1984 Sony Ruling. As such, de-encrypting software is lawful, available and does not require most people to understand it as files made available have already been de-encrypted. Prosecutions against developers have failed and as these are non-commercial providers and in free circulation, there is no target to go after in the courts once the technical lock-breaker is released.

May rightly suggests that DRM, soft and hard, has put many people off using commercial products which embed them. This may well have encouraged people to use copyright infringing services that do not carry such malware. This sits at odds with claims that users prefer the ease and safety of legal services. If such services embed malware on your computer to survey your online activities, and potentially damage your hard drive while interfering with other software and violating your privacy, they are hardly safe or easy. May points to iTunes' and Sony's use of hard DRM, but since 2007, both have stopped doing so. For all the advantage Apple gained by only allowing iTunes to play on its iPod MP4 playing platform, the simple fact that this inhibited those with other players from using its service limited its sales. It is the largest legal download site, but was still dwarfed by restriction-free P2P services. It was only the existence of such unrestricted services that persuaded the major record labels to allow Apple to sell downloads in the first place, and Apple's agreement to use DRM was a compromise with the majors which Steve Jobs was always keen to abandon.

DRM does not work technically. If it was hoped its threat would persuade people not to file-share, this has also failed. May notes that with the introduction of greater surveillance, the recorded incidence of file-sharing appeared to decline marginally. At least highly publicized campaigns of legal actions have seen immediate dips in the use of those services being targeted. Whether this is due to increased lawfulness or a decline in the use of services that are easy to monitor is hard to prove. Earlier campaigns simply encouraged migration to less visible services whose use was not then being monitored. Once this service became a target, measures of its use would be increased and the cycle would begin again.

The problem with format capture: closure versus exposure

The ability to profit from copyright is not simply in the ability to capture content and prevent others from gaining access to it. To lock away content would be as profit inhibiting as to let it circulate freely. Those who seek to profit from copyright require a combination of circulation and control. The advent of the iTunes downloading service is a case in point. As May (2007b) points out, the major record labels worked together to see off the threat of digital audio tape by jointly refusing to release any music on DAT. In the case of file-sharing, the widespread circulation of music through copyright infringing services, and the existence of MP3 players to listen to it on, meant such a closure strategy was not available. Record companies were resistant to licensing the sale of their music through a third party, but as their content was already in circulation, it was preferable to work with a copyright upholding actor like iTunes. Initially iTunes agreed to use DRM to prevent iTunes being played on machines other than the iPod they were downloaded onto. However, Apple's MP4 player, the iPod, did not have such electronic inhibitors. Competing with unrestricted players the iPod would have died at birth if it had restricted itself to playing only material from iTunes. Surveys by Apple (Jobs 2007) show that well over ninety per cent of music held on iPods are non-commercial file-sharing downloads. With only two per cent of iPod capacity being filled with iTunes, the remainder must be made up of content from CDs burnt onto individual iPods in what is referred to as format switching (the equivalent of time shifting using a video recorder). By 2008, the iTunes service had established itself as the dominant supplier of legal downloads, and any record company whose work was not being made available through it would have been marginalized. Apple was, therefore, able to lift its DRM restrictions and the record companies were in no position to resist.

Jobs (2007) noted that while requiring iTunes to develop the FairPlay DRM system to protect their content, the record labels sold DRM-free CDs. He argued that his company's sale of two billion protected downloads was dwarfed by the sale of twenty billion unprotected CDs in the same period. Jobs's claim was that his business was being inhibited by such protection, especially when he was losing sales from users of other MP3 and MP4 players; users of other download services unable to put these on to his iPods; and from those able to get free content from the Internet via unprotected CDs uploaded on to P2P networks. EMI was the first to withdraw its DRM from digital sales, including via iTunes, in April 2007 (BBC News 2007). Universal Music made the same move just after EMI. Time Warner announced in December 2007 that it would begin selling DRM-free music downloads from its catalogue via Amazon, while Sony BMG was the last of the big four to abandon DRM in early 2008 (Holahan 2008).

Something only alluded to in Jobs's (2007) announcement of his view that DRM was redundant, was that Apple's FairPlay DRM system had been broken anyway. Jon Johansen, on the pretext that he had a dislike for closed systems, had broken the source code that prevented iTunes from being played on other machines (Levine 2006). Repeated patches and updates had been routed around and, as such, iTunes's claim to have DRM in place was increasingly untrue.

The abandonment of DRM reflects the contradictory position faced by record companies and online distributors: wanting, at the same time, to control their product and to gain maximum circulation for it. Even if the record companies had managed to impose a uniform and functioning DRM system on their CDs and downloads, it would have been necessary to avoid all airplay on digital radio to prevent their music reaching its audience in a format they could record without paying for it. If it were not for the fact that all DRM systems have been broken anyway, perhaps locking down digital radio would have been the next logical step, but as 'time-shifting' technologies in video recording are lawful it is likely that such a legal and technical strategy would have been no more successful than the previous routes have been.

Managing the horror

Steve Woolgar (1988) refers coming to terms with and seeking to limit the consequences of the inability to provide absolute foundations in the production of scientific knowledge as 'managing the horror'. His concern is with the rhetoric of damage limitation rather than with explanations of why some stories carry the day and others do not. In the context of technologies, such as digitally recorded music, the commercial and the shared, the horror lies in the inability to generate 'technical solutions' to social confrontations. The music industry has sought various means to secure their position as monopoly supplier of recorded music. In the context of peer-to-peer file-sharing providing for free what they would seek to charge for, the attempt to produce technical locks to secure their legal property rights has been a priority. Yet all attempts to provide such security have failed. This might suggest an intrinsic technical limitation: that locks are always intrinsically insecure. Yet, while partially correct, the assumption that locks are physically inferior to the force brought to bear to break them assumes an inevitability that is not justified. That all locks have been cracked in this domain reflects the willingness of many at the cutting edge of computing to devote themselves to the act of breaking down barriers to the free flow of information. That Apple's FairPlay was reverse engineered so very easily, as was its DVD equivalent, highlights the vulnerability of even the largest corporate research and development budgets when faced with a hacker culture and a global Internet file-sharing community prepared to defend and celebrate the actions of those programmers willing and able to perform the next great leap forward – and to make it available to the world. Nevertheless, it should not be assumed that file-sharers have the monopoly on innovation and success. Just as grand claims regarding surveillance and encryption on the part of the music industry serve to 'manage the horror' rather than cure it, so claims by file-sharing providers such as The Pirate Bay to be on the brink of introducing blanket encryption for the whole Internet represents rhetorical management of the horror of detection and prosecution, rather than an actual watertight technical solution to the threat. Of course, as Collins and Pinch (1998) point out, rhetorical management can bring about the desired outcome just as well as any physical force. Whether or not the various sides to the dispute over file-sharing have convinced the rest of society, and in particular the key demographic categories of the population who traditionally bought most recorded music, becomes the key battleground. The music industry has been decidedly unsuccessful in persuading their core audience that they cannot get a cheaper and better service from peer-to-peer services relative to commercial ones. With falling sales leading to reduced prices, many still go out and pay for what they could get for free. The combination of legal, technical and cultural prohibitions is having some effect.

The dialectic of technology

Alvin Gouldner (1976) refers to the dialectic of technology as the potential for emancipation and domination within any technical artefact. Technology has no necessary consequences but is rather taken up, used and modified in the conduct of various practices and conflicts, which during their course may well challenge and change the positions, identities, investments and interests of parties to such relations. A false dialectic of technology hinges on whether technology is neutral or infused with the character of its social origins. Both sides of this debate hold some truth. The formation of artefacts carries traces of the goals of their originators but this does not determine use, especially as different users will modify the technology in ways that reflect their own intentions, even while such intentions may be themselves influenced by beliefs held about the potential of the new artefacts and how they are being used by others. Grint and Woolgar (1997) and Latour (2005) suspend the distinction between technical and social networks. They emphasize the intrinsic fusion of each with the other, such that social interests and technical functions can never be teased out as separate categories. Castells (1996) draws attention to how technological developments gain some autonomy such that they rebound with a force seemingly from outside the existing everyday world. These two positions are closer together than might appear. Castells is not suggesting technology is autonomous from society, only that the technology field is not reducible to other domains of social interaction. The social domain is itself divided into various competing and collaborating groups, the boundaries of which are in some ways opened up by new technical affordances but which also play a part in encouraging some possibilities over others. Kirkpatrick's application of Feenberg's 'dual aspect theory' (discussed in Chapter 2) can usefully be applied here in overcoming either/or constructions of technological impact and/or social shaping, while attention to the use and counter use of similar artefacts, as described in this chapter, also helps overcome the view that technology has either no significance or necessary effects.

Lewis Mumford's (1934) *Technics and Civilization* charts the rise of the European machine age from the mechanical clocks and the printing presses of the late medieval to early modern 'eotechnic' period to the 'paleotechnic' Faustian age of coal, steam, Newtonian physics, capitalism, urban concentration and the industrial factory; with its subordination of all organic life to power, efficiency and logical order. In this work Mumford perceives a dialectical tension between the mechanization of life within rational technical systems and the potentially liberating power of technology in relation to both ignorance and want. He envisaged the emergence of a third 'neotechnic' stage of development based on electricity (1934: 221–4) and communications technology (1934: 239–41) that would afford a return to life and work on a human scale, even if this possible application would have to be fought for in the face of ongoing forces of concentration and control.

Mumford's later work was more pessimistic about technology. Both volumes of his *The Myth of the Machine* (1967 and 1971) set 'the megamachine' and its cult of 'homo faber' against a rather elliptical playful spirit of 'homo ludens'. Ancient Egypt's human megamachine without machines, the systematic organization of slaves by priestly engineers for the glory of death and the sun god Ra finds itself reincarnated in the US/Soviet megamachines of the cold but total war, and their 'sun god', the atom bomb. By this time Mumford had lost his earlier belief in the potential of the new technologies of electrical power and information to enable a neotechnic return to life on a human scale, condemning computers as the ultimate extensions of the megamachine's surveillance system – the all-seeing omnicomputer eye of Ra. It is remarkable, therefore, to note the very dialectic of 'authoritarian and democratic technics' (1964) that Mumford was so much a partisan within, is so very forcefully manifested today in the one technology he rejected as being monolithic. The very computer network set up by the cold war 'Organisation Man/Eichmanns' (1971: 276–8), in their bunkers/pentagons, to immunize themselves from the consequences of the horrors they were programmed and willing to unleash, now affords the greatest liberation of communication in human history.

The ancient megamachines were brought down by new humane prophets – Abraham, Buddha, Hesiod, Lao-Tzu, Jesus and Muhammad – who condemned the cults of power, only for the sun god to rise again after Copernicus reset the sun at the centre and sent man spinning from the centre of the universe towards X (Mumford 1956, discussed in Miller 1989). The Internet is not a Dionysian anti-hero in mythic combat with today's megamachine. However, it certainly affords the practices of those who would resist centralized power in the name of human freedom. Mumford might well have approved, although if Jonah had simply sent the people of Nineveh an email from inside the belly of the whale Mumford might have felt cheated. We will have to work hard to avoid the negative and to realize the positive potential of our situation. Technology will not set us free. However, neither is it bound to enslave us. Mumford saw himself very much as a Jonah figure (Miller 1989: xiii–xviii), predicting the worst in the hope that it might thereby be avoided. In highlighting the beneficial affordances of the Internet in promoting decentralized communication and in sharing culture, this book seeks to redress the balance; highlighting the positive potential in the hope that it might thereby be achieved.

Conclusions

William Bogard's (1996) 'simulation of surveillance' captures the mythic character of technical solutions to social conflicts. Bogard calls his approach 'social science fiction', a study of the fantasy life of technocracy, the computer's dream of perfect information, only of course the dreamers are the technocrats who make the claims not the machines they make claims about. Today's anxieties about the immoral character of anonymous social interactions are not new; neither are the fears of its counterpoint, the rise of surveillance and control. The contemporary simulation of surveillance combines both fears into a vision of loss and return, such that people are persuaded that they are both prone to deviance but also being watched to keep them on the straight and narrow. Belief in the need to be watched and that you are being watched combine to simulate regulation. People who believe they are being watched behave themselves better than people who are being watched but don't know it. Literary and social scientific accounts of surveillance can be seen as performing a useful role in maintaining social control. Jonah here becomes a self-fulfilling prophet.

However, the computer's dream is dialectical, fostering both the belief in perfect information and that of perfect anonymity. The simulation of surveillance has its opposite, the simulation of encryption. Persuaded that they are not being watched, people behave as though they were anonymous – and in such numbers as to make such anonymity in many respects 'true'. This technical dialectic of surveillance and encryption is accompanied by a second, between the attempt to protect intellectual property while applying surveillance to those seeking to infringe IP, and the attempt to preserve a public sphere of freely circulating information while at the same time protecting such action from the surveillance set up to catch those doing so. The former dialectic operates on both sides of the latter – copyright holders and file-sharers using both encryption and surveillance, or at least the simulation of each, to forward their goals and practices.

Claims that technology can lock up informational goods and ensure copyright or anonymity are unsustainable. Compact discs, DVDs and commercial download services have all either abandoned the use of encryption-based forms of digital rights management or the systems used have been rendered toothless by a global network of hackers. The research and development departments of the worlds most powerful and advanced media and IT corporations have been turned over, often in a matter of days, whenever they release a new, revised or patched version of digital encryption into the hands of a network of amateurish geeks and playful informational anarchists. Claims that file-sharing networks can provide watertight encryption is equally questionable. Systems such as FreeNet, other services that use 'Darknet' techniques and The Pirate Bay's blanket encryption for the whole Internet may make life harder for those seeking to catch file-sharers, but there can never be total encryption as long as keys are distributed, and as long as sufficient time and effort are directed towards breaking into encrypted files.

Corporate surveillance and file-sharing community counter surveillance play off against each other. Attempts to embed software into users' computers when they download files is something that happens on file-sharing networks and when downloading from commercial sites. Both sides have drawn attention to the damage done to users' computers through the unwitting importing of spyware, malware and cookies. While early file-sharing services actively added such trackers, this is no longer common and the risk now comes from what other file-sharers might be adding to uploaded files. Commercial actors have been more active in adding such spyware themselves, but have run into considerable legal difficulty in so doing. As such, the claim – coming from each side – that the use of the other will damage your computer has an element of truth. The claim that commercial services are technically cleaner and safer is not true, so the suggestion that users choose between cost and security/ease of use is not correct. However, if some people are persuaded that this is the case, then the rhetoric of the content industries is having an effect; of course if users file-share because they fear the spyware being added to their computers by commercial providers more, then the opposite is true.

Technology is as much the problem as it is the solution. Just as technical solutions have fallen back on legal protections, such as the criminalization of counter technologies that evade encryption, so these legal protections themselves require cultural legitimacy. The cases of Jon Johansen and Dmitry Sklyarov highlight the inability of corporations to pursue hard-line interpretations of the law when to do so would cause significant bad publicity. To circulate informational goods in the absence of legitimacy and a strong basis of trust with those with whom you are exchanging, relying only on the existence of locks and threats is impossible. Legal threats are not enough either. The failure of cultural legitimacy is addressed in the next chapter.

7

Media Management

Introduction

Jessica Litman (1991) argues popular constructions of copyright rarely coincide with the actuality of copyright law. Authors and artists draw heavily upon the works of others. All lie between the fabricated romantic self-made artist with no debts and the accountant with receipts in hand. Creativity requires a degree of forgetting and all creative artists 'infringe' to one degree or another. Creative artists and publics alike, therefore, construct a myth of copyright in line with the reality of creative rather than legal practice. This myth is of something between a patent office and a censor, checking for plagiarism before assigning copyrights, such that the creative commons rules until artists formally seek legal protection. Litman points out that while copyright lawyers and scholars imagine creativity to be in some fashion fostered by rational calculations based on an understanding of the law, artists are not so motivated precisely to the degree that they do not know what the law actually entails. Artists create myths that reflect their own reality. Lawyers do likewise. This chapter explores myths being promoted by record and film companies and the counter myths set against them. As Litman's work would predict, artists and the public seem largely unconvinced. Not only that but, as Debbie Halbert (2005) suggests, resistance to the myths of copyright and patent being fostered by corporate lobbies is linking together into 'webs of dialogue' within movements of 'counter-globalization'.

The limitations of legal and technical forms of property rights protection mean that much of the success or failure of corporate attempts to prevent copyright infringing file-sharing lies in the ability to convince those liable to file-share that they will be caught, that it is technically impossible, and/or that it is wrong on ethical or cultural grounds. This has more to do with mass-media management than with the legal and technical realities of new-media. This chapter examines the attempts to manage media representation of both file-sharing and the attempts to regulate it. The attempt to link intellectual property rights violation with international terrorism is taken as one case study. This case highlights the process by which meanings of particular events and actions can be inverted by conflicting parties within a dispute. Attempts to stem copyright infringement in one realm (CD and DVD piracy) came to legitimize copyright infringement in another (file-sharing). File-sharers, through web-based discussion boards and blogs, inverted the claim that piracy funds terrorism. The claims about the pervasive nature of pirated material meant the only responsible action was file-sharing which, as no money was involved, ensured no funds got into the wrong hands. As well as discussing this inversion of mainstream media claims through new-media forms of communication, mainstream media claims are also examined in more detail. The attempt to link piracy and international terrorism involves numerous deceptive claims and associations. The pervasive presence of such stories requires an examination of the public relations work of the entertainments industry (Poster 2006), their representatives and campaign organizations, even while the reception of such stories remains open to a much wider range of influences and constructions. Other attempts to represent file-sharing as a moral threat to society have involved the claim that file-sharing is associated with illegal drugs, poor academic scholarship and criminality more generally. The generic category of 'piracy' is used to associate file-sharing with organized crime and with illegal immigration. Largely unsuccessful, and often highly counterproductive, attempts to associate file-sharing with all sorts of immorality and criminality have been more recently replaced with campaigns designed to persuade file-sharers that they will be caught and punished severely, again with ambiguous results.

The relationship between the content industries and the broadcast/print media is then examined in more detail. While traditional mass media give coverage to content industry representations of events, tensions exist that limit the pervasive distribution of a strong IP message. The extent to which content industries have been successful in lobbying government may in part also explain their unpopularity more generally. The chapter concludes with a discussion of 'ideology' in the twenty-first century. Is anyone persuaded? Are we all cynics now in the twilight of false-consciousness, or does a dominant ideology only really need to persuade the ruling elite, while the rest of society can be sufficiently managed with threats of punishment and the absence of a realistic alternative?

'Piracy funds terrorism and will destroy our society and your future enjoyment' (FACT?)

Before the advent of digital recording, compression and distribution, content industry anti-piracy press releases concentrated on the alleged poor quality of 'knock-off' copies. The above quote comes from a 2004 press release by FACT. This press release was part of a media management campaign involving music, film and software companies in the UK, US and elsewhere. The campaign sought to gain direct advertising space in the mass media as well as in cinemas and on products (such as messages on DVDs and CDs), as well as gaining indirect publicity through coverage of claims and promotional events as 'news' and/or 'infotainment'. The theme of this particular campaign was to link the damage caused to copyright holders' profits from unlicensed copying and the damage caused to society from terrorism. At a deeper level the campaign continued an older theme, which was to equate file-sharing with commercial piracy/counterfeiting. The distinction made in the above statement between '*our* society' and '*your* future enjoyment' may have been unintentional, but does hint at a perceived distinction between the world as seen by IP based corporations and the world as experienced by their target audiences. The attempt to associate piracy with terrorism was an attempt to find a legitimate source of cultural leverage so as to persuade the public that undermining corporate profits was wrong. This campaign was largely unsuccessful in that aim, although the reasons for its failure are complex.

While the above quote was used in direct advertising, most heavily in pre-film cinema screenings and on sale/rental DVD trailers, the multi-million pound promotional campaign involved the payment of celebrities, politicians and 'experts' such as police officers and piracy investigators whose statements were then packaged as press releases by FACT and other lobby groups, both in the UK and around the world, for take up within the news cycle of television, radio, newspapers and magazines. These press releases were designed to associate piracy, organized crime and terrorism. While going on very shortly afterwards to win an Oscar for her portrayal of Queen Elizabeth the Second, Helen Mirren had to be content with a large cash payment for her performance in a FACT press release in which she states: 'It is increasingly clear that the money people spend on fake DVDs goes straight into the pockets of organized crime and international terrorism'. The television presenter Jonathan Ross was also keen, for an undisclosed sum from the FACT spin-off lobby group 'The Industry Trust for IP Awareness Limited' (David and Kirkhope 2004), to inform the public that counterfeit DVDs benefit 'some very unsavoury individuals indeed'. Both quotes were picked up by terrestrial and satellite television as well as by the broadsheet and tabloid newspapers in the UK. These celebrity hooks were combined with statements from politicians. The claim that piracy funds terrorism was also backed up by statements from and about Interpol and from police forces around the world, all of which were said to support the claim that international terrorists had been linked to the distribution of counterfeit goods, including pirated music and film.

Parallel campaigns were under way in the United States, with many of its direct advertising films being subsequently shown or modified for release in Europe and elsewhere. On 13 March 2003 The United States House

Judiciary Committee's Subcommittee on Courts, the Internet and Intellectual Property heard evidence on the question of IP theft, organized crime and terrorism. Rather, it would be fairer to say that the congressional hearing heard evidence regarding organized crime, but heard none at all regarding terrorism. The hearing took evidence from four key figures: John Malcolm from the Department of Justice, Richard LaMagna from Microsoft, Joan Borsten Vidov of the company Films by Jove Inc., and Jack Valenti, president of the MPAA. Malcolm asserted the link between DVD counterfeiting, organized crime and terrorism but, when pressed, conceded that he knew of no concrete examples. 'It would surprise me greatly if the number were not large' he suggested, but could not give any further explanation for this than that these were all bad people after all. Malcolm sought to equate file-sharing networks with organized crime on the basis that they were international networks and they were enabling illegal activity. He was forced to admit that such networks were not profit making and so were fundamentally different from what most people, and the law, defines as organized crime, which refers to networks of professional, profit-oriented business criminals. LaManga simply outlined the extent of Microsoft's anti-piracy strategy, while Borsten Vidov explained her company's difficulties in Russia, where she claimed the state represented the most organized of all criminal networks. It was left to Jack Valenti to make the boldest assertions. Drawing upon a 2002 article in the US Customs Service newsletter entitled 'Financing Terror: Profits from Counterfeit Goods Pay for Attacks', by Kathleen Turner, Valenti declared:

> It states that the participants at the 1st International Conference on IPR hosted by Interpol in Lyon, France in 2001 all agreed the evidence was indisputable: a lucrative trafficking in counterfeit and pirate products: music, movies, seed patents, software, tee-shirts, Nikes, knock-off CDs and fake drugs accounts for much of the money the international terrorist network depends on to feed its operations. The article concludes that the new link between commercial-scale piracy and counterfeiting has redirected public attention in 2002, and law enforcement agencies like customs and Interpol are going after the organised crime syndicates in charge of what was too often viewed as a victimless crime. September 11 changed the way Americans look at the world. It also changed the way American law enforcement looks at Intellectual Property crimes. (Cited in Bagchi 2003)

While asserting that 'all agreed the evidence was indisputable', no evidence was forthcoming, though Valenti was correct in pointing out that after 9/11 all law enforcement agencies had made terrorist connections to their field of operations, as this often gained additional resources. That Valenti was seeking to make the same connection himself – to garner further state funding for his fight against copyright infringement – is not surprising. As will be pointed out below, the Interpol conference evidence was eventually revealed, and does not support the claims being made of a connection between music and film copying and international terrorism at all. Turner

(2002) evidences the sale of fake designer handbags in the funding of terrorism, but does not offer any concrete evidence for informational goods.

Valenti went on to flag up the problem of 'Internet Piracy', by which he meant file-sharing, and how the condition of the music industry showed the potential future of his area, the film industry, but then went on to focus upon DVD piracy and counterfeiting. In using the term piracy to refer to both file-sharing and the making of 'knock-off' DVDs and CDs for sale, Valenti allowed elected members of the congressional committee (Democrats and Republicans) to ignore the evidence and testimony given, and instead launch into strong attacks on all those branded as 'pirates' – all of whom were thereby tarnished by the association with organized crime and then with international terrorism. Ironically, the group most lambasted by the committee's elected representatives were peer-to-peer file-sharers, college students and teenagers, who had in no way been associated with organized crime or terrorism, but who perhaps represent the greatest threat to the corporate lobbies that finance legislators' election campaigns. Democratic Party Florida Representative Robert Wexler announced: 'If more American parents understood the connection between the pirating of intellectual property and organised crime, I think then there'd be a much more effective public relations response in our own country to better appreciate the disastrous ramifications' (cited in Gross 2003). Why American parents? Children and young adults living with their parents are the last major bastion of cinema attendance, at least for Hollywood products, and they do not represent the core market for DVDs, legal or otherwise. They are, however, a core group involved in file-sharing. Wexler went on to suggest that government-funded public service commercials should be made and distributed to 'highlight' (or perhaps better to create) the linkage between piracy and terrorism, on a par with the associations made between illegal drugs and terrorist funding. Texas Republican Representative John Carter suggested it would be good to imprison some college students and then publicize it.

> I think it'd be a good idea to go out and actually bust a couple of these college kids … If you want to see college kids duck and run, you let them read the papers and somebody's got a 33-month sentence in the federal penitentiary for downloading copyrighted materials. (Gross 2003)

Just such a flurry of 'public service commercials' and well publicized legal actions were not long in coming. This campaign of media management coincided with the legal and technical campaigns documented in Chapters 5 and 6 (see also Haugland 2003).

The campaign to associate copyright violation (whether for file-sharing, piracy or counterfeiting) with 'international terrorism' lasted little over a year and the direction shifted after 2004. The insinuation that in the aftermath of 9/11 Islamic terrorists, in their opposition to American cultural dominance, would engage in the discounted circulation of the very cultural products – Western music and films – they would consider so very degraded and contemptuous could not be sustained. Complaints in the UK to the Advertising Standards Authority in 2004, and similar complaints in the US in both the media and academic journals, led to greater clarity as to what FACT and MPAA were suggesting. Initially in the UK, FACT representatives claimed they could not reveal the specifics of terrorist connections, implying that this would undermine ongoing investigations. When it was pointed out that this meant that no firm evidence had yet been tried in court, FACT went on to produce their one piece of confirmed evidence. This was the case of a group of Northern-Irish paramilitaries convicted of DVD piracy. Given that this was after the Good Friday Agreement it was not clear whether these were terrorists at all or rather former terrorists who, in the absence of violent conflict, had turned to other criminal activities. There had been a threat made to blow up the offices of Northern Ireland's Anti-Counterfeiting and Racketeering Unit, though this did not ever take place. The Advertising Standards Authority rejected the claim that FACT had wilfully misled the public in its statement that 'piracy funds international terrorism' on the grounds that this one case sustained the claim (Advertising Standards Authority 2004). The evidence from Interpol, and the claim that police and anti-terrorist organizations around the world all agreed that there was evidence linking terrorism to piracy, all boiled down to cross-referencing of reports of this case. Whether or not the convicted former paramilitaries were best described as 'terrorists', whether the term 'international terrorists' best described them, whether the claim that 'piracy funds international terrorism' could be justified on the basis of a single case, and whether it was appropriate, at a time when audiences would have been most likely to associate the term 'international terrorism' with Al-Qaeda, for FACT to point out that they were not making such a connection, were all set aside by the ASA. As far as they were concerned, it was not possible to prove that FACT had acted with the deliberate intention to deceive. Oliver Burkeman (2004) quotes terrorism finance researcher Rita Katz as stating: 'I have never found, in any of my investigations, any terrorist attacks financed by the grey market [in pirated DVDs]'. Burkeman suggests that the overextension of claims made about a link, in the absence of evidence, came eventually to undermine the credibility of lobby groups on both sides of the Atlantic (see also Grosso 2003 and AndTea 2006). These claims were being made around and just after the 2003 invasion of Iraq and the subsequent discrediting of various claims made regarding weapons of mass destruction and imminent threats used to justify the war. Cynicism was rife.

Jean Baudrillard (1995) and Paul Virilio's (1984) suggestion that 'information war' blurs media propaganda and physical conflict to the point where audiences are unable to detach themselves from the urgency of the threat message bombarded at them, would appear to overstate the capacity of the media to persuade. Even the acceptance of the message does not ensure such an acceptance produced the desired behavioural outcome. An amusing subversion of the MPAA/FACT campaign to associate piracy and terrorism circulated globally on websites and blogs. This was the suggestion that if pirated DVDs were truly funding terrorism and/or organized criminals, and if, as lobby groups had also claimed, pirated and counterfeit DVDs representsed up to one-third of all physical sales – with such copies often sold in shops as well as just in the street – surely the only way to ensure money did not get into the wrong hands was not to pay any money and to download such material from the Internet for free. Another line was to suggest that tax revenues from legitimate sales would fund state terrorism in response to the non-state terrorism funded by illegitimate sales so – again – the only responsible route was to file-share. One ironic blogger, mimicking the language of the corporate lobbyists, wrote the following: 'Because you're not paying tax on the download, tax that would've been used in The War Against Terror. Actually, if you download movies instead of going to the cinema you are a terrorist! Wink.' By the end of 2004 cinema adverts making the claim that terrorism was linked to copyright violation were being greeted with rounds of hysterical laughter and verbal abuse. The campaign was dropped. In June 2004 Valenti testified before the United States Senate Committee on Foreign Relations that:

> According to Ron Noble, the international police network's secretary general at the first Global Congress on Combating Counterfeiting in Brussels last month, 'Interpol believes there is a significant link between counterfeiting and terrorism in locations where there are entrenched terrorist groups'. How much of the revenues flow to terrorists is hard to measure, but doubtless it is there. (Valenti 2004)

Even by this stage such statements, based on one person's reference to another person's claim regarding the opinion of another group of people, were beginning to sound stale. Valenti's final sentence rather summed up his approach. In the absence of evidence just believe it anyway. Sadly for Valenti, his target audience didn't. Having held office for four decades, he retired the following year.

Intellectual property theft is the new street drug

In 2003 Ken Fisher posed the question 'Is P2P the next "drug war?"' (Fisher 2003). With the attempt to link the war on terror with the war against file-sharing largely dead by 2005, Fisher came to the view that far from being constructed as the next war on drugs, the MPAA was attempting to construct its war on copyright infringement as the old war on drugs, with pirate/counterfeit DVDs being presented as 'the new drug on the street' (Fisher 2005). Fisher observes the rather obvious fact that organized criminals engage in profitable crimes, and those who engage in the sale of illegal drugs will no doubt take part in the manufacture and sale of pirated or counterfeit music and film if there is a profit to be made. In the year after the campaign to associate copyright theft with international terrorism the emphasis turned towards the links between various forms of organized crime. Most US citizens were not persuaded either by the reality of a link between 'piracy' and terrorism, or its significance, but the link between copyright and drugs is potentially more persuasive at both levels.

> But tying piracy to drug trafficking is a fantastic move, because if you're just loose enough with the rhetoric, you can basically draw a line from Sally making a mix-tape to Sally mixing drugs and ending up in the methadone clinic. The MPAA's terrorism rhetoric seems to have largely disappeared with the retirement of Valenti. It looks like it may be time for a new yarn. (Fisher 2005)

Lobby groups around the world began releasing stories to the press concerning drugs raids in which caches of illegal CDs and DVDs were also found. As Stuart Hall et al. (1978) point out about 'mugging', it is not that the events being highlighted did not happen; rather it is the decision to make such acts the focus of attention, and the fashion in which they are constructed as being indicative of a deeper threat to the fabric of society, that is significant. Did such a campaign persuade parents to stop their children file-sharing? Alternatively, did this campaign encourage parents to tell their children to file-share, as this would ensure no contact with DVD-dealing street traders pushing illegal drugs? Would association between drugs and DVDs make the latter more or less attractive? Again, the scope for subversions of dominant messages such as 'Drugs are Bad!', and 'Piracy equals Drugs!' make it hard to gauge how such a campaign would be read by target audiences. Who was the target audience anyway? Parents, legislators, law enforcement agencies, or young people? Certainly the same message would have been very differently received by such a diverse range of viewers.

Intellectual property theft and illegal immigrants

In testimony to the US Senate Foreign Relations Committee, Jack Valenti (2004) sought to highlight the danger to European markets for US film and music corporations. He catalogued police raids in Pakistan and Russia which, he claimed, highlighted the production of pirate and counterfeit products destined for the Western European market. He suggested that the expansion of the European Union, and its consequent opening up of borders to ten new 'accession countries', was going to increase the trafficking routes and weaken the existing border controls. The suggestion that counterfeit goods and illegal immigrants go together presents a double threat of pollution to 'our' society. As was noted in Chapter 4, Isabella Alexander (2007) parallels associations made in 1900 between pirated sheet music and supposedly Jewish organized criminal gangs operating across Europe and controlling the underworld in London with today's claims. Similar suggestions are routinely made today in anti-piracy commercials which seek to link people trafficking, the importation of sex workers, and the importation of counterfeit and pirated CDs and DVDs. One anti-piracy advertisement, placed on DVDs, posters and buses featured rats pouring out of sewers.

Intellectual property, identity theft and student plagiarism

Another equation being put forward on both sides of the Atlantic (by FACT, The Industry Trust and the RIAA and others) is that between identity theft in the form of plagiarism and intellectual property theft in the form of copyright violation. The distinction between identity theft and intellectual property theft can be highlighted in the distinction between piracy and counterfeiting, the former simply copying content for sale, the latter seeking to present itself as being the official output of the authorized copyright holder. The attempt to equate file-sharing and the copying of words from someone else in a student essay without referencing is deeply spurious. The equation has enabled the above organizations to claim that they are working with schools and colleges in the fulfilment of educational goals, while at the same time seeking to gain the cooperation of schools, colleges and universities in prohibiting students from using their educational computer networks to file-share anonymously. As Snapper (1999) argues, plagiarism is the attempt to pass off someone else's work as one's own, so to engage in identity theft and intellectual property theft. Selling counterfeit CDs and DVDs made up to look like originals is identity theft and IP theft. Downloading music from the Internet may infringe copyright but is not identity theft and, therefore, not plagiarism. A student who fails to cite their sources and thereby gives the impression that certain ideas are their own is engaging in identity theft and, therefore, plagiarism. Educational institutions should be encouraging the free circulation of ideas on the condition that users do not seek to claim such ideas as their own original thoughts. They should encourage students to take and use what they can, to acknowledge their sources and to build something new from the fusion of what they found. Allowing lobby groups to enter educational institutions in order to equate learning with consumption of purchased products is misguided. When students around the world are increasingly expected to pay fees for their education, teachers already face difficulties seeking to persuade them that they should appropriate ideas rather than simply pay for the end result. Promoting a pay-for culture in education by equating identity theft and intellectual property theft would make this situation even worse. Pedagogically speaking, free libraries – and using them – is good.

In 2008 the record industry in the UK began funding the charity Childnet to 'help' teachers and parents 'educate' children into respecting copyright (Cellan-Jones 2008). The charity focuses upon safety, though the only danger is the threat of legal action by the charity's funders. In the United States the RIAA has produced media packs for schools entitled:

'What's the Diff?: A Guide to Digital Citizenship', which provide schools with role-play games designed to 'educate' junior high school children into the belief that file-sharing is dangerous and immoral (Howe 2004). Cellan-Jones and Howe agree that both schemes are hopelessly biased and doomed to fail as neither has any connection to the reality and beliefs of those they are allegedly aiming to communicate with. However, the aim may be merely to gain greater access to schools and university campus computer networks, through which to spy on students and, thereby, attempt to bypass any effort to win over their 'hearts and minds'. Another charity called Film Education, sponsored by the UK film industry, promotes the message that plagiarism and intellectual property theft are one and the same, alongside a range of other activities aimed at moulding the UK curriculum and qualifications of 14–19-year-olds in line with the promotion of strong IP protection (Film Education 2008).

Mark Poster (2006: 87–115) highlights a double meaning in the use of the term identity in current media campaigns. The first is a notion of identity as self-possession: the self-aware, self-directed person, the agent or actor. Poster links this to Locke's ideas of self-possession as the basic property from which other property rights stem through the investment of self in things. This idea of identity is distinguished from a second conception, that of self-identification: the ability to prove that you are who you claim to be, something bound up with facial recognition, signatures and fingerprints, and with innovations today such as DNA testing, retinal scanning, blood tests etc. In the realm of computing, Poster suggests, the increased incidence of identity theft highlights the growing tension between person and persona, self-identity and self-identification. He highlights the rise of crimes concerning identity theft, something which was newly legislated for in a number of countries in the late 1990s and which, therefore, saw an exponential rise in the number of recorded incidences after that time. The development of usernames and passwords, which are claimed to protect the identity of computer users, are as much tools of surveillance to identify users. Poster also highlights US media campaigns that focus attention upon victims of identity crime. The theft of personal information to gain access to bank accounts, to create credit accounts in the name of the victim, or to gain a passport for example, are publicized to increase awareness of virtual identity theft. In the USA, poster campaigns have sought to link identity theft with terrorism, smuggling and people trafficking, while FACT in the UK sought to link such crimes with file-sharing and piracy. This aims to equate intellectual property theft with identity theft but, as Poster points out, IP and ID are two different things. It is easy to feel sympathy for someone whose passport details have been cloned or whose bank account has been emptied. There is a greater shared feeling that these people have been robbed than is the case in relation to copyright infringement. The attempt to equate the two forms of violation may have the effect of garnering sympathy for copyright holders. In highlighting the suffering of those who have had their virtual privacy and identity violated, while at the same time seeking to introduce greater invasions of such identity and privacy (such as will be discussed in the following two sections), content industry representatives run the risk of garnering the very hostility against identity violators that they seek themselves to foster and harness.

Intellectual property theft and airport security myths

On 10 July 2008 an alleged leak was made to a technology website of supposedly secret plans to introduce searches for illegally downloaded material as part of airport security checks. The leak coincided with the completion of the 2008 G8 Summit of heads of state from the world's largest eight economies, and the releasing of their 'Declaration on the World Economy'. This makes mention of discussions regarding the development of a new Anti-Counterfeiting Trade Agreement (ACTA), which would require states to give over greater resources to defending the economic interests of intellectual property rights holders. The 'leaked' document suggested that in addition to greater resources being devoted to catching international counterfeiting gangs, a further option would be to introduce random searches at airports of the contents of MP3 and MP4 players such as iPods. This message seeped into press and television coverage. The UK conservative broadsheet *The Daily Telegraph* (Simpson 2008) noted research by the British Music Rights group which suggested the average UK teenager has 800 illegal downloads on their MP3 player, while then going on to cite a representative of record labels saying the practice of 'scanning' iPods and phones was unworkable. The former research discerned what is legal and what is not on an MP3 player by simply asking teenagers to give a number. Airport security might not find this strategy very useful. The problem, highlighted in *The Guardian* (Arthur 2008a), lies in attempting to confirm the legal status of a music file, while at the same time seeking to manage the flow of human traffic in and out of airports. The next day the technology website GIZMODO hosted a discussion forum on the viability and ethics of the proposals. While two people supported the ethics of clamping down on copyright infringers (using the argument that those with nothing to hide have nothing to fear), all the dozens of other respondents condemned the idea as unethical. More significantly, all those that commented on the manageability of such a project, in the context of an airport, derided the plan as unworkable. Given that most music, even iTunes, is now DRM free and that in some countries format shifting individual CDs on to personal MP3 and MP4 players is legal, the notion of 'scanning' a player is meaningless. There are no definitive signs that would make some fictive detector 'bleep' when it came across a file that had been downloaded from a file-sharing site rather than copied from a CD. That airport security has been heavily challenged to meet even its primary security functions in an age of terrorist threats, and when traffic volumes have led to difficulties enough in managing human flows, the suggestion that staff would take time to check the contents of music players was dismissed as baseless propaganda. While it might be assumed that some people reading about airport security checks might be scared into deleting copyright infringing downloads, at the same time the story further added to a general discrediting of such stories among those participating in file-sharing networks. With mainstream media coverage sceptical at best, with cited representatives of venture capitalists and record companies decrying the plans, and while geeks with an eye for the workability of such proposals laughed on the sidelines, it might well be suspected that the 'leak' was the work of those seeking to promote file-sharing simply on the grounds of undermining the credibility of its critics. However, with G8 leaders on hand to give their seal of approval, the suggestion could not be dismissed as merely the work of a playful provocateur.

Media scopes: the next big 'clampdown' – July 2008: via ISPs

Following on from the suggestion that society be asked to condone random searches of personal data at airports in order to check for unlicensed music files, sceptics asked why airports? The suggestion of random stop and search powers at airports, in some vague way linked to general airport and border smuggling fears, died a quick death but was soon replaced by a more general suggestion that such stop and search powers be extended across the whole of society, in the form of a compulsory agreement between copyright holders and Internet Service Providers. At the same time as stories of airport security checks for unlicensed music were being filtered (rather unsuccessfully) into the mainstream media so too were suggestions that, once again, we were on the brink of a new breakthrough – something that would wipe out file-sharing. In early July the BBC ran news bulletins with the headline 'Illegal downloaders face UK ban'. Once again, 'leaked' documents, this time from the Department of Culture, Media and Sport after consulting with 'stakeholders' in the UKs creative industries, suggested that new powerful laws were on the brink of being brought into force, laws that would compel Internet Service Providers to hand over the identities of those suspected of file-sharing – on the basis of the size of the files they were uploading and downloading – to the content industries and/or to the police. The initial coverage given to such claims was itself countered by the Internet Service Providers Association who claimed they were no more responsible for what people did with their Internet accounts than was the post office for what people wrote in letters. The BBC's coverage of the story began with the strong claims of the music industry but, with the range of other corporate voices in play, did not provide wholehearted support. *The Times* also began with supportive coverage, but went on to cite doubts and criticisms. Having challenged the viability of such a strategy, the BBC gave over considerable coverage to the Chief Executive of the BPI and his defence of the planned clampdown.

The impact of earlier coverage (see Chapter 6) on the development of the story was significant. Early coverage in the spring of 2008, given over to the Internet Service Provider Virgin Media and its agreement to send out warning letters to users suspected of copyright infringing file-sharing, had rather an unintended consequence. The scheme, which Virgin had devised in an agreement with the BPI, was designed to show ISPs getting tough with their own customers, and generating a flood of departures and threats of departure from Virgin's Internet service. By mid 2008 Virgin Media were at pains to tell the BBC's *Newsbeat* (the scaled-down version of the news designed for the BBC's youth services and popular music channels) that there was '"absolutely no possibility" of taking legal action or banning Internet users as part of a campaign against illegal file-sharing on its broadband network' (Reid 2008). Earlier reports that file-sharers faced the prospect of being banned from the Internet and prosecuted were dismissed as misrepresentations of earlier policy discussions.

For Internet Service Providers to clamp down on their customers would require a blanket introduction of the practice so that no individual provider would see its market share drop relative to competitors who did not toe the surveillance line. For this to be achieved, it would be necessary to bind all ISPs around the world – something that is not within the power of any legislative body. Given the criticisms levelled at Internet companies that have made even minor concessions to repressive regimes, the likelihood that such companies as a whole will agree to alienate their customer base in such an extreme fashion as would be the result of agreeing to police every transaction is remote. The case of Virgin Media's agreement with the BPI to send 800 letters to customers seemed, at first, a victory for the music industry. The backlash against this move, however, in the absence of the political will to introduce extreme measures to compel all ISPs to act as Internet censors, led to media coverage that told a very different story: of a climbdown and of a media content industry grossly at odds with new-media and new technology companies.

When, eventually, the UK government's Department for Business Enterprise and Regulatory Reform did intervene to require UK ISPs to make a deal with the content industries, this deal remained in the shadow of previous developments. On 24 July 2008, the BPI announced that it had signed a Memorandum of Understanding (MoU) with the six largest UK ISPs to work together to address file-sharing. Initially, media coverage of the BPI's press release (BPI 2008b) presented a picture very much in line with the BPI's representation of events. Central to this line was that those whose Internet accounts were to be reported to ISPs by the BPI were illegal file-sharers, that the new deal would start with warnings, but would progress towards punishments for repeat 'offenders'. On that day *The Times* reported that 'Parents will be punished for children's net piracy' (Sabbagh 2008a) with the prospect of being 'blacklisted' for their children's downloading of music. *The Guardian* (Sweeney 2008a) reported the three strikes and out policy that the BPI had been advocating: first step, education/warning letter; second step, suspension; and third step, disconnection. *The Independent* reported the three strikes and out proposal as well as the idea of a charge to all Internet users to allow free downloads (Morris 2008). It soon became clear that this reporting was far from accurate. Later the same day, the BBC's Charles Arthur (2008b) pointed out that the Memorandum had required the dropping of any suggestion of a levy, a three strikes and out system or any kind of blacklist. ISPs signed up only to distribute letters to users warning them that content industry representatives had identified their IP addresses as accessing sites known to facilitate file-sharing. ISPs refused to reveal to the BPI the identities of such individuals or the content exchanged on such sites. Charles Dunstone, chief executive officer of Carphone Warehouse and an outspoken critic of earlier plans, sent an email to the BBC in which he wrote: 'It is not our job to tell customers what they should or should not be doing but we believe it is in their interests to warn them that they are being accused of wrongdoing' (cited in Arthur 2008b). This amounted to saying ISPs were actively seeking to tip-off users that copyright holders were investigating them. A spokesperson for TalkTalk was cited as saying:

> If rights holders think a copyright infringement has occurred they can use legal means to attempt to prosecute the individuals concerned. TalkTalk will continue to act in the best interests of its customers and will fight any action which prejudices customer rights and privacy. (Arthur 2008b)

Even on the day the BPI issued its press release, three of its six supposedly 'understanding' collaborators were actively distancing themselves from the suggestion that the new agreement would have teeth. The other three said nothing to indicate they would go further in cooperating with the BPI. The other three big ISPs, BSkyB, Orange and Tiscali, each have commercial interests in the free circulation of content (the former owning MySpace, the second distributing ringtones and other music via its telephones, and the latter in general competition for new-media revenues).

Sabbagh (2008b), again in *The Times*, reported that copyright holders would be able to monitor users' IP addresses when they were logged onto file-sharing networks, while at the same time not actually scanning the content of what was being shared. This was cited as evidence that file-sharers will be caught, but that privacy will not be invaded. Monitoring of flows rather than content meant users could only ever be suspected of infringement by such methods, rather than this being proven. Without ISPs revealing real world identities and content the BPI's position was a bluff. No evidence, no chance of getting the names, still having to go to court if some kind of sanction was to be sought, the Memorandum was getting diluted almost by the hour. By 25 July only *The Independent* was presenting the BPI line (Bland 2008), not least as a result of the criticism it had taken the previous day for suggesting the continued viability of the levy idea, something none of the major decision makers (the BPI, ISPs and government) continued to support. All three key players and the other newspapers turned on *The Independent*, and the next day its story conformed to the BPI line regarding 'illegal file-sharers' and the prospects for three strikes, slowdowns and discontinuation (despite government rejection of all three). *The Times*, which also continued to run with the three strikes and out angle, however, also ran a story outlining all the ways by which the new scheme could be circumvented. Online station ripper software, hidden directories, deeper encryption, online sound recorders, external hard-drives and registration with non-compliant ISPs all shot holes in the scheme, even if the cooperation between content industries and ISPs could be achieved in locating and identifying users of existing file-sharing networks (itself unlikely). Moustrous and Sabbagh (2008) suggest: 'Whatever the technique, everyone agreed that the latest effort of the music industry to protect itself would be defeated by an army of teenage computer geeks willing to try'. They cite one hacker as saying: 'That's all that your efforts result in, dear music industry … Stronger, hardier weeds that you can never kill. You lose. You just don't know it yet.' The authors then go on to mention a new deal between Universal and BSkyB, and point out that the latter is part-owned by the same parent company as the newspaper they were writing in, as if that might be of significance – which no doubt it is. From relative compliance with the BPI press release's line a week before, by the end of July *The Guardian*'s John Sweeney (2008b) was highlighting the government's distancing of itself from the BPI over an open letter sent by the latter to the six ISPs it had signed up with, threatening them with litigation if they did not move beyond the MoU, which the BPI saw as merely a starting point for ongoing collaboration and enforcement. The Business Minister, Baroness Vadera, who had brokered the MoU, wrote an open letter back to the BPI's Geoff Taylor expressing her disappointment at his outburst. From early success, within a week the media coverage of what had started out as a major breakthrough for the 'war on illegal file-sharing' had collapsed in disarray, acrimony and the discrediting of yet more claims as to the legal, political, technical and cultural capacity of the established content industries and their representatives.

What all this media coverage highlights is the relative weakness of media management. Despite the very best efforts of the music industry – to control the story, to persuade audiences that file-sharing is wrong, impossible, linked (via the common use of the term piracy) to organized crime, terrorism and drugs, and likely to lead to punishments – none of the dire warnings seem to have been successfully communicated. How can such a pervasive failure of cultural leadership be explained by an industry whose very rationale is in the production of mass-circulation culture?

The mass media and new-media

Given the position of the film and music industries at the heart of producing popular/mass culture, it is curious that they have been so 'hegemonically' unsuccessful. It is certainly not from any lack of trying, or from a lack of resources. Huge amounts have been spent in advertising and in generating publicity. Many of the world's leading celebrities, from both genres, have been used in commercials and press releases. More actors have been used than musicians in these publicity events. Whether either group is convinced, it appears that actors are at least better at giving the impression of being so, even if neither group has been very successful in doing much convincing. Unlike actors, many musicians have actively proclaimed their support for copyright violating file-sharing (as will be seen in the next two chapters). This inability to present a coherent argument, even by the people supposedly best able to make the case and who are meant to be the very individuals the content industry claims to be fighting to protect (the starving/struggling artists), further frustrates attempts to frame the mass media debate, let alone new-media discussions and behaviour.

Jurgen Habermas's (1989[1962]) examination of commercialization in eighteenth century European print media, with its shift from being a vehicle for political challenge to being a means of promoting depoliticized consumerism, is easy to cite when evidence suggests such commercial pressures are being applied to new-media, and for good enough reasons. When Rupert Murdoch acquired MySpace or when commercial or government interests are said to have gained leverage over the ranking or exclusion of sites on search engines such as Google (Kirkpatrick 2008) or Yahoo, it is only right that critics stand up and warn that we have seen this sort of thing before. However, we should not read events, or Habermas, as a one-way street. While having a star cast of 'talking heads' onstream, good mass media access as well as the resources to generate the research, authoritative statements and other news which easily and conveniently fills up air-time and column inches do appear to enable coverage, they do not ensure stories will be framed in terms that make such investment in media management advantageous. There is limited value in being able to get a story into the news if that story is only to be framed in such a way that leaves you looking worse than if it had not been brought to light at all. As Anderson (2004) suggests, crude content analysis might rank the ability to get cited but, unless all publicity is truly good publicity, such success may well be pyrrhic.

While this chapter has evidenced the failure to frame mass media coverage, the continued extent of file-sharing suggests such media campaigning has also failed at the level of effect, though this attribution is more problematic. One valuable future research project would be to investigate the appropriation of anti-piracy advertising in forms of widely circulated online parodies, their popularity being evidence of both the widespread awareness of such messages and the equally widespread dislike, inversion and/or dismissal of their content.

As has been shown, content industry publicity material does get picked up in the newsroom cycle but tends to be countered by claims from other corporate bodies, whether these be governmental or, more typically commercial, IT and communications providers. Significant economic differences exist within the technocratic elite and not only within the media/new-media/entertainment sector. As Beck (1992) suggests, when experts from within the technocratic elite cannot agree, at least when such disagreement spills over into the public discrediting of each others' claims, the consequence is a contradictory message and ongoing media controversy. It can be seen, above, that the framing of media coverage of file-sharing has largely been through the voices of powerful economic and political actors, those with corporate publicity machines and ready access to the mass media cycle of news production. As such, the voices of file-sharers are rarely heard, though they are not totally excluded. However, even when given a voice, this is in reacting to new measures and never in outlining how they feel events should be presented. It is necessary to visit the blog sites and discussion groups attached to and beyond the mass media channels to pick up these voices.

Because six-and-a-half million alleged file-sharers in the UK, and hundreds of millions around the world, have no corporate representative, it is not surprising that they are not represented in the mass media as are corporate bodies structured in such a hierarchical fashion as to parallel the top-down/centralized character of mass media. As Gitlin (2003) suggests, any attempt to find a voice for an anti-hierarchical form of subversive behaviour, a voice that could speak through a medium fundamentally alien to the very nature of those it claims to speak on behalf of, would most likely be a fabrication by the mass media itself: an interlocutor moulded in its own image, playing a role in a dialogue between elite representatives. Today's mass media representations of file-sharing are the result of contradictions between content providers, new-media service providers, government legislators and the mass media industry itself, which has a significant commercial stake in what it is at the same time reporting.

It is not enough to point out that BSkyB may have differing commercial interests to the members of the MPAA, as Rupert Murdoch's media empire includes both BSkyB and Twentieth Century Fox, one of the largest Hollywood production and distribution companies and hence a major contributor to the MPAA. This empire also includes *The Times* newspaper group and one of the world's largest ISPs. While keen to profit from its television and film making content via Fox and Sky television, the empire also includes MySpace, whereby hundreds of millions of dollars of advertising revenue are generated selling access to the eyeballs of users attracted to the site by the free content put there by other MySpace users. Sony Corporation similarly owns Columbia Studios and Sony Music, a string of other subsidiary content providers, at the same time as being one of the largest producers of the very mobile phones, MP3 players, computers, stereos and other digital devices that make file-sharing and digital rights infringement both easy and attractive. Time Warner owns Warner Brothers Studios, America On-Line (AOL) and the television companies HBO and CNN. It can, thereby, cover disputes between its own Internet Service Provider and film studio via its own television channels, just as Rupert

Murdoch can. Virgin Media, as part of Virgin Group, is, ironically, one of the least conflicted, being no longer as involved in either music production or distribution as its origin as a brand might suggest. Vivendi, which owns Universal Studios and a string of record companies (though not Universal Music), is the largest mobile phone provider in France and a number of other locations. It is also currently moving into large-scale Internet service provision. Universal Music is owned, along with the television network NBC, by the giant General Electric. Every passing day witnesses changes to the configuration of the players, their relative stakes in each others' markets and each others' subsidiaries. Similarly, the ongoing legal actions being brought by each of these players against one or more of the others for allegedly unlawfully damaging each others' business interests, would require daily updates. These daily updates, suitably edited, make up the metaframe in which file-sharing is represented in the mass media. The diversity of voices that make up today's mass media may all speak with a similar corporate accent, but such similarity does not prevent them from arguing with each other – and in public.

Given the current uncertainty concerning the viability of traditional mass and new-media based commercial strategies, conflict exists not only between companies but also within companies and corporate groups of companies, within and between sectors, as well as around the boundaries between fields, such as film, music, television and computer games. The failure of the film and music industry to frame the mass media debate on file-sharing should not lead to any reassurance as to the democratic pluralism of our television and newspapers. Outsider voices are seldom heard, and never allowed to frame discussions. Rather, the mass media give an interesting reflection of the current state of dispute within technocratic and corporate elites. A transnational capitalist class (Sklair 2002) may be developing but such a class remains divided, not only in competing with each other, but also in defining the future strategies, obstacles, targets and alliances they will be competing over. The fundamental problem for Sklair's analysis of such a group as a *class in itself* is the very problem experienced by such an emergent group of highly mobile, internationally educated symbolic manipulators. Unable to predict which way things will turn out, it is not possible to identify let alone act with certainty in accordance with one's own best interests. Betting on uncertain and often divergent outcomes produces highly contradictory strategies, investments and proclaimed beliefs.

Spreading conspiracies

Fredric Jameson (1991) suggests conspiracy theory is the poor man's cognitive map, a short cut to explain complex patterns of association in the absence of the evidence to explain such regularities. The ongoing attempts to foster such conspiracy theories in relation to file-sharing, piracy, counterfeiting, terrorism, illegal drugs, illegal immigration, organized crime and much else besides have become the stock response of the content industries in their attempt to stem the moral indifference felt by most people towards their diminished profit margins. Sadly, from their point of view, their conspiracy theories have largely failed, in part for being too grand but in another sense for being too modest.

In the first instance, and for the most part, each and every one of the grand claims made by the recording and film industry as to the nature of copyright violation has been subverted on the grounds that the evidence presented did not back up the bold claims being made. This is a combination of two things. First, objectively, the claims made in relation to terrorism, organized crime, drugs, plagiarism, airport security, new and draconian clampdowns, encryption and surveillance have all overstepped the bounds of what might reasonably be claimed to have been true. However, and perhaps more significantly, subjectively, those most likely to file-share were least likely to believe anything the content industry was saying, and actively sought to challenge, subvert and invert whatever messages were given to them.

Mark Poster (2006) provides a fascinating illustration of the outright cynicism fostered in the worldview of new-media savvy students and bloggers in the United States, the place most likely to be receptive to the claims of Hollywood studios and the big recording companies. Poster tells the story of a playful web-designer who liked to fabricate pictures of the Sesame Street puppet Bert in various incriminating situations (relaxing on Adolf Hitler's boat, standing on the grassy knoll when Kennedy drives past, sitting beside Osama Bin Laden). As Poster tells the story, just such an image of Bert sitting next to Bin Laden, and placed on the web, was then incorporated by an Indonesian poster maker, when asked to produce a placard design celebrating the Al-Qaeda leader. As such, a poster containing multiple images of Bin Laden, one of which has him sat next to Bert from *Sesame Street*, was reproduced all over the world and could be seen in various newspaper photographs taken at 'anti-American' rallies from across the Islamic world. Or so Poster tells the story. Poster was interested to know what his students would make of this curious recruitment of a US children's television character into the propaganda war against the US-led invasion of Afghanistan. Was it an accident? Was Bert being used to invert cultural imperialism? What Poster found was that the vast majority of his students assumed the whole thing had been made up as a joke. His students assumed the media was never to be trusted. They believed what they wanted to believe, however conservative, radical or indifferent that might be. In such a climate, tall tales from the content industries, along the lines of the 1950s Red scares (Turner 2003) are unlikely to persuade.

Yet, for all the difficulties encountered in making claims that were too big, the content industry was also caught out for offering conspiracy theories that were dwarfed by the biggest conspiracy theory of them all. Countless millions of people have now seen the grainy face of Jack Valenti starring into the camera on Airforce One as Lyndon Johnson takes the oath of office just hours after the murder of John F. Kennedy. Valenti, a White House aide in 1963, was until his death in 2007 a Washington insider, an operator at the very heart of things. While Valenti sought to persuade the world that his industry was the victim of innumerable criminal, political and terroristic conspiracies, he was himself the focus of even grander conspiracy theories. One obituary to Valenti wrote: 'If only Lee Harvey Oswald had valued cheap movie downloads more than the future of the free world' (OzJuggler 2007). Valenti's appearance as the longest running operator in Washington made him the object of all manner of conspiracy claims, not least in relation to the apparent ability to get what he wanted for his organization. To his critics he appeared to be able to pull all the strings. Yet he was not invincible. The conspiracy theories about him rather overstated his power. He was not actually very successful in his campaigning to persuade the public. He had lost the action taken in 1984 against the Sony video recorder, and had been relatively unsuccessful in stopping file-sharing. He was more successful shaping laws than in getting them enforced. While keen to sign up to the War on Terror back in 2001 (Walsh 2001), Valenti's relationship with the Bush administration was poor and, as a lifelong Democrat representing an industry that largely backs the same party, Valenti and Hollywood showed little enthusiasm for a reorientation of its output towards Neo-Conservative epics of American greatness – not least as such films would be unprofitable even at home let alone in the global marketplace. While some propaganda films and series have been made, and while eventually Hollywood agreed to send their blockbusters free to US soldiers in Afghanistan and Iraq, those of a Republican disposition suggest Valenti was keen to make demands on the state to uphold his members' interests, but never more than frosty when it came to turning Hollywood over to the war effort (Teicholz 2002). At least being the centre of a conspiracy theory made him seem powerful. His legacy may be to have helped make file-sharing seem more powerful by the same means.

Conclusions

Given the position of the music and film industry in the production of commercial culture it may at first appear odd that they have been so very unsuccessful in framing the media representation of their problem with file-sharing: to represent file-sharing as wrong, technically limited and also highly likely to end in successful prosecution. As was seen in Chapters 5 and 6, while able to frame elements of law to favour their interpretation of events, the content industries have still found it hard to make such legal changes effective. Similarly, while able to generate a large amount of publicity through press releases, conferences and events, as well as producing and paying to distribute large amounts of anti-'piracy' advertising, the content industries have been unable to frame news in their favour. They have also failed to generate advertising messages which either stick or persuade.

Attempts to frame copyright infringement as a crime linked to terrorism proved unsuccessful, while the link with organized crime was as likely to encourage file-sharing as it was to discourage the purchase of counterfeit DVDs. The linkage between plagiarism and copyright infringement raises more doubts than it does evidence, while recent attempts to suggest new security measures at airports and tough new measures through Internet Service Providers did more damage than good, as they highlighted powerlessness and marginality rather than strength and cooperation. The development of new technologies, and the way these have been taken up and used, place the music and film industry in a position where they are vulnerable not only to being bypassed by their traditional customers, but also either bypassed or bought up by other sections of the media, entertainment and technology sectors. The legal and technical limits faced by the content industries, such that attempts to clamp down on the Internet are resisted by other commercial actors, can also be seen in the resistance within mainstream mass media. Mainstream mass media orient to dominant actors. Conflict between such actors prevents any closing down of coverage around a clear 'frame'.

Failure to close down debate, at least in terms of substantive frames such as terrorism, organized crime and new surveillance, may be to ignore another framing device. This is the continued use of the term 'piracy' to refer to the spectrum of activities from peer-to-peer file-sharing to counterfeiting. Legally speaking 'piracy' refers to making unlicensed imitation copies of copyrighted material for sale, but ones which do not seek to pass themselves off as licensed productions. The attempt to pass off copies as originals is counterfeiting. File-sharing is neither piracy nor counterfeiting. Mass media representations of copyright infringement have picked up the content industries' recurrent use of the term 'piracy', often in an uncritical way that accepts and uses its blanket association. This can be seen as a framing success, a higher level frame, even where so many lower level frames have failed. This is, however, a double-edged sword, just as was the ironic acceptance of the terrorism association with 'knock-off' DVDs by those who then concluded it would be safer to file-share. The Pirate Bay, in its explicit acceptance of the pirate frame, openly inverts the negative associations given to piracy, and takes this term as a symbol of rebellion against corporate authority and its attempts to police the Internet. Given the romantic associations made about piracy in both popular music and film, the ability to equate all copyright violation with piracy is potentially a very hollow victory indeed.

As was witnessed in Congressional hearings, where Jack Valenti's testimony seemed eagerly accepted by those disposed to its content despite being disbelieved by the media and public who seemed disposed to reject it, and as shown by Mark Poster's study of his students' beliefs, people believe what they want to believe and reject what they don't want to. As has been suggested in relation to the dominant ideology thesis, it is only really the dominant groups that seek to rationalize some kind of justification for the status quo, and even then not always with great success (Abercrombie et al. 1984). Media coverage of file-sharing presents a contradictory message and audiences read this in many different ways. Sloterdijk's (1984) distinction between fatalistic cynics and challenging cynics may be usefully deployed in mapping relations of belief, passive dismissal and playful inversion.

The way that, first, mass media coverage reflects within 'the cultural system' (Archer 1989) conflicts within and between economic and political institutions, or in Archer's language 'social structures'; second, the way such representations are received, interpreted and/or believed rejected by audiences in different locations within the sociocultural world; and third the internal coherence or contradictory character of media messages – these all constitute key elements in any account of the role of 'culture' in social life. Yet the relationship between culture, social institutions, identity and motivated actions is not identifiable outside of particular empirical cases. First, the coherence of 'cultural systems' is always, at least in part, a matter of interpretation for actors, as is the relationship between representation and social structure (Presdee 2000). While the 'technical systems' of the network society offer certain 'affordances' which Castells characterizes as 'morphogenetic structures' as they condition the possibilities for action within the sociocultural domain, the scope for interpretation 'afforded' by 'cultural systems' such as mass media are far more open ended. It is easier to recode the message than it is to recode the medium. The mass media do have morphogenetic structural characteristics in the form of news cycles, source hierarchies, editorial priorities and advertiser/owner/governmental influences. These condition the first and third elements above, yet their causal scope relative to the second element (whether anyone believes) is weaker. Law, as a cultural system, sits between new-media technology and mass media 'effects'. The 'weight' of precedent, statute, organization and roles within the legal process has greater 'morphogenetic' structuring impact than mass media, but less than does the protocol structuring the Internet. But this is all contingent. As Chapters 5, 6 and 7 have shown, what is more significant than relative differences in the integration of cultural systems, social structures and individual actions/beliefs is the common failure of technical, legal and media strategies to regulate sociocultural practices that challenge dominant social structures.

8

Creativity as Performance: The Myth of Creative Capital

Introduction

As discussed in Chapters 4 and 5, intellectual property rights law developed differently in different countries but draws upon a common repertoire of ideas concerning the defence of creativity; in particular in the realm of the arts this has taken the form of claims about the Romantic genius. This defence of property rights on the basis of promoting creativity can be questioned not only in its selective account of Romanticism, but also in its claims concerning the centrality of the artist in what copyright actually defends. Following from the discussion in Chapters 3 and 6 of creativity in the open-source and hacker movement, this chapter examines the relationship between creativity and reward in the music business. That most returns from recorded music go to record companies and other management, promotional and production-related professionals rather than to the performing artists, and that greater returns are gained by almost all musicians from live performance, challenge representations which place the role of the 'recording artist' above that of 'performing artist'. The decision by The Beatles to stop touring in 1966, and the subsequent recording of the first 'concept albums' by The Beatles and The Beach Boys, marked a watershed in the representational balance between performance and recording, with the latter increasingly presented as the thing itself – the product – and the former as the means of its promotion. This model represents the world as seen from the point of view of the 'recording industry'. Technological determinist accounts (the rise of the studio album driven by increasingly sophisticated technology), and globalization accounts (the expansion of markets) are deployed to neutralize the shift in priority.

This chapter challenges both the priority of recording over performance in the experience, practice and livelihoods of musicians, and the explanations given for the priorities of record companies. In short, existing models of recording and copyright express a corporate conception of creativity as 'property'/'capital', as an object that can be externalized and thereby alienated from the practices of its embodied production. In challenging monopoly protection the practices of file-sharers threaten/promise to undermine the recording industry's priority of recording over performance. With the loss of monopoly protection undermining the profitability of creative 'capital' ('intellectual property'), and as open-source and hacker practices challenge the idea that creativity is best fostered through corporate models of ownership, this chapter will conclude with a discussion of creativity as performance and interaction. This discussion draws upon the work of Lee Marshall (2005), Mark Hansen (2006), Brian Holmes (2003), Timothy Warner (2003) and Steve Albini (1994), among others.

Artists should get paid like everybody else, right?

Hi, I'm Jack Black. You probably know me from my movies and music. That's why you'll understand why what I'm about to talk about is very important to me. PIRACY. Look, super mega rock gods and super stars are just regular dudes like you guys. We punch the clock. We put on the pants, and then we blow peoples' minds. That's how we make a living. And then these pirates come and they steal all our Internets. I don't know how they do it. But these pirates can bust into our entertainers' homes, make us walk the plank, steal our rocking tunes and leave us broke. And you know what that means. No cash. No inspiration. No inspiration, no rocket sauce. No rocket sauce, no kick ass rock 'n' roll, or movies. Is that what you want Mr Long John Silver? What's your parrot going to listen to when you go toe to toe against the English armada? Jazz? I don't think so! Don't be a douche … stop piracy. This is Jack Black! (Black 2008)

This broadcast, by the actor who played the inspirational professor in the film *School of Rock* (2003 Paramount Pictures: Director Richard Linklater) seeks to avoid the mistakes of previous campaigns, which sought to ram home the message about criminality, and instead seeks to suggest that the music and film loving public should think of the poor artists who will lose out if they download for free. The message is delivered with hyperbole and irony rather than threats and exaggerated claims to objective fact. Interestingly, the suggestion is made that artists are both 'regular dudes'

119

who 'punch the clock' and creative artists who need some special inspiration to create their art. On the one hand, it is suggested that artists do and should get paid, like regular workers, and at the same time that they need motivational payment to foster creative innovation. This tension is that between wages and royalties. In one scenario, artists are workers who need the security of a regular income to allow them to do their jobs. In the other, artists are said to be motivated by the profits that can be made on the sale of copyrighted goods such as music and film.

This chapter examines the claim that artists are appropriately rewarded under current copyright-based business models, either as workers with a secure income or as creative entrepreneurs living from the profits (royalties) drawn from their intellectual property rights. The evidence suggests that neither is the case. If artists are not being reasonably rewarded either for punching the clock or from inspirational royalties on their 'kick ass rock 'n' roll or movies', this is more the consequence of the business models currently in operation than it is of the challenges to such models from copyright infringing file-sharers. As is suggested in numerous parodies of current anti-piracy commercials, the real pirates/criminals may well be the music and film industry itself. One such parody toys with the acronym obsession among lobby groups and released its parody under the authorship of the Music and Film Industry Association of America (MAFIAA).

'Perhaps on the rare occasion pursuing the right course demands an act of piracy, piracy itself can be the right course' is the closing line from the film *Pirates of the Caribbean* (2003 Disney Pictures: director Gore Verbinski). If the music and film industry can rely upon one of their creations, Jack Black, to campaign on their behalf; they have also created another, Jack Sparrow (the lovable pirate captain played by Johnny Depp), to popularize the counterpoint. As another anti-piracy parody circulating on the Internet puts it: 'Hollywood hates pirates; unless they're Johnny Depp'. Who are the real pirates? This chapter suggests that the content industries themselves best fit that description.

Creative industries?

The BPI's *More than the Music: The UK Recorded Music Business and Our Society* (2008a) begins with an iconic photograph of John Lennon alongside the line: 'Imagine life without music'. The report then puts forward the following proposition: 'The UK has more buyers of CDs per head than any other country in the world. As a result we have a thriving music scene which benefits all of us.' The suggestion is clear, no record sales would lead to no music scene and no music scene would lead to no music. For all the contradictions in John Lennon's song 'Imagine' – with a suggestion for us to imagine no possessions coming from someone who had just accumulated rather a lot of them – the juxtaposition of John Lennon's face, reference to his most famous lyric, and the claim that without profit and property we would live in a cultural equivalent of Rachel Carson's (1962)

Silent Spring (wherein the use of pesticides led to the death of all the birds) is highly problematic. The suggestion that high sales cause a vibrant music scene may be turned on its head and it can be argued (see Chapter 9) that the rise of free music downloading has in fact led to a huge rise in money available for live performance. For all its questionable logic, the BPI report is interesting in its attempt to naturalize the business model whereby property leads to profit, which leads to creativity, prosperity, charity and social benefits of all kinds. The report goes on to list a range of supposed beneficial results of a profitable recording industry, right the way down to contributions made to the school curriculum. 'Participating schools were provided with resource packs, including a CD-ROM with original lesson plans and activities. These explored contemporary music and the music business itself, encouraging debate around topical and controversial issues, such as music file-sharing' (BPI 2008a: 12). One assumes the CD was free.

The UK Department of Culture, Media and Sport's February 2008 report, *Creative Britain: New Talent for the New Economy*, highlights the tension that exists between content producers and content distributors.

> A recent London Business School study noted that 'Content distributors (studios, record labels, publishers) are bigger and more powerful than content creators. As a result, distributors capture much of the value that producers of creative content generate'... Although the relationship between producers and distributors is usually mutually beneficial, the continued success of the creative industries depends on clear terms of trade and the robust regime of intellectual property regulation. (DCMS 2008: 50)

The assumption that the relationship between intellectual property creators and copyright holding distributors is 'usually mutually beneficial' is neither questioned nor substantiated, but the suggestion that 'terms of trade' between them should be clear highlights the often murky and problematic nature of contracts between artists and the companies they sign up with. The report highlights that the routes into the creative industries often involve working for free or next to nothing in the hope of future success. The creative industries are said to be notorious for their poor payment of creative talent and that this may be deterring creative individuals from entering the field if they don't have relative wealth and security to start with. That the companies involved in capturing creative content and then extracting commercial value from it stand as powerful gatekeepers to the field makes it hard for creative producers to make a living without them, even if they face significant difficulties doing so within such industries. This construction of 'mutually beneficial' – such that the benefit is mutual irrespective of the relative advantage and disadvantage between parties to an interaction, as long as the weaker party has no realistic alternative – means extreme exploitation can be described as mutually beneficial as long as the alternative is obscurity and/or unemployment.

The suggestion that content distributors play an essential role in 'capturing' and 'maximizing' the potential value of creative works will be challenged later in this chapter. This is not questioned by the DCMS report. Rather they are concerned, first, that the return to artists is so often poor, and second that copyright infringement is eating into even that which might be then returned to artists: 'Online IP infringement, in particular, continues to grow. If creative artists cannot make a living as a result of their work, then our creative industries will not thrive' (DCMS 2008: 50).

While hinting at the potentially exploitative nature of relations between artists and content industries, the DCMS report focuses upon helping not challenging existing elites. In relation to the notorious problem of young artists being paid nothing by the industry that seeks to harness their talent, the government's proposal is to pay the young artists themselves. The proposal to create thousands of apprenticeships in the creative industries will see the government paying young people for what they note the creative industries do not pay for themselves. On the other hand, in relation to online copyright infringement the government proposes to get even tougher, looking to further legislative, technical and cultural actions to reduce its incidence. This includes the proposal to introduce lessons on intellectual property at every level of the school system, with assessment on the topic being introduced into examinations at various levels and in various subject areas. The report suggests that IP is 'poorly understood' by young people, by which is meant that young people do not think about IP the way the government and business leaders think they should. Given the government's own admission that the content industries are so poor at paying young artists for their creativity, it is ironic that they should imagine young people would conclude that IP protection really does reward young talent, when it doesn't. Suggesting that children need to have IP protection exams to 'help' them agree with the content industries' view of the world may create interesting future conflicts. That companies who don't pay their new talent will get government grants while file-sharers who don't pay these companies will get threats, again highlights the assumptions built into government reports. 'Stakeholders' within the current business model get to define their practices as natural and necessary. Whatever challenges them is defined as damaging and even criminal. The copyright and royalties system that justifies not paying artists and the prosecution of those who seek to share informational goods is naturalized in the DCMS report, and in the statements of content industry lobby groups such as the BPI, RIAA and MPAA, even while it is being resisted, challenged and surpassed by new practices and business models that will be discussed in Chapter 9. For now it is important further to explore the question of whether the current business model rewards the very artists the industry claims it is 'capturing' the value of in order to encourage.

The problem with music today

Steve Albini (1994) exposes the mythology surrounding music industry contracts, advances, recoupable expenses, royalties and copyright. Albini suggests too many young bands still believe the only way to make it is to sign to a 'major label'. He illustrates the balance sheet of what might appear at first to be a lucrative million dollar record contract. A band, until now signed to a small independent label and which has gained some degree of critical attention, hires a manager to build their reputation and connections within the business. The manager gets them in touch with an A & R person from a major label, who offers them a 'deal memo' in advance of a formal contract. This memo is legally binding, and prevents the band signing with anyone else, so they are not in a position to negotiate the conditions of the subsequent contract they sign with the 'major'. They hire a lawyer, but this is standard industry practice so the law offers no protection or escape, even if it will incur a fee. The independent label will require paying off, a fee that will be taken out of royalties, as will the manager's percentage and the lawyer's fees. The band's million dollar record deal ties them up for four years and a specific number of albums. The new signing means the band gets better promotion and distribution, and this means they can play larger venues with better merchandising and publishing deals. Assuming sales of a quarter of a million albums per year, by the end of the first year the band will still owe the record company money. The royalties garnered on sales will not cover the advance plus the producer's percentage and advance, the promotional budget and the buyout from the independent label. Meanwhile the cost of recording, making a video, album artwork and band equipment consume almost the whole of the advance, while the label also charges the band for all tour-related expenses. This is said to promote the album. While the label offsets all this expense, and the manager and agent take their percentages, the band lose money on the tour even though everyone else gets paid. After manager's and lawyer's fees have been taken out of merchandising and publishing advances, the band may just about have made as much money as if they had been working less than half time in a convenience store, 'but they got to ride in a tour bus for a month'. After all the non-recoupable costs involved in physical production and distribution are paid, the record company makes a gross profit of over seven hundred thousand dollars on three million dollars worth of sales (a quarter of a million sales at twelve dollars each). The next album will be worse, for the band, as they did not even repay their advance first time, so the label will insist on a greater recoupable promotional and production budget. Also, the merchandising and publishing advances have already been paid. Albini (1994) concludes that: 'Some of your friends are already this fucked'. Sales of the magnitude suggested here are rare. Only a handful of artists achieve them. Hence, most artists don't even make the minimum wage achieved by Albini's unfortunate winners.

Albini's analysis bluntly outlines the point made by the DCMS, that content producers and content distributors occupy diametrically opposed positions of strength within a royalty-based system of supposed payment, though it also undermines the notion that the relationship is mutually beneficial (except, of course, for the bit about the bus ride). Of course, the band could have sold more records if they had only tried harder or been better. If sales of a quarter of a million are considered insufficient to warrant a part-time sales-assistant's wage, something seems amiss with the model. As will be pointed out below, the vast majority of musicians with major label recording deals do not make a living wage from royalties. The BPI (2008a) is keen to highlight the number of people who do make a living in the music industry. Few of them are artists, and how little goes to artists may in part explain how there is so much left over to pay the secure and substantial salaries of lawyers, managers, manufacturers, promoters, engineers, company executives and numerous others besides.

The 'Love Manifesto'

> June 14 2000. Today I want to talk about piracy and music. What is piracy? Piracy is the act of stealing an artist's work without an intention of paying for it. I'm not talking about Napster-type software. I'm talking about major label record contracts. (Courtney Love 2000)

Six years on from Albini's calculations, the prices have changed, but not the overall analysis. Love's hypothetical band are more successful. Their first album sells a million copies, and hence 'goes platinum' in the US. Due to the additional promotional and distribution costs added on to the artists' bill by the record company, and given the tax now being paid by the band who are now earning enough to pay tax, this group having sold a million albums are now earning the same as full-time employees at the same convenience store that Albini's band (after selling only a quarter of a million albums) were earning the equivalent of half-wages in. The fourfold increase in fictional sales sees the profits of the record company rise over eightfold to over six-and-a-half million dollars. The artists have reached reward levels somewhere in the region of semi-skilled retail employment. And, as Love points out, the artists have signed over the reproduction rights to their work for increasingly long, effectively perpetual, periods. She also points out that artists who do not achieve US scale 'gold' and sometimes even 'platinum' sales (i.e. half a million and a million respectively) will usually end up in debt to their record companies, and that in the United States it has been made increasingly difficult to declare bankruptcy to get out of the kinds of contracts that lead to such situations in the first place.

Love points out that only around thirty albums a year go platinum in the United States, while there are some thirty-two thousand releases. While hundreds of thousands of Americans make some money from music, only around fifteen per cent of these do so as their primary means of making a living; for almost all of these the greater part of their income is from performance not royalties. If high volumes between gold and platinum sales are required to make a basic living, and given the tiny numbers of artists who do achieve this level of success, it is clear that for all the billions of dollars being paid by customers, and the hundreds of millions of dollars being made in profit, the record industry is a horrifically ineffective mechanism for rewarding creative artists.

Love suggests artists would be better off giving free access to their music online and asking for 'tips' from those fans who like what they hear. If the present arrangement keeps audiences and their money as far away from artists and their pockets as could be imagined, artists have little to fear from 'pirates' other than those they have already signed contracts with. Love supports enforcement of copyright, but just not into the pockets of companies that don't pass it on. She would want to sue anyone who 'stole' her music, but would rather start with her record company Universal, than with her fans. 'Since I've basically been giving my music away for free under the old system, I'm not afraid of wireless, MP3 files and any of the other [new] threats to my copyright' (Love 2000). Having paid record companies for promotion and distribution access, the possibility of removing the need for such 'gatekeepers' is a blessing for artists. However, the question of how artists will establish relationships with fans that will see them making a living from their music may be just as problematic as trying to make a living wage from a one million dollar record label advance. This new economy will be explored in Chapter 9. This chapter simply points out that for all the potential problems in such a new economy, it should always be recalled that the established model was, in reality, nothing like the rosy image presented by those who profited from it.

The emperor's new sword revisited

Given that the situation in the United States and the United Kingdom is one in which artists rarely get paid a living wage, lose control over their intellectual property, and have this set against almost all the fixed costs of the industry which claims to protect them, it is curious that it is these two countries that lead the world in the dissemination of stronger IP protection regimes, premised upon the idea that only such systems as the US and UK have will ensure creativity and security in the future. Are things better elsewhere? As Holmes (2003) points out, things are no better in France (see Chapter 5). In a country that also prides itself on its love of artists across the creative spectrum, France's composers' rights organization had approximately one hundred thousand members in 2003. Only those who earned more than five thousand euros per year from musical royalties were allowed to vote in this organization, meaning only two-and-a-half-thousand people had votes. In other words, only two-and-a-half-thousand people earned the equivalent of unemployment benefit, and these were considered the privileged elite. Holmes goes on to point out that of this tiny number of dubiously privileged artists, only around three hundred musicians in France made their living primarily from royalties. This fraction of one per cent of all French musical composers who were able to make a modest living from the sale of recorded music are, like their opposite numbers in the US and UK, characterized as the wellspring of national and global culture, yet the laws that have been passed in their name do not reward even them in any significant way. For the over ninety-nine per cent of others also seeking to live from their own musical work, recording rights are of near minimal benefit. Holmes concludes that free distribution of recorded music would ensure an audience for many more of these artists than does the current system, and that income from such performances would pass revenues to artists much more readily than having revenues pass through the hands of large corporations. Though a myriad of protective layers claim to be helping the artist, while typically helping themselves at the artists expense, the possibility of making a more direct relationship with audiences via new-media and live performance offers to combine new means with the most established means of interaction. This threatens the current regime of the musical economy, a regime that takes itself to be natural and necessary. If this natural and necessary character were true, such threats would be threats to the very foundation of musical life, and this is the claim being made by the status quo – or at least those benefiting from it. As this chapter suggests, such claims are simply false and should not deter anyone from exploring the possibility of alternatives.

> Most artistic types are generous, open-minded, inquisitive people who sincerely believe in freedom. John Cage is remembered as saying: 'I don't know what art is, but I'm sure it doesn't have anything to do with the police.' Yet artists are increasingly forced to keep the company that Cage refused, by accepting payment through the copyright system – the linchpin of 'immaterial imperialism'. (Holmes 2003)

If Holmes is right, and if Albini and Love are correct also, regarding the levels of reward given to artists through the royalty system, it might be suggested that artists are not increasingly forced to keep such company, as such company does not bind them with any material reward. Whether immaterial imperialism can bind artists in other ways will be explored below. Regarding rewards from royalties, the vast majority of musical artists are forced to be free by the very absence of significant payment. Those with a little more 'success' are shackled to debt-inducing contracts. A very tiny layer rise above this and 'make a living'; precarious, often more modest that the image of a 'rock star' suggests, and with only a limited duration.

David Baskerville (2004) notes that while there is no standard royalties rate, the range is typically between ten and fifteen per cent of 'retail' (a contrived term which sounds better than it is, as it is sale price minus an array of historical and technically redundant deductions that make the amount closer to the price sold to the distributor/retailer than the price paid by the customer to the retailer). Producers usually take three per cent of 'retail' in addition to their upfront costing. While Baskerville suggests that 'major stars' can negotiate marginally above this the scope to achieve such leverage is limited. Typical multi-album deals will include escalators that start below ten per cent and ascend to twelve per cent for the first album if it sells over a million copies. As this is very rare, the royalties, minus recoupable costs will often leave the artist in debt, which ties their hands in relation to future release negotiations. Baskerville writes:

> many attorneys argue that the recording company in this situation sees profits long before the artist's royalty account is recouped ... In fact, fewer than 15% of recordings recoup. Almost all recording companies include a clause in the contract making costs accrued on all recordings recoupable out of royalties on all recordings ... This language, called cross-collateralization, makes it difficult for the artist's royalty account to ever be recouped or 'in the black'. (2004: 172)

Geoffrey Hull (2004: 143–9) provides a similar picture of the royalties system, which while having improved from the 1950s to the present still remains a mechanism by which gold discs often translate into bounced cheques (2004: 148). The contractual parameters of recoupable costs, modest percentages and deducting significant percentages from sales volumes for unrealistic risks of breakage and returns, all leave artists impoverished even when their labels make a profit on their work. As such, given the findings of Holmes, Baskerville and Hull, Albini and Love's stinging assessments of what typical record deals can amount to might very well be unduly optimistic. By all accounts, the system is not stacked in favour of the artist. What Hull identifies in the USA, Richard Bagehot and Nicholas Kanaar (1998) illustrate in the UK: a system designed to minimize the rate and the amount returned to the artist, while maximizing the costs that can be off-set against such royalties.

The shift 'back' from recording to performance

Alan Krueger (2004) analysed the returns to the music industry data collection agency Pollstar in the United States. Pollstar records prices, venues and sales of tickets for popular music performers. Krueger sought to strip out problems associated with the increasing quality of data by recording only artists with a high enough profile. He used *The Rolling Stone Encyclopedia of Rock and Roll* (October 2001 issue) as a benchmark as, he estimated, bands with a high profile were more likely to have had Pollstar listings even in their early years, when data collection tended to miss out less successful artists. What Krueger found was that while concert prices rose roughly in line with inflation up until the late 1990s, after this time, concert prices began to rise far more steeply. Krueger dates the start of this rise in 1997, but his data shows that the period from 1996–99 merely brought rises back into line with a fall in the rate of increase in the period from 1993–96. The really steep rise begins in 1999. Krueger notes that the early acceleration (1996–99) coincides with the advent of readily available CD burners, while the most pronounced jump (after 1999) coincides with the advent of file-sharing. Krueger applies what he calls 'Bowie Theory':

> This model was anticipated by the rock & roll singer David Bowie, who predicted that, 'Music itself is going to become like running water or electricity' and he advises performers, 'You'd better be prepared for doing a lot of touring because that's really the only unique situation that going to be left.' (Quoted from Pareles, 2002.) Hence, I call this hypothesis Bowie Theory. (Krueger 2004: 28)

The so-called theory is that as people spend less on recorded music, so they have more to spend on concert tickets, and so artists have less incentive to cap prices in the expectation that some revenue lost through under-pricing concerts will return to them in the form of greater record sales. Krueger writes:

> Each band has some monopoly power because of its unique sound and style. So my hypothesis is that, in the past, when greater concert attendance translated into greater artists' recording sales, artists had an incentive to price their tickets below the profit-maximizing price for concerts alone. New technology that allows many potential customers to obtain recorded music without purchasing a record has severed the link between the two products. Moreover, only the very best artists received royalties anyway, so this phenomenon can explain why dispersion has increased. (2004: 36)

This last point refers to the finding that prices for the most successful artists have risen far more than is the case for less successful ones. However, overall, even while Sherwin Rosen's (1981) economics of superstars (the winner takes all tournament conditions that characterize global informational commodities among others) tends to polarize the returns to artists, Krueger notes that this does not explain an overall increase in revenues to artists from concert receipts in recent years. This, he suggests, can best be explained by Bowie theory: the decline in competition for revenues between potentially complementary goods, i.e. recordings and live performance. Krueger calculates that where recording sees the split between artist and label as 15/85 (with the artists bearing a greater proportion of costs from their far smaller share of the revenue), in performance the split between artist and promoter is reversed, while costs are shared more equally. All in all, except for a tiny number of superstars, the collapse in the market for recorded music is a blessing for musicians. While tensions exist over interpreting the effect of file-sharing on sales and prices for recorded music (Liebowitz 2003, 2004a, 2004b; Oberholzer and Strumpf 2004), Krueger's analysis suggests that it would be in the interests of artists for such an effect to be negative.

Krueger (with Marie Connolly 2006) goes on to show that in 2002, of the thirty-five most successful musical acts in the United States only four made more money from recording than from performance, and overall income from touring exceeded that from recording by a ratio of 7.5 to 1. The authors note that while total US recording sales in 2003 amounted to $11.8 billion, recorded concert ticket sales amounted to $2.1 billion (though this latter figure is likely to be a significant underestimate). Despite record sales dwarfing ticket sales, as a source of income for artists the reverse is true. The shear inefficiency (or simply the grossly exploitative character) of the recording industry as a mechanism for paying performers is starkly revealed in this seemingly perverse reversal. Krueger and Connolly cite the work of Zhang (2002), who calculated that file-sharing represents both a more efficient and a more equitable method of music distribution when combined with greater scope for making a living from live performance. They conclude with reference to Gopal et al. (2006) who suggest that in time file-sharing will even erode the inequalities characteristic of the winner takes all economics of superstars, though this does not seem to have happened yet.

The term 'back' in the above subtitle is perhaps misleading. It is rather the case that for the vast majority of musical artists the primary source of income is, will be and always has been, live performance. As the above examples demonstrate it is not the advent of digital downloads that have brought about a move away from well-paid recording artists towards hard-working performers touring their work to make a living. It has always been thus except for the tiny handful of artists who sell gold, platinum and even diamond albums – and even for many of them, overall revenues from recording rights have always been small relative to average earnings in the wider society and when compared with their own income from performance and associated merchandising. The mythology of the 'recording artist' can be traced very specifically to the year 1967 and the release of The Beatles' *Sgt Pepper* album. This album was in part a response to the band's decision in 1966 not to tour again after Beatle mania in the United States had meant poor quality amplifiers could not project the sound of the music over the screaming of the fans, and was also a response to the release a year earlier of The Beach Boys' album *Pet Sounds*. Whether *Pet Sounds* or *Sgt Pepper* should be seen as the first ever concept album is debatable, but the release of the second album, a recording phenomenon never to be 'performed' live as such, but rather created solely for record release, saw the birth of something new. The decision not to tour and to release pure studio creations founded the idea of the artist as a recorder rather than a performer. While The Beatles' sales did generate huge fortunes for its members, for very few others was the career of the recording star ever more than a myth, backed up by live performance to make a living. Robert Sandall (2007) points out the current economics of music, which has seen the relative price of recorded music fall, while the prices people are willing to pay for live performance has 'rocketed'. However, it should not be forgotten that the underlying reality for artists has always been performance and not recording based. The decline in CD sales revenues in recent years has had virtually no impact on the incomes of artists, even though it has dented those of major record labels. The rising demand for live performance, and the increased willingness to pay high prices for such performances, has benefited artists far more than royalties ever did. Musicians are better off when they get paid to do a 'shift' on stage than they are waiting for a return on their music as 'capital', dead labour seeking a return as an investment.

Just as every good social science student knows, you cannot draw a causal explanation from a simple correlation between two variables. This, of course, has not stopped record companies making the strong claim that copyright infringing digital downloads cause the suppression of physical sales and legitimate downloads. By the same logic, it should be argued that the declining revenue from music fans to record companies being directly correlated with their increased willingness to pay, and to pay more, for live performance means that file-sharing has led artists to be better paid. Of course, this cannot be proven directly, and is certainly not an argument you will hear among the 'stakeholders' who advise the government in framing policy and legislation. If, however, beyond correlation it is possible to demonstrate the existence of the mechanisms or processes that explain the relationship between correlates and their temporal sequence, we do move one step closer to causal sufficiency. Few artists made a living from royalties before file-sharing; many are making a bettter living from live performance after its advent. This blunt fact supports the argument that the commercial sale of recorded music as it is currently configured is an exploitative, inefficient and redundant vestige of the pre-digital age. Can there be any rationale for the continued existence of the major record labels? Five elements compose the argument for such a continuation. These will be explored in the following section of this chapter.

The declining value of investment

It might be asked, given all the evidence put forward in this chapter already, why any musician or band would sign a contract with a record company. If the signature on such a deal requires that you hand over eighty-five per cent of the sale value of your recorded music to that company, while undertaking to cover the cost of your production and promotion from the remaining few per cent, in addition to paying the costs of management, lawyers and others from such royalties – and this tends to leave you in debt to the very company that is taking such a huge percentage, while you struggle to make a basic living – why would anybody even pick up the pen? One argument is that artists are simply ignorant of the facts and remain convinced by the mythology of the industry, and its tiny crust of wealthy recording artists. I will return to this 'false consciousness' hypothesis later. It is problematic, in its simple terms, but when set in the context of material constraints that pressure artists to sign with major record labels if they want to reach an audience, it may well be true that artists faced with little alternative cling to a belief most know is highly unlikely to come true for them.

The material constraint argument, put forward by record companies to justify their existence is simple. Talent needs capital investment to reach its potential. Such investment is required to foster creativity and to bring it to the world in a form that can generate profit, and thereby income for the artists. In this model, capital is an essential part of the creative process. There are five dimensions to this argument, which are: 1. the production function; 2. the manufacture of physical product; 3. distribution and sales; 4. promotion and publicity; and finally 5. publishing and associated rights management.

The production function

Steve Albini's claims regarding the current state of the music industry (in 1994 and to this day) carry credibility within the musical field because Albini is a well-respected musician and producer. If musicians mistrust the calculative nature of the industry suits and the industry suits distrust the temperament of artists, the producer straddles the boundary – at times trusted by all parties, although sometimes seen by all as representing the other side of the coin. The producer was traditionally both recruiter and recorder, bringing in new talent and moulding it in the studio to create the sound that would then be packaged, marketed and sold to the world. The most legendary producers were the founders and owners of the studio-empires they worked in. This was the case at Tamla-Motown, under song-writer, producer, founder and studio owner Berry Gordy Jr (George 2003, Posner 2005); Sun Records, under its founder, owner and head producer Sam Phillips, is also taken as a paradigm case in point (Crouch and Crouch 2008). Phillips is often credited with the very creation of 'Rock and Roll' while Gordy has been similarly credited in moulding 'Soul' for a mass black and white audience. The same ambition, to create a new sound, would be true today within many small, independent record labels, typically driven by producer-based values of discovery and creation. However, across time and in the particular development of companies as they grow, the producer function becomes separated from other elements within the organization, not least as this 'entrepreneurial' function is largely at odds with the other functions, functions that require very different skills. Gordy's downfall and Phillips's sale of Elvis Presley for a fraction of his value are often cited as evidence that a genius producer is not always the best person to preside over the company accounts.

In larger record companies the producer would, traditionally, still com-bine the role of going out and finding new talent and working with them in the studio. Studios would employ someone like Phil Spector (who had orig-inally performed and then created his own label before working for other bigger labels, see Wolfe 1966, Brown 2007, Ribowsky 2007) or Trevor Horn (Warner 2003) on the basis of their track record in finding and building new, commercially successful sounds. As Peter Martin (1995) points out, the position of the producer – whether in recruiting, recording or in both – has a significant degree of autonomy only as long as what they do continues to generate a roster of profitable products for the remaining arms of the company to package, promote, sell and manage. This track record is closely monitored, and the careers, budgets and contracts of producers rise and fall accordingly.

Interestingly, Martin (1995: 248) points out that in recent years, the producer function has been increasingly outsourced and subdivided, thereby externalizing the risk of this entrepreneurial function to the remaining, more bureaucratic, functions of the organization. Albini, for example, is an independent producer. He is not employed by a record company, but rather receives payment in terms of percentages of sales, recouped from the artists' royalties. Albini also hires his studio time direct to artists in return for a set daily rate. Major labels seek to insulate themselves from low selling records, even while claiming they need to retain revenues from high selling recordings to cover the supposed losses made on the 'failures'. Whereas in the past the studio producer worked for the major label, today they increasingly occupy a position similar to that of artists.

Meanwhile the other dimension of the producer function, going out and finding new talent, has also undergone a transformation that similarly insulates the bureaucratic functions of the major labels from the entrepre-neurial function of risk-taking with new artists. Whereas in the mid twen-tieth century (from the 1950s to the 1980s) record companies underwent a series of cycles of concentration and competition, periods where larger companies expanded and took over the field and ones where new com-petitors entered and exploited new possibilities (Peterson and Berger 1975, cited in Martin 1995), the late twentieth century has witnessed what Frith (1990) calls a complementary model. Here, small independent labels undertake the entrepreneurial producer function of finding new talent and working with them in the development of their sound and their audience. If successful, artist and repertoire (A&R) producers from major labels will take an interest and either buy out the act from the independent label or simple buy up the label. Typically, this buyout cost is recoupable from the artists' royalties. In this way major labels insulate themselves from the cost of the artists' early development. While the cost of buying a semi-established act from another label is greater than the cost of signing an unknown act directly 'from the street', this additional cost is recoupable. Better to make large bets at short odds with the artists' future royalties than to bet small on long odds with your own money.

In splitting the production function and externalizing both parts, record companies increase the security of their investment, and reduce the time in which returns are expected to be made. Buying experienced artists from independent labels means they can be 'launched' fully formed almost as soon as the ink is dry on the contract. An established audience, existing studio experience, time spent performing and an offsetting of production costs against royalties does make the life of a major label more secure, making it easier to calculate production runs and promotional budgets.

However, at the same time, externalizing both the recruitment and recording aspects of the production function, does mean that labels who practice such outsourcing and insulating cannot then claim that these production functions represent essential dimensions of their role in the creative process. As such, except in relation to fully manufactured in-house acts, the producer function can be ticked off the list of reasons why a creative artist would sign a deal with a major label. Such an artist would have already had to undertake such work either themselves or with an independent label before being signed to a major. The major label cannot turn around in years to come and claim they made those early investments. Precisely because they did not take those risks, they cannot later claim the credit, or at least they have no legitimate grounds to do so even though they routinely do.

Digital technologies are often credited with enabling someone with a half-decent collection of software to produce music in their bedroom at a level equivalent to that recording studios would have struggled to produce only a few years ago. Making demos has become much easier, and gaining studio time to carry out self-production is also cheaper than ever before, with the price of mixing desks reducing significantly. Nevertheless, just as a guitar may cost a fraction of an average weekly wage in most advanced economies, that does not mean many people can actually play one, let alone expect to get paid for so doing. The studio producer function is still highly prized, and 'self-production' may well require hiring a professional producer to capture, mix and master the recorded sound. The increased tendency of major labels to outsource such work means that even the claim that quality requires more than bedroom or garage demo mixing does not validate the continued utility of such companies. The debate over the value of professional quality studio production relative to newly available self-production is not one I am qualified to enter into. Debates concerning under- and over-produced studio recordings, the relative merits of live recordings and other sources of distortion versus the cleanliness and precision of professional production, are ones in which technique blends with notions of authenticity into what are often really preferences. Do these preferences themselves reflect positions within the musical field of production? Such preferences are a fascinating topic for sociological research with only limited work already undertaken. As such, for now, it is only my opinion that Sir George Martin's reworking of many famous Beatles' tracks for the 2006 *Love* album was chronically over-produced. As someone writing a book about file-sharing I would say that, wouldn't I? That my ears are still ringing from the distortion and volume imbalance from the live performance I went to yesterday, might lead me to the opposite conclusion, but stubborn prejudice still convinces me that it was great. While MP3 compression enables cheap reproduction, and initially enabled only this, today's greater memory capacity or the use of the MP4 format allows far greater sound quality, if desired, and even the static crackle of vinyl can be digitally captured.

The manufacture of physical product

This section may appear not to require writing. Anyone with access to a computer can now burn their own CDs. The 'recording industry' started with the development of the gramophone and the phonograph in the late nineteenth century (Martin 1995: 238) and required the production of physical records to store information which would then reproduce sound when played on suitable player. Such records and record players could not be made or adjusted by the customer. They were costly to produce, with high initial fixed costs and then small marginal costs per unit of additional production. The price of the first copy was greater than the cost of turning out the rest of the batch. Customers could no more make their own copies than they could make their own cars or houses or other capital intensive goods. Presses were large, expensive and technically precise machines. While there was a pirate industry in the production of unlicensed discs, such a practice was restricted to large-scale criminal organizations or music business insiders (Marshall 2005).

The development of audio tape, and in particular the audio cassette, changed the nature of production dramatically, both enabling the widespread availability of pirated copies of commercial releases and bootleg recordings of live and studio recordings otherwise not available, and allowing home recording for the first time. Perceived at the time as a major threat to the recording industry, bootlegging and home taping are largely seen today to have helped the music industry. Bootlegs were largely providing material that was not otherwise commercially available and tended to fuel interest in the official output of those artists who were having their out-takes and live events circulated without permission. Marshall (2005) suggests that there was even collusion to promote such alternative material getting 'out there'. Home taping was perhaps the greater potential threat as it was commercial material that was being taped. However, the relatively poor quality of such copies meant they were never seen as a direct substitute for 'the real thing', the commercially packaged record. The tendency for tapes in general to be seen as a cheap alternative to vinyl meant that those unable to afford many records would home tape, but when they could afford to they then went on to buying records. In retrospect it seems that home taping created a new generation of music fans who, when economic conditions allowed, went on to buy more music than ever before.

That new surge in music buying was in part explained by the advent of the CD. Home taping in the 1970s and early 1980s was displaced by the rise of the CD after 1982 and the development of recordable CDs shortly afterwards. The CD allowed the same quality of reproduction from commercial copy to home burnt copy as has been passed from the original master to the purchased recording. The record industry was, in effect, giving away its master copies. The advent of digital compression was at first seen as equivalent to taping, capturing only a low resolution version of the original recording, but as file capacity has improved, this claim has become less viable. File-sharing today delivers high quality copies without the need for the traditional physical manufacture and packaging function of record companies. As such, it can be suggested that where the producer function of major labels has been outsourced to freelance producers, independent labels and artists themselves, the physical manufacture and packaging function has been outsourced to the audience. The second foundation for the continued existence of major labels appears also to have withered. Audiences and artists do not need an intermediary physically to package the music for it to be transferred from one to the other.

Of course, it can be shown that many people prefer to have their recorded music packaged. The album is so called because in the past recordings were packaged with each song or piece on a single one-sided disc located in a book of discs resembling a photo album, The term has stuck, even if the physical function of such packaging is redundant. That one hundred thousand people chose to buy Radiohead's 2007 album, *In Rainbows*, in its deluxe box-set physical format at the cost of forty pounds a copy, and then millions more bought the standard edition in shops, despite this album being released first online and at whatever price the downloader felt the work deserved, says two things. The first is that physical formats are not, of necessity, going to be killed off by cheaper forms of distribution. As such, the major labels could cling to the fact that many people will want more than a download. However, the second thing Radiohead's release showed undermines this comfort. If audiences are prepared to buy a physical product from the artist, despite having the option to download it for next to nothing, there is really no need for artists to rely upon record companies to protect their intellectual property. Radiohead's standard shop release was a distribution deal with an independent label, not a royalty-based deal with a major. Generating even a modest income from online sales or live performance would cover the radically reduced costs of physical production, and if a more direct trust relationship between artist and audience can generate greater returns to the artist than can sales mediated through highly inefficient and ill-trusted record labels, why sign? Chapter 9 explores the alternatives that are currently being developed.

Distribution and sales

A great sound, nicely manufactured and packaged is all well and good but, sat in a crate in a warehouse or in someone's garage, it is not going to realize any financial value. Getting work into the hands of potential buyers traditionally involved a distribution network that would see physical product being placed in record shops for potential buyers and available to order for those making specific requests for works they have heard about. To establish this supply chain involves not only the ability to get product into shops but also the ability to get payment from the shops back to the company, and supposedly then to the artist. Even if artists could trail around every record shop in the country, or the world, and even if a large number of those shops took their record to sell, it would be nearly impossible to collect the money. Major record labels might be venal and self-interested, arm-twisting, contract manipulating, money grabbers but that might be just the kind of organization you want to be working with when trying to leverage payment from reluctant shops, whose willingness to pay the next final demand may only be realistically achieved if the threat of withholding a whole swathe of profitable material is held over their heads.

Of course, when the likely return to the artist is minimal, getting the product into the shops and sold may be of little direct financial benefit, while the real advantage lies in building an audience and gaining a reputation. In this sense, a distribution network that may be equally poor in securing a direct financial return to the artist but which gets the recording to a wider audience, without the restrictions imposed by a system of distribution which requires a large chain of intermediaries to be paid before the audience gets to be exposed to the artists' work, might be considered superior. If low and medium volume sales produce negligible returns to the artist, such artists would be better off financially if their work was distributed freely or cheaply online. With this option could come the expectation that such exposure and low cost would increase audience size and relative spending power for live performances, and for associated merchandising which might include physical recordings.

For established artists who could expect high sales volumes, the case of Radiohead suggests a wide fan base does not require a major label distribution network to engender willingness to pay. For both new acts and established artists the distribution of physical product, once considered an essential function of the record label, is becoming redundant in the digital age, at least in its own terms. The Internet provides a far more efficient means of distribution, one that does not require major label investment to facilitate. Again, a central plank in the defence of major labels is being undone. If audiences have been prepared to download for free, this cannot be used as a defence of the traditional model of physical product being sold in shops. If audiences do not feel the moral obligation to pay for recordings, a belief that is encouraged by the view that what they pay in the shops does not go to the artist anyway, defending the value of physical distribution is to miss the point. The key to the future of music will lie in refounding the relationship between audience and artists. Whether this is done through the renaissance of live performance, or in new modes of distribution where trust and legitimacy supplant purely legal and technical methods of enforced payment, or some combination of both, remains to be seen. Belief in the essential necessity of yesterday's modes of production, manufacture and distribution is waning, even if it is doing so more slowly in the offices of major label executives than it is among artists and audiences.

The promoter function

The previous three sections have pointed out that in terms of production, manufacturing and distribution the major record labels' claim to be serving essential functions – investments that would otherwise not be carried out, and hence which are crucial for the future of musical creativity and the careers of artists – are simply not true. In relation to the role of the major labels in what can be called the promoter function, the claim that major labels are the key means by which artists are able to gain exposure (whether on radio, television, and in the music press, as well as being able to secure slots playing at prestigious events and locations, or with other successful or rising artists) is true, at least to a significant degree. Whereas in relation to the three previous functions criticism focused upon the false claim that major labels do essential work, in relation to the promotion function criticism should be focused upon the control such corporations hold. It is precisely because major labels monopolize access to a number of key promotional channels that they can still control the market. Even without their help in production, manufacture and distribution, an artist might still feel compelled to sign a contract if that was the only way they felt it was possible to gain significant radio, television and press coverage, and to secure valuable performance opportunities.

As Peter Martin (1995) suggests, the practices that once governed access to promotion have in large measure been rendered illegal. It is unlawful in most countries to pay directly to secure airplay for artists, or to offer various kinds of bribes such as first refusal on new material by established artists in exchange for adding the work of new artists from that label to the radio station's playlist (for example). However, to get around this legal prohibition on such explicit bribery (often referred to as 'Payola'), major labels typically resort to paying independent 'promoters' and 'pluggers' to act as intermediaries. Paid substantial amounts of money to get results and given a degree of discretion in how they get those results, such intermediaries continue to ensure that major labels secure almost exclusive access to mass media promotion, even while maintaining a nominal distance from such media channels. It was almost unheard of for an artist without a major label record deal to gain a high ranking in national charts, though this has started to happen with the inclusion in chart calculations of digital downloads that bypass the need for a physical distribution network.

Significant media exposure has been crucial to the development of subsequent record sales and for bookings for the kinds of large venues from which large revenues flow. While some inroads have been made into this promoter function by new-media channels that do not have major label money determining (if only at a distance) their editorial policy, it still remains the case that major labels can hold the keys to relative fame over the heads of artists who might, in relation to production, manufacture and distribution, feel that they do not want to sign a record deal. Claims by major labels that their investment in promotion is crucial to the future success of the particular artists they invest in may well be true, but this is not the same as saying that such artists, and artists in general, benefit from such a monopolistic situation wherein not being signed up to one of the gatekeepers means you are likely to remain in relative obscurity. It is only the existence of such monopolistic control that requires artists to operate within its terms. If the dismantling of the first three supposed functions of major labels outlined above led to a reduction of the financial flows necessary to maintain monopoly controls over promotion, it would not be in any way to the detriment of artists and audiences as such. It is likely rather to benefit those artists whose talent attracts an audience in more open conditions of exposure, and to benefit audiences with an interest in something slightly more diverse than the safer bets most commonly promoted by labels whose primary motivation is to secure a sufficient volume of sales to enable them to afford the next round of promotional work. As Martin (1995: 252) notes, a major label requires a tenfold greater number of sales to cover its costs relative to an independent label. Such high volumes rarely see significant returns to the artist, yet are seen as necessary to fund the high levels of publicity that give such material their sales potential. To ensure such sales, the product rarely deviates from what executives consider to be sufficiently similar to everything else that is currently popular. As Billy Bragg pointed out (personal conversation, December 2007), a total monopoly over recording and promotion such as operated in the Soviet Union through the Melodika Label encouraged a tendency towards repetition and conformity. Conditions in contemporary monopoly capitalism are not identical. Neither are they entirely dissimilar. A defence of major labels and their profit margins on the grounds that they engage in risky investment and thereby deserve to reap the high returns justified by such risk taking is again undone by even a cursory examination of their monopolistic practice in relation to the promoter function.

Publishing rights and the management of wider rights

Twenty years ago, Simon Frith (1987) argued that record labels, and in particular major labels, were no longer primarily involved in the business of selling physical product but were, rather, engaged in the management of a 'basket of rights' around music: performance rights, recording rights, rights in composition as well as publishing rights, merchandising, and other tie-ins and promotional deals (such as product endorsements and advertising appearances). Twenty years on, in the midst of ongoing struggles to control the sale of physical goods, and where such sales still represent the primary source of income for record companies if not for the artists they claim to represent, Frith's claim may appear not just premature, but entirely incorrect. Despite falling CD sales and prices, physical sales still represent the bulk of record companies' revenues. Digital music sales equal only ten to fifteen per cent of physical sales (Kirton et al. 2008) and, despite various efforts, record labels' control over performance and merchandising revenues remains contested, and limited in overall amount and as a proportion of overall revenue. Publishing rights is a little different. Yet there is some truth in the suggestion that managing intellectual property rights in music is more than selling physical product. Precisely at a time when it is increasingly difficult to stop individuals downloading music for personal use, so it becomes more attractive to go after revenues in public and commercial settings. This may be from shops, pubs, clubs and restaurants playing music as part of the creation of an atmosphere they hope customers will themselves pay to enjoy. It may be in gaining payment for music played as part of television and film production. It may be for music played in advertisements. These sources of revenue become increasingly attractive. As accessing music for personal consumption becomes increasingly easy and, despite very significant limits, increasingly anonymous, so the open and public use of such material makes it easier to locate and its commercial character makes it easier to justify charging for. Also, the profitable nature of such venues and media outlets and outputs means the per-unit revenues that can be gained are larger. As such, being easier to locate, easier to collect and larger per-unit income, it is not surprising that such revenue streams are now seen as a lifeline for major labels otherwise facing increasingly difficult and diminishing returns in their, until now, core business. As such Frith's claim may indeed, one day, come true.

However, revenues from publishing have historically gone to artists through publishing companies independent of record labels. While the composition of 'publishing' revenues changed over the course of the twentieth century, from mainly sheet music sales to rights in mechanical reproduction and broadcast/synchronization with visual media, until the 1980s it was almost universal for artists to assign publishing rights to a separate company than the company releasing their recordings (Hull 2004). The rise of record companies over the course of the last century rather eclipsed the significance of publishing, and while publishing rights cover a range of areas – radio and television airplay; use as background music in television programmes, advertising and film; the playing of recordings in public venues; cover versions; and elements of live performance payments – the capture of such income remained problematic and limited in all but record sales until recently. Hull (2004: 92) notes that between 1909 and 1978 publishing rights remained at two US cents per record (single or album) and has only marginally out performed inflation since then, the statutory rate being eight cents in 2002 (with most publishers accepting six). Such amounts are split, after various deductions, evenly between publisher and artist.

However, digitization has increased the scope for monitoring play in public venues and on radio, and there is now more television, film and advertising that requires background music. Just as the 1980s saw major reorganization and concentration in the recording industry, so major labels embarked upon a comprehensive acquisition of music publishing companies. Hull (2004: 72–5) documents the rise of such integration. The major record labels now own all the music publishers in his listings of the largest of such companies across the major music genres he examines.

While publishers' back catalogues and new acquisitions are lucrative assets with long profit tails relative to the short duration of profitability typical of most recordings, and given declining CD sales and prices, publishing rights are still only a modest part of most record companies' revenues (EMI being perhaps the exception here). However, bringing publishing companies 'in-house' has one very important advantage for record companies, relative to others, that of cross-collateralization. If an artist fails to recoup an advance made on future royalties, a record label can recoup from publishing rights instead, but only if the artist is signed to that record company's publishing arm. As has been pointed out already most artists end up in debt to their labels as they are only paid a royalty based on a small percentage of net sales, while the full cost of production, promotion and equipment is set against this small percentage. In the past such debts were never repaid and, though the artist rarely saw a return on their recording rights, they did receive a small amount from publishing. With the incorporation of publishers by record labels, and through the principle of internal cross-collateralization, even this is now taken by the label. The birth of the so-called 360 degree contract was born here, and was only later extended to include merchandising and direct payment for performance.

Radiohead's decision to release their 2007 album, *In Rainbows*, through a publisher independent of their old record label (EMI) was all the more significant as it was set against the backdrop of twenty years of relentless incorporation of publishers by major labels.

Whether new artists would sign a contract with a major record label simply to have their publishing rights managed, when this could be done more cost-effectively by a lawyer working for a fee, remains an open question. It is unlikely that this alone would secure the long-term viability of major labels, which would require continued domination over the fourth function: the maintenance of monopoly control over promotional channels. If a sufficient number of established artists break away from the traditional record company model, and thereby create momentum for alternative channels of promotion both to exist and to function, the resources necessary to maintain today's existing monopoly will not remain available. If this further expands the space for new acts to find an audience without the majors, the emerging cracks in that fourth pillar may lead to a total collapse of the current major label business paradigm. For the sake of artists and audiences, we can only hope that the analysis presented in this chapter is correct.

At the start of this section the question was raised as to why artists would sign contracts when the reality of artistic work in the current business model is so far removed from the ideological representation. It might be assumed that in a celebrity culture (Rojek 2001, Turner 2004, Cashmore 2006) everyone else buys into the myth of instant fame and fortune, even if we see through it. It is not necessary to assume artists are simply duped into believing the false promises. As this chapter has pointed out, even armed with a full knowledge of how things are for most artists, the capacity of major labels to control key elements in the promotion of artists would still make it hard to avoid the conclusion that except by signing a contract with a major the doors to the kingdom of heaven – or just modest success – will remain barred. It is not necessary to assume ignorance, rather it is the absence of alternatives that may hold artists to a contract they may be fully aware of the problems with. The really interesting question will be how artists come to perceive their choices in conditions where alternatives begin to emerge. These alternatives have been in part created by new technical affordances, and by the actions of audiences and artists – some established and others emerging. As such the alternatives are not simply an external reality confronting artists but opportunities that have been created, spaces that have been opened up. However, once in existence, the willingness of artists to take chances on alternative models, relative to sticking with traditional paradigms, will determine their future viability. When the band Radiohead chose not to renew their contract with EMI, and rather chose to release an album independently, the band Coldplay, who were still under contract with EMI were forced to explain their willingness to go along with the old game. In an interview for the BBC's listings magazine, *The Radio Times*, Coldplay's singer likened the decision to stay with their label with continuing to live in your grandfather's house. It was a bit restrictive, but they liked the old man and they felt he'd been kind to them in the past. This spin on their contractual obligations at least avoided the impression of having to live with their parents because they were legally prohibited from leaving. Faced with new possibilities, artists will have to make choices not always available in the past, and justify actions that would have once been written off as unpleasant but unavoidable necessities. The outcome of such choices may help clarify the power of celebrity dreams relative to material realities, even while the power to make such choices offers the scope to challenge both.

Creativity as embodiment and performance?

Disputes over the sources of creativity parallel those over the very meaning of the term. Claims for the creativity of: 1. compositional genius; 2. expressions of heritage, tradition and community; 3. intersubjective emergence from interaction between performers; 4. intersubjective emergence from interaction between performers and audiences; and 5. the complex technical division of labour which can combine technique and other resources in a structured form – these all maintain they hold the aesthetic 'high ground' of producing 'originality'. No doubt each account of 'origin' holds particular appeal for those located in positions for which that account gives greater credit, even while simultaneously all five accounts might be accepted as having some validity.

For fifty years the recording industry has successfully equated its position in relation to the technical division of labour with the lion's share of recorded sales revenue. The far smaller percentages paid in royalties to artists for, first, composition (equating roughly with personal genius) and, second, performance (equating roughly with intersubjective emergence between performers), reflects the relative success of different parties to record contracts to define the value of their contribution. The contribution of heritage, tradition and community has been largely unrewarded. The value of interaction between musicians and audiences has been valued in relation to 'live' music, whether directly or in 'live recordings', yet this valuation has been at odds with the primacy of the studio recording, and of course the audience typically do not get paid. With the relative decline in profit margins from recorded music, and with the increasing revenues being generated by live performance, so definitions of creative value will no doubt also shift in their weighting of priorities.

The apparent irony of global digital media, that in making recorded sounds universally available they might thereby increase the value – both material and aesthetic – of those forms of expression that remain scarce and/or unique, is explored in Mark Hansen's (2006) new philosophy for new-media. Drawing upon Henri Bergson's embodied materiality, Hansen offers an account of experience in digital cultures wherein the performance of seemingly immaterial forms (and music might be taken as a case in point here) creates new meaning. It is my suggestion here that as live performance takes on a greater significance in the musical economy, so constructions of creativity will come increasingly to value that originality which emerges in such interactions, relative to that which might occur in a recording studio for example. This is not to say, objectively, that one interaction is intrinsically more creative than another. Rather, it is to identify what is felt to be more valuable by particular groups at particular times (see Fonarow 2006).

If audiences are willing to pay more today for something particular, precisely because recordings offer no such distinction, it is not that creativity as such should be equated with singular non-repeatability. The scope to coordinate investments or instruments through structured production regimes and/or structured notation and scoring of time can facilitate creativity, and a 'live' performance involves a huge array of prior organization. The recent rise in popularity of live performance and its equation with the meal, while the recording becomes only the menu, reflects a preference for one conception of 'creativity' over other perfectly legitimate and authentic forms. Hansen's conception of the embodied virtual captures the seeming incongruity of such a heightened valuation of the unique experience of presence and participation in performance in an age of globally circulating images and sounds. Such a revaluation coincides with the interests of musicians who have always tended to make more from performance than from recording, and challenges the interests of recording companies for whom the opposite has always been the case. This only reinforces the conclusion that what is bad for the established music business model may, in fact, turn out to be good for musicians.

Conclusions

'Money isn't everything, but no money is nothing!' (popular expression). This chapter has highlighted the chronic failure of the existing system to reward artists for their work, either as labour or as creative capital. The claim that 'pirates' are robbing artists of their rewards better describes the practices of major record labels than it does the actions of file-sharers. While major labels claim that the war on file-sharing pirates is a war in the defence of artists, it should be noted what file-sharers might otherwise have paid for recorded music was never likely to have ended up in the pockets of artists, so it is not the artist who is being robbed – at least not by file-sharers. If major labels wish to point out the correlation between file-sharing and the decline in their profit margins, it should also be pointed out that the rise of such peer-to-peer distribution of recorded music which potentially bypasses such companies is also correlated with a significant rise in the revenues generated by live musical performance, which has itself benefited artists more significantly than any loss in what were only likely to be trivial royalties. Even the financial losses of the major labels can be said to benefit artists, as such diminished profits decreases the capacity of major labels to monopolize promotion, something that has often forced artists to sign onerous contracts for the promise of exposure. The outsourcing of producer functions to artists, independent labels and to freelancers, the outsourcing of manufacture to audiences, and the inefficiency and redundancy of physical distribution networks leave the promoter function as the key 'bottleneck' by which major labels continue to seek to control the relationship between artists and their audience. While revenue streams from publishing and other rights management offer new and potentially rising flows of income, whether these will continue to flow through record labels will be largely determined by the struggle currently going on to maintain power in the fourth domain, that of promotion. If this monopoly is significantly disrupted, in part due to new affordances in the first three functions combined with alternative channels in the fourth, it is likely that the major label's days as significant players in the musical field are numbered. The next chapter explores 'alternative business models' and 'alternative cultural practices' that are already challenging the status quo.

9

Alternative Cultural Models of Participation, Communication and Reward?

Introduction

While it is one thing to highlight the theoretical contradictions within the idea of 'intellectual property', along with the legal, technical and economic tensions that exist within the music industry as it currently exists and which are exposed by the practices of file-sharers, it is still worth asking whether copyright infringing file-sharing is simply: 1. a relatively insignificant parasitic practice; 2. a substantive threat to cultural innovation; 3. a subversion that reinforces dominant versions (as was/is the case with bootlegging); or 4. a prefigurative practice that embodies new and progressive forms of social interaction, reward and motivation. Another, fifth, scenario also exists: the colonization of the musical field such that music becomes the free content for an advertising funded appropriation of new-media by established old media corporations. Through an examination of the use of file-sharing by musicians, promoters and audiences this chapter examines the possibility of a music business/culture that does not depend upon intellectual property rights. Could/does such a business/culture exist? Could/does it innovate? To what extent are these questions answered in the here and now by alternative practices and in part by the reality of a musical performance culture and economy that does not fit the recording industry's account? This chapter suggests that the answers are very much in the affirmative and that alternative futures can readily be identified in prefigurative practices in the present. This chapter examines current realities, highlighting six case studies (two emergence stories, two continuing success stories and two cases of artists who are no longer at the peak of their celebrity). Using the axes of trust and proximity, four 'ideal typical' futures are then mapped out. The future of music will fall somewhere between these polarities.

Five interpretations of file-sharing

Perhaps file-sharing is just another flash in the pan, a mildly irritating phenomenon for the recording industry which, rather like home taping, can be condemned as parasitic but which, in the long run, will have no lasting negative effect. Recorded music revenues have fallen heavily in the years since Napster, but perhaps this was just a correction after a decade of reformatting, where sales were boosted by the replacement of vinyl back catalogues with CDs. Prices have dropped to reflect competition with free downloads and fear of file-sharing has led major record labels to accept online service providers such as iTunes. Legal, technical and media campaigning may one day stem the tide, and business confidence in its core market will return. This scenario, while possible, remains unlikely. Legal, technical and cultural failures to stop file-sharing have all been widely recognized as such. Declining revenues and profits make the core strategic business of buying up all major promotional space (in various media and by various direct and indirect means) less feasible. This has opened up possibilities for artists to break from established controls.

Given the weak returns to artists from a royalties-based system of payment, and with revenues lost to recorded music being more than compensated for by increased revenues for live performance, the claim that file-sharing will substantively threaten creativity seems dubious. While challenging one mode of allegedly rewarding creativity (one that rewards the complex division of labour within major record labels, if not often the artists that are signed to such labels) it should be noted that this form of organization is more focused on a particular mode of realizing value in creative works than it is on fostering such innovation. As Chapter 8 pointed out, major labels tend to insulate themselves from the entrepreneurial risks of creative innovation in the early stages of artists' careers and tend towards a conservative reproduction of success once acts are signed. Repeating a winning formula is only one definition of the creative process.

Might file-sharing act to relegitimate the music industry, injecting music with a rebellious edge that audiences want but that major labels cannot provide? Will file-sharing do today what bootlegging did in the past (Marshall 2005)? To the extent that bootlegs were mainly studio out-takes and live performance not otherwise available commercially, they did not threaten the commercial sector in the way file-sharing does. File-sharing is a part of a new emerging relationship between artists and audiences. However, it is unlikely to be one that accommodates established interme-diaries. As the six case studies that follow will suggest, file-sharing may offer scope for a new musical economy, whether in refocusing attention on live performance as the primary source of revenue generation (which for artists it already is) or in requiring new formations of trust between artists and audiences to foster payment for recorded material.

Finally, while condemned as economically damaging by established inter-mediaries, the free circulation of cultural works offers scope to established media businesses. The possibility of music as free content being used to draw audiences to media channels and platforms is very attractive to both advertising-based media corporations and those in the electronics industry. Businesses like Sky, Sony, Time Warner, Vivendi, Disney, Samsung, Microsoft, Apple, General Electric, Toshiba and Philips all see the potential to profit from audiences attracted to free content. We may witness the decline of established sectoral elites. Whether this will then produce a more democ-ratic musical culture or one more fully integrated within corporate control remains to be determined.

Music today: myth and reality

It is worth reiterating that a royalty-based system of paying artists has never been successful at rewarding and securing any but the tiniest number of artists. It is not the advent of file-sharing that has taken us from a golden age of well-paid artists to a situation where only a fraction of one per cent of those receiving royalties actually make even a basic income from them. That was the case before file-sharing and it is still the case today. What has changed is the possibility of doing things differently. Until now access to a large audience was tied to major label domination of the avenues of pro-duction, manufacture, distribution and promotion, with the latter the key to getting heard. Artists were in a weak position if they did not sign the con-tracts offered and these contracts reflected this relative weakness. The pos-sibility of reaching an audience by new means is potentially threatening. Reaching by electronic means runs the risk of reaching the world, but having no capacity to force those reached to pay. Also, the absence of editorial control means all voices are shouting at once and so everyone is equally unlikely to be heard. If old monopolies over promotion restricted access and subordinated artists to labels who controlled that access, how might artists negotiate successfully in conditions where such restriction has been replaced with overcrowding? The following six case studies seek to map out the field of possible positions, resources and strategies.

Six case studies

The six case studies discussed below are not an exhaustive or representative sample of artists. They are selected because they are examples of alternative pathways which challenge the conventional model of becoming or staying successful in the music business. Two cases are of bands that became successful using new techniques that might seem to threaten the status quo. Two are examples of bands which are in the period after their greatest 'star' exposure, and who have adopted alternative methods of distributing their music online in such a way as to bypass the need for a record company and yet still make an income from music – perhaps even a greater living than would have been afforded had they relied on royalties as a proxy for a pension. Finally, two of the case studies are of artists at the peak of their success, or at least at the very pinnacle of the global recorded music business, who have chosen to adopt alternative modes of distribution of recorded music, again without recourse to a major label. Two other potential case studies, those of Prince and Paul McCartney who chose to give albums away through tie-in deals with a newspaper and coffee shop respectively, were not chosen as 'alternative' models in the context of new digital technologies, but these examples should be kept in mind as we go on to discuss the scope for a colonization of the musical field by other commercial fields. The six cases chosen are not conclusive proof that what they show to be possible will inevitably come to replace the status quo. They do, however, allow an exploration of practices that prefigure positive alternative futures for artists without record companies at all levels of their careers and thereby refute the common proposition that a future without today's major labels would be a future without musicians or new music.

Arctic Monkeys

The Arctic Monkeys (BBC News 2006, Domino Records 2008) came to prominence in January 2006 when their first album, *Whatever People Say I Am That's What I'm Not*, sold almost one hundred and twenty thousand copies on its first day, and over one-third of a million copies in its first week. This made it the fastest selling album in UK history, dwarfing the combined sales of all other albums in the UK top twenty that week. The parents of the band's lead singer, Alex Turner, were both music teachers and, with their help, the band was able to record 'demo' CDs of a reasonable quality using home recording and mixing equipment. These were given away for free at early performances from 2003 until 2005. Limited supply meant that fans burnt copies and put the music up on the Internet to be shared. The band have claimed that they did not even create the MySpace page from which countless thousands of fans downloaded their music, and that they were surprised to find audiences able to recite their lyrics back to them with such proficiency. This may well be false modesty. It may be true. Whichever is the case, the consequence of free distribution of Arctic Monkeys' music online fuelled the creation of a large fan base, leading to large venue bookings even prior to their signing a recording contract with Domino Records towards the end of 2005. The release of their first album was brought forward a month (in January 2006) amidst suggestions that the label was afraid that leaked copies circulating on file-sharing sites would undermine sales. While the Arctic Monkeys signed with a relatively 'independent' label, and so cannot be accused of having 'sold out' to a major label completely, their label does have distribution deals with major labels in some territories, and the attempt to fend off competition from file-sharing has led to criticisms from fans whose identification with the band's focus on live performance and free distribution of their recordings was seen to have been betrayed.

Interestingly, after the commercial release of their first album, the band's next release was a deliberate attempt to avoid the standard courting of radio play in the attempt to promote sales. The EP, *Who the Fuck are the Arctic Monkeys?* contained no short and catchy single. The title and the content (both in length and language used) ensured that the music received very little air time. The band's presence online meant this deliberate rejection of radio as a medium to gain publicity did not hamper sales. The album and subsequent singles entered the UK charts at number one. This case illustrates how a band was able to produce its own recordings, have this manufactured and distributed, and generate sufficient promotional exposure to bypass both major labels and radio stations, and generate significant performance income from large venues even before signing a record contract. This band did sign, but with an independent label. It can be suggested that the Arctic Monkeys broke the stranglehold of major labels in four out of five of the functions outlined in Chapter 8 (production, manufacture, distribution and promotion), while their eventual label seems to have cut deals over publishing in some territories at least. Having achieved the first four functions without a label it has been suggested the band has been, at least in part, incorporated within the established music industry model when it did sign. As the band has not signed with a major, this 'incorporation' is only partial. All the five functions that major labels claim justify their existence, and their claim over the lion's share of recorded music revenues, have been challenged. Many artists who witnessed the success of the Arctic Monkeys have sought to extend this challenge.

Enter Shikari

Formed at around the same time as the Arctic Monkeys, Enter Shikari followed a similar pathway (Youngs 2007, Enter Shikari 2008). Recording their own demo CDs in one band member's converted garage/recording studio, and building a fan base through extensive touring, the distribution of their home-made CDs, and with their music widely circulating for free on the Internet, the band's reputation was built without the need for external promotion, such as via radio play or advertising. The band's style builds upon audience participation and makes a virtue of its 'live' qualities. As such, their early recordings were only ever secondary, never seeking to distract from the main event, that is, the live performance. Youngs (2007) describes the band's attitude to the audience as seeing them as the fifth member of the group, rather than as passive spectators. It is claimed the band played over five hundred concerts between 2003 and 2008. As with the Arctic Monkeys, the Internet enabled the band to disseminate its sound and build a following for its live shows. This capacity to attract an audience itself attracted promoters, and the band were able to gain dates at many of the most prestigious festivals and largest venues, again with virtually no radio play and no record deal. They became only the second unsigned band to play the London Astoria in late 2006.

At this point the band were offered contracts by a number of major labels, but these were refused on the grounds that such contracts would require signing away copyright and reduced control over the direction of the music, while at the same time the benefits were relatively small. As the band had produced their own work and were able to promote themselves well enough online, this left only the manufacture, distribution and publishing rights. The band created its own label, Ambush Reality, which exclusively handles the band's production, manufacture, promotion and rights management. They then signed a deal with a distributor called Vital, who have paid Ambush Reality upfront for promotion rights, and who themselves take a fee to distribute physical recordings. As such, the band pay for the various functions to be performed and retain the remainder, inverting the standard relationship between artist and label. The band retains control over the creative process and on the copyright to their musical recordings. The band's Official Web Forum announced in 2007 that, to promote their US tours, it would be necessary to sign a contract with a major label. However, the deal was in fact with a relatively independent label, Tiny Evil Records. Nevertheless, signing a deal again raised the question of whether the band had been forced to conform to the mainstream model in order to get the kind of publicity in America they had been able to generate for themselves in the UK through the combination of self-managed touring and self-managed production and distribution. Simply putting music online was not enough to become known if you don't know the terrain.

Simply Red

The band Simply Red have their origins in the late 1970s Manchester punk and alternative politics/lifestyle 'scene', with their previous incarnation The Frantic Elevators. When this band split up in 1983, its lead singer Mick Hucknall's new project was named Simply Red after his red hair, football team (Manchester United) and political orientation. The band's style combined romantic ballads in various jazz, soul and funk moods, with political critiques of the then government of Margaret Thatcher. The new band was signed to Electra Records and went on to produce a string of highly successful singles and albums. Increasing commercial success brought increased critical questioning of their 'mainstream' sound, extensive use of covers, and for Hucknall's increasing sense of his own celebrity status. In 1991 Hucknall claimed the band was really a solo project, and the rather fluid character of the band does suggest that it is really only Hucknall's backing group, which seems somewhat at odds with the singer's professed socialist outlook. In 2001 Hucknall and Simply Red left their second record company East West to produce and release their own music through the website 'simplyred.com'. With the success of Napster, and with the court action that would close it looming, Simply Red were the first 'established' band (i.e. one that had been under contract with a significant record label) to abandon this established model and use the Internet to go direct to their fans. Unlike the Arctic Monkeys and Enter Shikari, for whom the Internet acted to help create a fan base, for Simply Red – a band who were beyond the peak of their 'chart topping' celebrity status -- the Internet represented a way of maintaining both their audience and the income stream from their recorded music. The seeming incongruity of the DVD of the band's concerts in Cuba alongside luxury romantic concert packages (hotels, roses, chocolates and a concert) being marketed on their website, as well as the full range of back catalogue materials available in physical and download format and the usual array of merchandising, can be set against the claim that the band have successfully taken control of the means of their musical production and have thereby set up their own form of online socialism, as distinct from the anarchy of file-sharing and the capitalism of the established business model. Whether socialism can exist in one website is perhaps too big a question to be answered here. What is interesting is that reliance on fan loyalty to buy from the artists what might be downloaded for free from file-sharing sites means that Simply Red has maintained revenues without resource to the kinds of legal actions that have alienated many fans from traditional record companies and their artists. The band is set to split up in 2010, after 25 years in existence. Their Internet-based self-ownership model has shown itself to generate a substantial return to artists who have moved beyond the peak of their celebrity, something the established royalties system rarely does.

The Charlatans

The Charlatans (known in the US as The UK Charlatans to avoid confusion with a 1960s US band of the same name) formed in 1989 and released their first single through their own record label, called Dead Dead Good Records. This truly independent release earned the band great respect and no money, and they subsequently signed with the more commercially successful independent label Beggars Banquet, and then with the major label Universal. Though gaining significant critical acclaim and widespread exposure when with Beggars Banquet, and having made money from a string of high profile live events, the band claimed to have made no money from its recordings while working with this independent label, and they decided in 1998 to sign with a major (Universal). In the period with Universal the band explored a number of new sounds and styles, much to the dismay of their new label. Universal wanted to cash in on the commercial potential of the band's essential 'English Indie' sound. Ironically, it was only towards the end of the band's six years with Universal that their sound returned to something close to their signature style, by which time their label considered this to have lost its mass appeal. The band believed their label was not promoting them and the label felt they were not producing the kind of music needed to warrant a large promotional budget (i.e. music that would sell in large volumes if it was sufficiently plugged). The band were released from their contract in 2004, leaving Universal with rights over a raft of material which they have packaged variously for sale.

The band signed with the Sanctuary label in 2005, a subsidiary of a larger, but still not quite major, label: Rough Trade. Sanctuary went bankrupt in 2007, leaving the band free either to sign another contract or, as they did, to release their music in a new way. The Charlatans were the first band to release a single and then an album, for free download, via an online radio station – in their case Xfm. Both the single and the album were called *You Cross My Path* and, initially at least, the band claimed there would be no physical release. The recorded music would stand as promotional material for the band's live shows, which had always been the band's primary source of income (as is the case for most performing artists). Nevertheless, a physical album was released through the record label Cooking Vinyl in May 2008. The release was a distribution deal rather than a standard contract, with the band retaining copyright. Fans who had downloaded free copies still wished to buy physical copies, especially in the knowledge that their money was going primarily to the artists rather than to the label. The use of a distribution deal meant that the label gets paid to distribute, rather than taking the full net price and only paying the artist a percentage royalty. Again, this model is premised on a trust in the audience, who, despite free alternatives, choose to buy from the band.

The Charlatans' manager Alan Magee was reported in the *New Musical Express* (2007) as saying:

> Why would you volunteer to join the army for 10 years unless you had no choice? Record companies are kind of like the army – very regulated. We were really excited when Xfm got behind us and were as enthusiastic about the download as we are. They are the first people to embrace music for the people. The band will get paid by more people coming to gigs, buying merchandise, publishing and sync fees. I believe it's the future business model.

Radiohead

On the same day as the above interview with Alan Magee, the band *Radiohead* announced on its website that its new album would be released on the Internet, not for free as such, but for as much as those downloading it thought it was worth (with a 45 pence card handling fee). The album, *In Rainbows*, was released on 10 October 2007. Early claims, later denied, suggested that 1.2 million downloads were made on the first day, but it later appeared that this figure was for the period up until 31 October 2007 (Buskirk 2007). Buskirk cites data from the online survey company Comscore which suggested only thirty-eight per cent of these people paid anything beyond the required handling fee. This still meant the band received over two-and-a-half million dollars in less than three weeks, with all revenues going to the band not to any record company as they had declined to renew their contract with EMI. The Comscore data suggested that the average payment of those who had paid was six US dollars. The 'honesty box' download option remained open until 10 December 2007. On 3 December a limited edition box set became available for eighty US dollars or forty UK pounds, while at the end of December 2007/1 January 2008, a standard CD was released through the independent record label XL Recordings in most territories worldwide, but through other distributors in Japan, USA, Canada and Australia. These were all exclusive licensing agreements to distribute, with the band retaining copyright and the label being paid a fee per unit for its distribution of physical product. Cam Lindsey (2008) cites Warner Chappell, Radiohead's publishers, who claimed by 15 October 2008 the album, *In Rainbows*, had sold three million copies. They claim that 1.75 million standard CDs were sold to that date and one hundred thousand copies of the box set, leaving again, the recurring figure of 1.2 million downloads having already been sold. This figure did not include free downloads from either file-sharing sites or the band's own website, but did include downloads from iTunes and Amazon. Much quoted across the old and new-media was Warner Chappell's claim that despite the majority of downloads being for free the value of the 'pay what you want to' sales had generated more revenue for the band than the band's total earnings from their previous album *Hail to the Thief* (2003). This previous album had been selling for five years, while the honesty box had closed after two months.

Despite 'the pay what you want to' scheme, physical sales remained high, and the licensing agreement meant returns from these sales again went largely to the band. Not only did an honesty box generate more money than a copyright enforced royalty payment system, it also made no discernable impact on the band's physical sales. As mentioned in Chapter 8, Radiohead's decision to release *In Rainbows* through a publisher, not a record company, struck out against the preceding incorporation of the music publishing industry by the major record labels. However, the specific conditions of the release, i.e. the band's retention of revenues from sales while the publisher continues to receive their share of publishing rights in those sales is something other bands have achieved through distribution deals with record companies. Whether or not a band works with a record company, the crucial transformation lies in the retention of copyright. Returns in recordings based on mechanical publishing rights have not changed significantly. Publishing rights in mechanical reproductions (record sales), performance (broadcast, covers, recordings played in public venues and in live venue performance) and in synchronization (background in television programmes, advertising and film) have always been more equitable than royalties for recording rights.

Madonna

Two days after Radiohead released *In Rainbows*, the magazine *Marie Claire* announced that Madonna was to leave her twenty-five-year-long relationship with the Warner Music label to sign a new contract with the concert promoter Live Nation. The new deal, alleged to be worth sixty million UK pounds, would give Live Nation a share of the artist's merchandising, recordings, performance revenues as well as publishing and image rights. *Marie Claire* (2007) noted the artist's huge recent concert revenues and her more modest record sales as background to Madonna's decision to sign with a promoter rather than a record company.

> Live Nation, however, has been pushing to broaden its business reach, and with this sort of deal it could send a signal that it has a 21st century model for how the business of music could be handled after the advent of the digital revolution over the last decade. (*Marie Claire* 2007)

The deal turned on its head the plans put forward by major labels for so-called 360 degree contracts. Such contracts, which sought to offset losses resultant from declining recording revenues by means of labels securing a share of performance, merchandising and other rights, exposed the widely known fact that revenues from performance were growing while those from recording were in decline. Live Nation, which manages over one hundred music venues across the United States, and others worldwide, realized the potential of such a shift and sought to turn the tables on established labels. Why sign over a share of performance rights to a recording company which cannot secure its profits by what it allegedly does best, when you might rather sign over a proportion of your recording rights to a live performance promoter who can at least make their side of the business pay? Madonna was only the first big name to sign. As the most profitable female performing artist of all time, and as someone keenly aware of the decline of recording relative to performance on her balance sheet, this particular material girl was significant. Others were to follow, U2 being the next most famous. By October 2008, however, the viability of the Live Nation model was coming into question. A shortage of credit and boardroom conflict over how much to offer megastars to jump-ship had left Live Nation without the money to pay artists to defect, and without a functioning recording arm to deal with production, manufacture and distribution (McCormick 2008). Live Nation had to offer significant numbers of shares to artists such as Madonna, U2 and Jay-Z to honour their commitments, while bands such as Oasis, who were themselves out of contract, re-signed with Sony BMG, despite approaches by Live Nation. Oasis still held on to the hope that their money would be made from high volumes of record sales, rather than from performance, and Live Nation were apparently unable to convince the band or its management that they could distribute and promote recordings successfully. Live Nation resorted to the same licensing agreements with external distributors that bands such as Enter Shikari, Radiohead and The Charlatans had made for themselves, except with reverse 360 degree contracts to ensure that a large percentage of whatever came back from such deals would go to Live Nation, not the artists.

General discussion

The six case studies discussed above highlight a range of different strategies for artists in the musical field seeking to adapt to, use and modify the free circulation of music on the Internet. Arctic Monkeys and Enter Shikari rose to prominence, in large part at least, through the free sharing of their music by fans, in each case with the explicit encouragement of the groups, though in different ways in each case. Radiohead and Madonna have adapted to the weakening of the established record company/contract/ royalties model, which each attributes to file-sharing but in very different ways. Radiohead have sought to engage with the question through a strategy of relegitimation of recording sales, while Madonna has shifted emphasis to live performance. Both have abandoned the major labels they had previously signed with, as neither could offer them the returns available from either direct online sales and licensed sales of physical recordings, or from a deal with a live promoter. Both have adapted in ways that maintain their positions as current musical superstars. The Charlatans and Simply Red have used new-media to sustain their positions within the musical field after they had ceased to be 'today's' superstar celebrity artists. Both bands have similarly bypassed, in large part, the traditional record contract/label/royalties model, in taking their music directly to their audience online.

These six cases highlight the alternative possibilities for making a living and making a life in the music business. Two show how this can be done at the start of a career in the field, two in the positions of current superstars, and two from the position of being beyond that stage. The defence of the current contractual/royalties/major label model is not only open to challenge in relation to its five core legitimating functions (i.e. production, manufacture, distribution, promotion and rights management/ publishing). The weaknesses of these five legitimating claims were demonstrated in Chapter 8. The suggestion that complaint is merely sour grapes is challenged when it is noted that the current system fails artists at all levels of career and success. If new talent feels exploited, they are told to work harder as the system is designed to benefit superstars. If superstars seek to bypass major labels they are accused of stripping their labels of the resources necessary to support new talent. If both new artists and superstars complain, it is suggested that at least the system provides a 'pension' for yesterday's talent, as was the image created by Wordsworth and Twain when pushing for extended copyright terms. It is only when we examine the position of new artists, established superstars and those who are no longer at the peak of celebrity together – and examine alternative business models at all these stages within a musical career – that the defence that 'someone else benefits' falls down. The six cases taken together illustrate that whatever stage an artist is at, alternatives to the current record company contract/royalties/copyright model exist, and offer greater artistic freedom and material reward. The case of Live Nation, where an alternative player (a large concert promoter) has sought to substitute for existing record labels, but who then introduced a variation of the same 360 degree model of payment which has dismayed so many artists already, may show that not all alternatives are as potentially attractive. In this case, the alternative may not turn out to be quite as 'alternative' as was first envisaged. The extent to which other cases above contained elements of engagement with old models (such as in signing royalties based contracts for foreign markets, or, in the case of Arctic Monkeys, signing a standard royalties-based contract across the board, even though with an 'independent' label), or engagement with established players, even if by new rules (such as signing licensing agreements rather than royalties contracts with record labels for distribution), should prevent us from assuming a total transformation has or will occur overnight. Nevertheless, the case studies illustrate how alternative possibilities exist and are being created. The fabric of the established order is fragile, to say the least.

We should pay particular attention to the diversity of the above alternative possibilities. The Charlatans and Madonna, in very different ways, have adapted to the rise of file-sharing and the decline in record sales with an emphasis upon live performance. Arctic Monkeys and Simply Red have maintained, in very different ways, an emphasis upon the sale of recorded music (whether by means of conventional royalties or through online sales at fixed prices). Enter Shikari and Radiohead have encouraged fans to download their music for free or for as much as they wanted to pay, so challenging the priority of recording over performance in making a living, even while at the same time making very good returns on the money that fans chose to pay them directly for recordings. Simply Red and Enter Shikari have created their own record labels. The Charlatans and the Arctic Monkeys have signed contracts with independent labels. Madonna and Radiohead have abandoned record labels and have instead distributed their music through deals with their promoter and their publishers respectively. Madonna and the Arctic Monkeys have royalties-based contracts for their recorded music. Simply Red and Enter Shikari primarily release their own music while having signed licensing deals in some territories. The Charlatans and Radiohead have licensing agreements with record labels for all their physical sales.

Madonna appears to have adopted the most extreme model of profit maximization. Radiohead's seemingly radical move has generated the next greatest income for the artists. After them it is likely that the Arctic Monkeys are the next best paid. It is not clear quite how Simply Red's long tail (their near quarter-century-long accumulation of a fan base) compares to Enter Shikari's new popularity in terms of income generation, or how this could be teased out relative to their alternative business models (though they are in many ways the most similar). The Charlatans' strategy appears to be the least commercial, and in this sense at least the most 'alternative'. Having said this, the relatively greater commercial potential of the other alternatives may make them more radically threatening to the existing record industry model. This leads us on to the question of possible futures.

Possible futures

The outcomes that emerge from the possibility of file-sharing are multiple. Particular responses have been outlined above. Here I wish to map the most specific possibilities that emerge from the circulation of digital music through file-sharing networks. First, there is the question of whether anyone will pay for recorded music when it is otherwise freely available. Can artists reconstruct the legitimacy (Habermas 1976) of selling recordings such that fans will pay even when the same work is available for free? The converse of this is whether artists will be able to trust fans. One axis of alternative business models then will be that of legitimacy/trust. Second, how will the existence of free music online impact on the significance of recording relative to live performance within artists' careers? Will the making, distribution and sale of recorded music remain a commercial activity or will it fade away, leaving an expanded emphasis upon live performance as the fundamental business of making money from making music? The second axis then is that of proximity and distance. Will the global distribution of digital recordings lead to intensified deterritorialization or forms of reterritorialization? It is possible to imagine four polarities within a typology of high–low trust/legitimacy (whether audiences choose to pay for recordings), and high–low proximity (the relative significance of mediated and live music). Table 9.1 provides a schematic outline of these alternative scenarios.

Table 9.1 *Alternative business models prefigured in current developments*

Trust/legitimacy	Proximity/Mediation Low proximity	High proximity
Low trust/legitimacy	Low trust/low proximity Field Colonization: commercial sponsorship, tie-ins and synchronization deals: e.g. The Feeling Delegitimation and deterritorialization	Low trust/high proximity Live Nation: The recording is the menu; the live event is the meal: e.g., Madonna and U2 Delegitimation and reterritorialization
High trust/legitimacy	High trust/low proximity The Honesty Box: Self-management online. Audiences pay despite free options: e.g., Radiohead and Simply Red Relegitimation and deterritorialization	High trust/high proximity The Best of Both Worlds: Free online builds live support and sell recordings as well: e.g., The Charlatans, Enter Shikari and Arctic Monkeys Relegitimation and reterritorialization

Field colonization (low truth/low proximity)

If audiences are able to gain recorded music for free, and do not then spend the money saved going to see artists performing live, the additional income and the channels through which they access free content will be an attractive site for advertisers keen to convert that saved income into sales for other goods. The channel MySpace was bought by Rupert Murdoch's News Corporation for this very reason. If artists migrate away from existing record labels, and then find that they cannot support themselves by means of performance or direct sales, they will either find themselves working as free content providers (as is the case on MySpace), or may have to enter purely commercial sponsorship deals advertising products, composing jingles, or allowing their music to be used as backing material for films and television. If the standard record label model is exploitative of artists, its demise could witness destitution or colonization for artists who would lose even the modicum of autonomy currently afforded the musical field by present arrangements. The royalty system preserves, if in an often damaging fashion, the distinction between pure business and aesthetics, the corporate suits and the creative artists. A low trust, low proximity future might leave musicians having to sell themselves directly into a market that has no pretensions to valuing music in its own terms.

Delegitimation/reterritorialization (low trust/high proximity)

Realizing that the audience are getting their recordings for free, but that they are still willing to pay to come and see the artist perform live (and perhaps even more willing or willing to pay even more), another scenario will be for artists to ring fence their work in both forms: continuing to seek maximum sales of recorded work through copyrighted downloads and physical copies, while maximizing revenues from performance by means of increased prices, larger venues and longer tours. The case in point here would be Madonna, along with other acts who have signed deals with Live Nation, whether for 360 degree management or only for performance and merchandising (such as U2). Proximity here refers only to the control of fixed territory, the boundary of a venue that can be policed and commercialized, in a context where virtual deterritorialization makes such regulation impossible for recordings. As such, high proximity here does not refer to intimacy or any strong sense of interaction with the audience, which may be more relevant to those artists who have pursued strategies that combine proximity with the reconstruction of legitimacy and trust.

Relegitimation/deterritorialization (high trust/low proximity)

Another possible future might lie in artists re-establishing trust relations with their audiences through the bypassing of traditional record companies and selling recorded music to those who are willing to buy it, even while allowing those who simply want to listen to it without paying to do the same. Mediated forms of direct relationship (mediated in the sense of the Internet and direct in the sense of cutting out the major labels) allow a greater flow and proportion of revenues from what sales do occur to go to the artist. To the extent that audiences who like the artist are willing to pay, even when the option exists not to, such a model of payment is based on trust not copyright enforcement. Radiohead's ability to make large returns from digital sales while still being able to sell physical product on top of this, and to have allowed audiences to pay what they wanted and still generated more money than they gained from their previous album which had been sold by conventional means, highlights the possibility of a high trust/low proximity scenario. By low proximity here it is simply meant that such a model does not rely on artists making up for decreased sales of recorded material by means of increased revenues from live performance. Radiohead does not directly illustrate this possibility, as they have successfully toured as well. Simply Red might better illustrate the possibility of continuing to make a living from a high trust relationship with their audience, even after the band splits up in 2010. At this point, the absence of live performance will, of course, leave revenues only from the direct sale of recordings by the band's own website/record label.

Reterritorialization and relegitimation (high trust/high proximity)

The Charlatans' latest studio album *You Cross My Path* can be downloaded for free from the online radio station Xfm. The band initially suggested they would not make a physical version for sale but, despite its free availability, demand was sufficient from fans not only for the album to be made, but for it to be stocked in almost all UK record shops. Despite giving the material away, fans still want to give the band their money. The Charlatan's original conception was that the album would promote live performance events, not generate additional income. Fans had other ideas and demanded to pay for both. This is an extreme example of reterritorialization, the focus on live performance being combined with relegitimation of the payment for recordings which come direct from the artists, and for which payment goes direct to the artists. In a similar vein Enter Shikari actively sought to give their music away in its recorded format, while giving primacy to direct interaction with their audience at live performance events. Recordings were only ever a secondary aspect. Nonetheless, the groups' subsequent creation of their own record label to distribute physical copies of work otherwise freely available has proved highly successful. That both *You Cross My Path* and Enter Shikari's album *Take To The Skies* can be bought over the counter in every UK high street makes the need for a major label distributing your work a thing of the past. The choice of the Arctic Monkeys to sign a fairly conventional record contract, if with a relatively independent label, may in hindsight appear a rather conservative move. The label's decision to bring forward the release date of their first album, for fear of file-sharers under-cutting sales, drew much criticism, and demonstrated a lack of trust in the band's fans. Given the band's earlier strategy of giving away free demo CDs, and the role this played in building their fan base, the perception that once signed to a label the band had become less connected with its audience may have had the very effect of damaging future sales which the actions were designed to head off in the first place. However, neither widespread file-sharing nor suggestions of selling out prevented the band's first album becoming the fastest selling record in UK history. Despite hints to the contrary, the Arctic Monkeys appear to have maintained their relationship with their audience, both as live performers and in their relations with an independent record company.

Conclusions

In relation to the initial suggestions made at the start of this chapter, it is clearly not the case that file-sharing is merely a minor irritation, nor is it proving to be a threat to innovation and the creative arts. The possibility of opening the door to non-music based corporate colonization exists, although this can be seen in the colonization of major labels by wider media con-glomerates, just as much as in the attempts to bypass traditional sector elites as they struggle to maintain their dominance. The extent to which file-sharing shapes and becomes part of new prefigurative modes of musi-cal career making, and the extent to which any such change comes to accommodate itself with various elements of the existing musical landscape (producers, publishing rights companies, distributors, labels – independent and/or major etc.), remains to be seen. What this chapter has highlighted is the extent to which file-sharing has come to shape and be shaped within a range of new practices that offer more freedom to artists, as well as greater potential to make a living whether from performance or from recording or from both. What this chapter shows most forcefully, however, is that far from undermining the potential to make a living from music, file-sharing has encouraged the development of new and newly legitimate relations between artists and audiences by which payment is offered rather than demanded. Low trust models of intellectual property rights management, whether through legal, technical or cultural forms of enforcement, compulsion and/or even threat, have failed. Yet, giving music away for free has gone hand in hand with a renewed willingness on the part of those who receive to then go out and pay more for what they could have taken for nothing, either in the form of tickets on a door or for recordings in one form or another (or both).

10

Conclusions

- Music and the network society
- Reflexive epistemological diversity
- Theories of the network society
- An essential outline of this book
- Versus 'the winner loses' theories of closure
- Attention to the open character of ongoing conflicts
- Capitalist glasnost and perestroika?
- The future is not what it used to be!

Music and the network society

This book is about file-sharing and the impact of digital media on the music industry. As this book has made clear, digital media have been taken up and their affordances applied within the musical field in such a way as fundamentally to challenge existing business models and enable new and alternative business models to thrive. As such, the music industry has been radically reconfigured in the context of the so-called network society. However, it is not enough simply to say that the relationship between audiences and artists, and the position of record companies has changed as a result of network affordances. It is also true that the recent history of the music industry represents a paradigmatic illustration of the nature and dynamics of the network society itself. While theories of the network society improve our understanding of the contemporary music industry, so it is also the case that examination of conflicts within the musical field helps us to make better sense of theories concerning the network society. This is for two reasons. First, the dynamic character of disputes in the musical field over the last ten years in particular draws our attention to the signif-icance of technology as well as to the limits of any determinist account of societal development. As will be pointed out below, while structural accounts of developments within technology, capitalism and global society provide some value, they obscure the significance of interpretive practices and resistances operating at various levels. Attendance to the empirical reality of the musical field helps bring such strengths and limits of grand theories of the network society into focus. Second, disputes over control and distribution of digital music are only the most manifest examples of a wide range of disputes over ownership and control of informational goods in a global network environment. Currently, copyright disputes are raging in the fields of motion pictures, digital television (in particular over the live streaming of sporting events), as well as over computer games and other software. Related disputes over patent protection routinely explode in the pharmaceuticals and agribusiness sectors and beyond. Put bluntly, the increasing significance of informational goods within the global economy, and in particular for the wealthiest countries in the world, means that conflict over control of such intrinsically mercurial cultural products is central to contemporary social life. What is happening in the field of musical production is then only the most manifest example of a fundamental characteristic of the network society in general. The increased scope for 'identity theft' in a virtual society should be distinguished from 'intellectual property theft' as such, although this distinction is blurred with the sale of 'pirated' designer goods. This book is thus about more than just the music industry in a network society. The music industry is emblematic of the network society.

Reflexive epistemological diversity

History is the graveyard of elites (Pareto 1991) and the graveyard for absolute explanations. That is not to say that such theories have no value but rather that their value is limited, both in time and in explanatory scope. Time weathers any account of social relations both to the extent that societies change and to the extent that such accounts themselves impact upon the actions of those being accounted for. Whether by means of self-fulfilling prophecy or through reforms enacted on the basis of knowledge presumed; or out of resistance to the constructions presented and/or applied, theories of the world undermine their validity to the very extent that they are heeded. In addition to this limit, there is a more epistemological limit. The world may be an ontological unity, but no account of such a reality 'out there' can ever hope to capture such a unity. Non-reductive science recognizes the diversity of epistemologies required to account for a range of levels of explanation (Midgely 1996, Rose 1997). Non-reductive social science also needs to recognize the value of 'reflexive epistemological diversity' (David 2005, 2008a and 2008b). Non-reductive social science has to resist the temptation of reduction either to structural (base) levels of explanation, or to its ironic inverse, anti-reductionist reductionism, i.e. the reduction of explanation to discourse/language and micro-level interaction. The history of the sciences, and in a more intense form the social sciences, has been one of ongoing differentiation and sub-field specialization. The temptation to reduce explanation only to the toolkit deployed within your own sub-field is, of course, always strong. Careers are made within fields and sub-fields, and peer-review means the community of your specific angle. The tendency towards what Collins and Yearley (1992) call 'epistemological chicken' – where to blink first, i.e. to concede explanatory power to another field, is to lose – makes 'reflexive epistemological diversity' hard to achieve, but it remains essential.

Theories of the network society

The purpose of this book is not to provide an absolute judgement upon the state of theories seeking to account for what has variously been called the post-industrial, information and/or network society. However, it is possible to centre discussion of what such theories achieve around the work of Manuel Castells for one particular reason, that his work sits comfortably or uncomfortably at the juncture of all the major factions of such theorizing. I propose that this positioning can be seen in relation to four main strands of thinking (critical theory, Weberian rationalization, post-structuralist discourse analysis and ethnography). Castells' account of the mode of development and its relationship with the mode of production reproduced a classical Marxist account of how the forces of production develop within capitalist relations of production, even to the point where they come to challenge those social relations as fetters. The network society is a capitalist society, but network technologies create new possibilities that are not simply reducible to the ongoing intensification of capitalist relations of ownership and control. Interestingly, this dimension of Castells' 'critical realism' stands in tension to the 'critical theory' of May, Habermas, Webster and Kirkpatrick and many feminists like Haraway, Plant, and Wajcman who, while also holding a structural account of power, tend to place greater emphasis upon the social and cultural relations of such power, rather than on the significance of the forces of production in disrupting it (see Webster 2006). Castells' work can also be located in its dynamic tension with Max Weber's rationalization thesis. In large and explicit part Castells' network society thesis is a rejection of Daniel Bell's 'post-industrial society' theory, itself an extension of Weber rationalization thesis, yet (with Himanen 2001) Castells draws extensively upon Weber's language of career, vocation and elective affinity when describing the hacker ethic and the spirit of informationalism. The hacker embodies the drive to extend technology, perhaps even to 'realize' its 'true' potential, whatever that might mean, driven by little more than simply the desire to take the next rational step forward. The relative autonomy accorded to the mode of development in Castells' account, however, which places him at times at odds with 'critical theory' and Weberian accounts, does bring him close to post-structuralists like Alexander Galloway and Frederick Kittler, and to an extent to Foucault – though, of course, Castells' theoretical anti-humanism and his attention to the determining character of networks is more structuralist than post-structuralist. Castells' attention to the relative autonomy of networks and their 'morphogenic' (causal) structuring of human interactions (which is of course akin to Galloway, Kittler, Foucault and others in that tradition) is tempered by his continued insistence that, for all its autonomy, the network society is still fundamentally network capitalism. In this regard he is particularly close to the work of post-structuralists like Deleuze and Guattari, and Negri, though they (unlike Castells) give more attention to opposition within such networks. Finally, Castells' attention to networks gives a sense of affinity with ethno-graphic and ethnomethodological approaches to interaction. However, Castells is explicit in rejecting an action-oriented conception of social networks, but it is precisely in this rejection, and in Castells' attempt to provide an account of network structures that his approach is weakest, and tends most towards determinism and reductionism – as has been pointed out by both action-oriented researchers and critical theorists. Actor network theory occupies an interesting position between the more action-oriented perspective and a more structural account of networks and of the affordances of technical arte-facts, both close to Castells' perspective. As such, I do not wish to endorse Castells' account; it is as problematic as it is useful. Yet its location in the field of theories makes it a practical centre for thinking in a more reflexive epistemologically diverse way.

An essential outline of this book

In essence this book has done three things. First, it provided a historical overview of issues related to today's conflicts over file-sharing. Second, the book outlines dimensions of this conflict as it currently continues. Third, the book outlines the contradictions and conflicts within established economic relations and the possible alternatives that are prefigured in the present. The first dimension is addressed in Chapters 2, 3 and 4, with accounts of the rise of the network society, file-sharing and intellectual property rights. Chapters 5, 6 and 7 detail the character of current conflicts in the fields of law, technology and culture respectively. Of course these fields are not discrete and developments in each condition and are brought into play in disputes within the other domains. Similarly, the distinction between today's established business models, the conflicts and contradic-tions that exist within them, and the alternative futures prefigured in the present is not absolute. It is precisely the contradictory and conflict-ridden nature of current relations of ownership and distribution rights that generate such alternatives. Critique emerges from the reflexive practice of those engaged in the conflicts themselves, and not from a detached standpoint. While this text deploys theoretical models to frame events, the distinction between theory and events is misleading, as events are themselves practices informed by highly articulate reflections and which also generate such theorization. This book constructs a number of typologies: where does creativity come from, what are the functions of record labels, what are the alternative futures for the cultural economy of music making, how can theories of the information society be organized, how has IP been constructed by different actors at different points in time? And there are others. Some typologies seek to make clearer relations between competing academic theories. Some seek to highlight relations between theories that directly operate in everyday practices. These are exercises in clarification, even if they are more than just storage devices. While judgements are made and justified, it should not be assumed that the purpose of this book is to provide a framework that explains reality. The theoretical ambition at work is far more modest. Rather, the purpose of this book is to explore a reality composed of multiple actors, and types of actors, explicable in a number of different ways and operating across a range of fields of practice, deploying and developing a range of resources, techniques, affordances, claims and interpretations of rules. Such complexity requires reflexive epistemological diversity. I do not seek reduction to any one level of explanation, and do not seek to impose an artificial closure, by which reality is put to bed under a seductively impenetrable theoretical blanket.

Versus 'the winner loses' theories of closure

The attraction of closure, the provision of an account that provides sufficient explanation as to be predictive of future outcomes (such as in a simple and closed system), is at one level obvious. If outcomes could be fully predicted on the basis of a sufficient number of independent variables, of course such knowledge would be useful in the extreme, for good or ill. An attendance to the many levels of explanation in play in the development of any significant social process does in part seek to come to terms with this need to provide many elements of explanation to provide an approximation of a sufficient prediction of outcomes. Yet reflexive epistemological diversity highlights two fundamental limits to any grand predictive social science. First, the triangulation of mixed methods does not simply provide a neat interlocking account, such as in a jigsaw puzzle. Different levels of explanation and their attendant epistemologies and methodological toolkits often clash as much as they complement. Second, diversity means complexity and complexity generates unpredictability even in fully causal models where all variables are known and controlled for. One element of such unpredictability is feedback, and one form of such feedback is the reflexivity of human actors in relation to the consequences of their own actions and the accounts provided for such actions.

The winner loses scenario occurs when the theorist claims to have provided a watertight account of events such that alternative outcomes are inconceivable. In explaining everything, the theorist contributes nothing, as their account cannot possibly be of value to anyone, as nothing can be done. Of course if such total theoretical prediction could be achieved, we would simply have to bemoan our fate in having seen it coming and having been powerless to do anything about it. But such predictive closure cannot be achieved. This book does not suggest one course of action or another, but very much highlights that the future will be determined by the choices made as to how to take up the challenges and opportunities of the present. This book, then, is an invitation to make the future we want. That future is not determined for us in advance. Nor is it determined by structures at work in the present.

Attention to the open character of ongoing conflicts

As has been shown in Chapter 2, the 'hope' of introducing theoretical or epistemological closure in defining or approaching the 'network society' is unrealistic. Post-structuralist attempts to reduce networks to discursive codes, ethnographic attempts to reduce networks to interpersonal interaction, critical realist and critical theoretical forms of Marxist attempts to reduce networks to the forces or the relations of production, and attempts to account for the present in terms of ongoing rationalization of society all fail to capture the full story. Chapters 3 and 5 show closure in disputes over file-sharing by means of legal mechanisms have repeatedly failed in conflicts of both interest and interpretation. Legal changes aimed at one outcome have only encouraged the development of alternative technical strategies and artefacts that sidestep (or are used to sidestep) such rules, even while different interpretations of rules concerning property rights and human rights are used to justify divergent outcomes. The rules are not the same everywhere, and even the interpretation of the same rules shifts over time and across jurisdictions. Similar dynamics in the technical realm were brought to light in Chapter 6, in relation to the cat and mouse interplay between surveillance and encryption. No successful closure can be sustained by either copyright holders or file-sharers as detection and protection systems constantly trump each other, and as each side can use the same devices and strategies to neutralize the advantage achieved by others in their application of the same tools and techniques. In the end, as with the law, technical applications lead to outcomes based on weight of numbers, and not on any juridical decree or mathematical algorithm.

If, as Chapter 4 explains, intellectual property is 'an old "man's" game', with established actors – whether individuals, states, genres or industries – claiming ownership of today's culture on the grounds of their actions in the past, so it is also a game that the young will always seek to break the rules of, claiming rights over today's culture in the name of the future. For all the resources accumulated and deployed by the 'old', they never achieve total 'closure', and the very means by which they rose to success – by breaking the rules that secured yesterday's elites – tend to haunt them for the duration of their fragile dominance. Today's dominant players in the music recording business and to a lesser extent in film are certainly painfully aware of the fragility of their position. As Chapters 7 and 8 make clear, attempts to generate a moral and cultural closure around a belief in the legitimacy and/or utility of intellectual property rights have failed monumentally. This is in part a failure to persuade audiences that file-sharing is wrong and in part a failure to persuade artists that copyright is in their interests. However, new corporate players, for whom free content is just one potentially profitable strategy, also appear to take the view that free content is something they can work to their advantage. Quite how these various failures will play out, and what successful alternatives fill the available space, remains to be seen. As this book has shown, it is in the study of the practices of actors – variously configured, enabled and constrained, in fluid oppositions and alliances – that a sociology of the network society can usefully develop, and in so doing shed light on a world we are all knowledgeable of and participants in and yet so often find ourselves estranged from (Presdee 2000).

Capitalist glasnost and perestroika?

Manuel Castells' attempt to document the rise of the 'network society' was written in the immediate aftermath of the collapse of the Soviet Union. Castells suggests (1998: 4–69) one powerful reason for the collapse of the Soviet system was its failure to adapt its 'statist' mode of production to the 'informational mode of development', the new forces of production which were revolutionizing the world – economically, politically and militarily – in the decades running up to 1991. The bureaucratic command economy in the Soviet Union had consolidated over decades the positions of apparatchiks – state and party administrators and managers, who were resistant to any challenge to their hierarchical structures of authority. Castells suggests (1998: 52–5) that Mikhail Gorbachev's 'perestroika' (restructuring) in the Soviet economy faced entrenched resistance to any criticism of party doctrine, the party, Gosplan, the military command, the intelligence service and interior ministry, industrial managers and state officials. As such the policy of 'glasnost' (openness) sought to legitimate questioning and a freer flow of information with the intention of enabling reforms and greater efficiencies. Nevertheless, as the nuclear accident at Chernobyl soon showed, the regime's tendency towards controlling information where possible soon resurfaced, even though total control had by then become impossible.

Seeking to retain control in the face of economic decentralization and an opening up of information flows, the 'statist' regime fought reforms but, in the end, was overcome by both the internal challenges to central control and the external challenges of a capitalist mode of production that had harnessed more effectively the power of the new informational mode of development (in economic growth, the rise of the Internet and, not insignificantly, in the development of powerful new weapons systems – including anti-aircraft missiles supplied by the United States to Afghan rebels, nuclear cruise missiles deployed in Western Europe, and the more mythic 'Star Wars' strategic defence initiative). For Castells (1996: 18–22) 'capitalist perestroika' was successful in surpassing the industrial, bureaucratic, centralized and hierarchical mode of development (the Fordist factory model of production), with an informational (dymanic, distributed and flat) 'network' mode of development. The Soviet Union, unable to overcome the resistance of its 'statist' elites, and crippled by the economic, political and military costs of an arms race it could not afford to keep up with, did not adapt. Rather, it collapsed.

While the death of Soviet 'statism' is assuredly true, the triumph of network capitalism's perestroika is less certain for two, related, reasons pointed at in this book. First, as Castells' critics have pointed out, capitalism is not as 'flat' and 'distributed' as Castells' network society model suggests. Second, the potential for such a flat and distributed mode of production (one that would extend the affordances of the informational mode of development most fully in the direction Castells suggests would be most radical and efficient) is precisely what threatens today's hierarchical informational corporations. Today's major record labels are only the most extreme examples. As was suggested in the first section of this chapter, and by this book as a whole, the music industry today is emblematic of the network society in general.

The future is not what it used to be!

The birth of Napster in 1999 came one year after the United States passed into law the Digital Millennium Copyright Act, a law that has been replicated the world over. The possibility of digitally sharing the world's culture, and intensification of attempts to criminalize such sharing, form the focus of this book. The last decade has witnessed a battle for 'glasnost' and 'perestroika' from below. A 'global multitude' of hackers, artists, geeks and music fans has faced the economic, political, technical, cultural and legal force of established, centralized and hierarchical institutions keen to maintain their positions of dominance and reward. Attempts to close down 'openness' and 'restructuring' from below, attempts to criminalize, prevent and condemn the free and efficient circulation of information, have all failed. Alternative forms of making a living from musical performance, alternatives that utilize sharing technologies rather than creating monopolies through the legal and technical fabrication of scarcity, are both more efficient in distributing more music to more people at less cost – and at the same time have facilitated better incomes for artists than are achieved through the copyright and royalties-based systems of today's major record labels. Sharing culture, and a culture of sharing, threatens profits not creativity. A dual war – first, to control scarce 'pre-industrial' raw materials (in particular fuel); and, second, to construct scarcity in and then to control 'post-industrial' informational goods – underpins the maintenance of today's global capitalism. This book draws attention to very real and ongoing challenges to one of the two foundations of today's dominant social order. How things work out remains to be seen. File-sharing, in making mediated reproduction truly universal, may return music to its live roots (or simply remind us that for most artists it never left). Such a revolution would be both a return and the realization of something new. File-sharing may be appropriated within a reconfiguration of elites or taken up as part of a more democratic and egalitarian future.

References

Abercrombie, Nicholas, Hill, Stephen and Turner, Bryan (1984) *The Dominant Ideology Thesis*. London: Harper Collins.

Adorno, Theodor (2002) *The Jargon of Authenticity*. London: Routledge Classics.

Adorno, Theodor, and Horkheimer, Max (1979 [1944]) *Dialectic of Enlightenment*. London: Verso.

Adorno, Theodor, Frenkel-Brunswik, Else, Levinson, Daniel and Sanford, Nevitt (1964 [1950]) *The Authoritarian Personality* (parts one and two). New York: John Wiley and Sons.

Advertising Standards Authority (2004) *Non-Broadcast Adjudications: The Federation Against Copyright Theft (FACT)*, posted 31 March 2004 online at: http://www.asa.org.uk/asa/ajuication/non_broadcast/Ajudication+Details.htm. Accessed 13 August 2008.

Albini, Steve (1994) 'The problem with music', *Maximum Rock and Roll*, 133; online at: http://www.arancidamoeba.com/mrr/problemwithmusic.html. Accessed on 12 September 2008.

Alexander, Isabella (2007) 'Criminalizing copyright: a story of publishers, pirates and pieces of eight', *Cambridge Law Journal*, 66 (3): 625–56.

Anderson, Alison (2004) 'Mass-media and environmental risks', in Matthew David and Carole Sutton (eds), *Social Research: The Basics*. London: Sage, pp. 49–53.

AndTea (2006) *MPAA Uses Unfair Rhetoric in their Ad Campaigns*, online at: http://andtea.wordpress.com/2006/04/06/20/. Accessed 1 August 2008.

Archer, Margaret (1989) *Culture and Agency: The Place of Culture in Social Theory*. Cambridge: Cambridge University Press.

Archer, Margaret (1995) *Realist Social Theory: The Morphogenetic Approach*. Cambridge: Cambridge University Press.

Arthur, Charles (2008a) 'The right to peer inside your iPod', *The Guardian*, 10 July.

Arthur, Charles (2008b) 'BPI and ISPs scramble for upper hand in publicity battle over file-sharing deal', *The Guardian*, 24 July, online at: http://blogs.guardian.co.uk/technology/2008/07/24/bpi_and_isps_scramble_for_upper_hand_in_publicity_battle_over_filesharing_deal.html. Accessed 13 August 2008.

Austen, Jane (1990 [1813]) *Pride and Prejudice*. Oxford: Oxford University Press.

Bagchi, Jeebesh (2003) 'File-sharing and piracy linked to terrorism?', *Commons Law*, posted 31 March online at: http://www.kuro5hin.org/story/2003/3/14/234939/956. Accessed 6 August 2008.

Bagehot, Richard and Kanaar, Nicholas (1998) *Music Business Agreements* (2nd edition). London: Sweet and Maxwell.

Banerjee, Anirban, Faloutsos, Michalis and Bhuyan, Laxmi N. (2006) *P2P: Is Big Brother Watching You?* Technical Report hosted at: http://www1.cs.ucr.edu/store/techreports/UCR-CS-2006-06201.pdf. Accessed 17 July 2008.

Bangeman, Eric (2008) 'RIAA sees a 99.6% capitulation rate from students at UT', *Ars Technica: The Art of Technology*, January 2008, online at: http://arstechnica.com/news.ars/post/20080129-less-than-1-of-u-of-tennessee-students-hold-out-against-riaa.html. Accessed 17 June 2008.

Barlow, John Perry (1994) *Notable Speeches of the Information Age*. Sebastopol CA: O'Reilly.

Barlow, John Perry (1996) *A Declaration of the Independence of Cyberspace*, online at: http://homes.eff.org/~barlow/Declaration-Final.html. Accessed 28 September 2008.

Baskerville, David (2004) *Music Business Handbook and Career Guide* (8th edition). London: Sage.

Baudrillard, Jean (1995) *The Gulf War Did Not Take Place*. Indiana: Indiana University Press.

BBC News (2003) *Teenager Wins DVD Court Battle*, 7 January, online at: http://news.bbc.co.uk/1/hi/technology/2635293.stm. Accessed 2 July 2008.

BBC News (2006) *Arctic Monkeys Make Chart History*, 29 January 2006, online at: http://news. bbc.co.uk/1/hi/entertainment/4660394.stm. Accessed 29 October 2008.

BBC News (2007) *EMI Takes Locks of Music Tracks*, 2 April 2007, online at: http://news. bbc.co.uk/1/hi/technology/6516189.stm. Accessed 18 July 2008.

BBC News (2008a) *Illegal Downloaders 'Face UK Ban'*, 12 February 2008, online at: http:// news.bbc.co.uk/1/hi/business/7240234.stm. Accessed 10 July 2008.

BBC News (2008b) *Net Firms Reject Monitoring Role*, 15 February 2008, online at: http://news. bbc.co.uk/2/hi/technology/7246403.stm. Accessed 10 July 2008.

Beck, Ulrich (1992) *Risk Society*. London: Sage.

Biddle, Peter, English, Paul, Peinado, Marcus and Wallman, Bryan (2002) 'The darknet and the future of content distribution,' available at http://www.crypto.standard.edu/DRM2002/ prog.html. Accessed 28 May 2009.

Black, Jack (2008) *Don't Be a Douche. Stop Piracy!*, online at: http://www.youtube.com/ watch?v=-LkWKvMCzqA. Accessed 12 September 2008.

Bland, Archie (2008) 'The Big Question: What is being done to tackle illegal downloading, and will it succeed?', *The Independent*, 25 July, online at: http://www.independent.co.uk/arts-entertainment/music/features/the-big-question-what-is-being-done-to-tackle-illegal-down-loading-and-will-it-succeed-876680.html. Accessed 13 August 2008.

Bogard, William (1996) *The Simulation of Surveillance: Hypercontrol in Telematic Societies*. Cambridge: Cambridge University Press.

BPI (formally the British Phonographic Industry) (2008a) *More than the Music: The UK Recorded Music Business and Our Society*. London: BPI.

BPI (formally the British Phonographic Industry) (2008b) *BPI Press Release: Government-Brokered Deal on P2P Represents Significant Step Forward in Tackling Illegal Filesharing*, posted 24 July 2008, online at: http://www.bpi.co.uk/news. Accessed 5 August 2008.

Brown, Mick (2007) *Tearing Down the Wall of Sound: The Rise and Fall of Phil Spector*. New York: Knopf Publishing Group.

Buckley, Peter (2006) *The Rough Guide to MySpace and Online Communities*. London: Rough Guides.

Bulgakov, Mikhail (2007) *The Master and Margarita*. London: Penguin Classics.

Burkeman, Oliver (2004) 'Terrorism actually', *The Guardian*, 4 February, online at: http:// www.guardian.co.uk/film/2004/feb/04/1. Accessed 14 August 2008.

Buskirk, Eliot Van (2007) *Comscore: 2 out of 5 Downloaders Paid for Radiohead's 'In Rainbows' (Average Price: $6)*, online at: http://blog.wired.com/music/2007/11/comscore-2-outmusic. html. Accessed 31 October 2008.

Canetti, Elias (2005 [1935]) *Auto da fé*. St Albans: The Harvill Press.

Carson, Rachel (1962) *Silent Spring*. Boston MA: Houghton Mifflin.

Cashmore, Ellis (2006) *Celebrity Culture*. London: Routledge.

Castells, Manuel (1996) *The Rise of The Network Society. The Information Age: Economy, Society and Culture Volume I*. Oxford: Blackwell.

Castells, Manuel (1997) *The Power of Identity. The Information Age: Economy, Society and Culture Volume II*. Oxford: Blackwell.

Castells, Manuel (1998) *End of Millennium. The Information Age: Economy, Society and Culture Volume III*. Oxford: Blackwell.

Castells, Manuel (2000) 'Materials for an exploratory theory of the network society', *British Journal of Sociology*, 51 (1): 5–24.

Cellan-Jones, Rory (2008) *Can a Charity Make File-Sharing Taboo?*, BBC Website 30 April 2008, online at: http://www.bbc.co.uk/blogs/technology/2008/04/can_a_charity_make_filesharing. html. Accessed 10 August 2008.

Coleman, Roy (2004) *Reclaiming the Streets: Surveillance, Social Control and the City*. Cullompton: Willan Publishing.

Collins, Harry (1990) *Artificial Experts: Social Knowledge and Intelligent Systems*. Cambridge, MA: MIT Press.

Collins, Harry and Pinch, Trevor (1998) *The Golem at Large: What you Should Know About Technology*. Cambridge: Cambridge University Press.

Collins, Harry and Yearley, Stephen (1992) 'Epistemological chicken', in Andrew Pickering, (ed.), *Science as Practice and Culture*. Chicago, IL: University of Chicago, Press, pp. 17–46.

Comscore (2001) *Global Napster Usage Plummets, but New File-Sharing Alternatives Gaining Ground, Reports Juniper Media Matrix*, 'Comscore', 21 July 2001, online at: http://www.comscore.com/press/release.asp?id=249. Accessed 1 July 2008.

Cook, Pam and Bernink, Mieke (eds) (1999) *The Cinema Book* (2nd edition). London: BFI.

Crouch, Kevin and Crouch, Tamja (2008) *Sun King: The Life and Times of Sam Phillips, the Man Behind Sun Records*. London: Piatkus Books.

Danay, Robert (2005) 'Copyright vs. free expression: the case of peer-to-peer file-sharing of music in the United Kingdom', *Yale Journal of Law and Technology*, 8 (Fall): 32–62.

David, Matthew (1996) 'Information: culture or capital?', *Radical Philosophy*, 79 (Sept–Oct): 56.

David, Matthew (2002) 'The sociological critique of evolutionary psychology: beyond mass modularity', *New Genetics and Society*, 21 (3): 303–13.

David, Matthew (2005) *Science in Society*. London: Palgrave.

David, Matthew (2006a) 'Embodiment and communication, genetics and computing. what does it mean to be human?', in Lauren Langman and Devorah Kalekin-Fishman (eds), *Trauma, Promise and the Millennium: The Evolution of Alienation*. Boulder, CO: Rowman and Littlefield, pp. 77–91.

David, Matthew (2006b) 'Romanticism, creativity and copyright: visions and nightmares', *European Journal of Social Theory*, 9 (3): 425–33.

David, Matthew (2008a) 'Sociological knowledge and scientific knowledge', *Sociology Compass*, 2 (1): 337–51.

David, Matthew (2008b) 'You think is real. I know he's only an actor!', *Current Sociology*, 56 (4): 517–33.

David, Matthew and Kirkhope, Jamieson (2004) 'New digital technologies: privacy/property, globalization and law', *Perspectives on Global Development and Technology*, 3 (4): 437–49.

David, Matthew and Kirkhope, Jamieson (2006) 'The impossibility of technical security: intellectual property and the paradox of informational capitalism', in Mark Lacy and Peter Witkin (eds), *Global Politics in an Information Age*. Manchester: Manchester University Press, pp. 88–95.

DCMS (Department of Culture, Media and Sport) (2008) *Creative Britain: New Talent for the New Economy*. London: DCMS.

Delahunty, James (2005) *Supreme Court Rules in Favour of Metro-Goldwyn-Mayer in P2P Case, in After Dawn*, 27 June, online at: http://www.afterdawn.com/news/archive/6571.cfm. Accessed 17 June 2008.

Deleuze, Gilles (1992) 'Postscript on the societies of control', *October*, 59 (Winter): 3–7.

Deleuze, Gilles and Guattari, Felix (1984) *Anti-Oedipus: Capitalism and Schizophrenia*. London: Athlone Press.

Deleuze, Gilles and Guattari, Felix (1987) *A Thousand Plateaus: Capitalism and Schizophrenia*. Minneapolis, MN: University of Minnesota Press.

Dickens, Charles (2007 [1854]) *Hard Times*. London: Penguin Classics.

Domino Records (2008) *Arctic Monkeys*, online at: http://www.dominorecordco.com/artists/arctic-monkeys/. Accessed 29 October 2008.

Dostoyevsky, Fyodor (2003 [1866]) *Crime and Punishment*. London: Penguin Classics.

Durkheim, Emile (1984a [1893]) *The Division of Labour in Society*. Basingstoke: Macmillan.

Durkheim, Emile (1984b [1898]) 'Preface to the second edition', *The Division of Labour in Society*. Basingstoke: Macmillan.

Electronic Freedom Foundation (2006) *How Not to Get Sued for File-sharing (And Other Ideas To Avoid Being Treated Like a Criminal)*, posted July 2006 online at: http://www.eff.org/wp/how-not-get-sued-file-sharing. Accessed 15 June 2008.

Eliot, George (2008 [1871–2]) *Middlemarch*. Oxford: Oxford University Press.

Enter Shikari (2008) *Band Profile*, online at: http://www.entershikari.com/about.php. Accessed 29 October 2008.

Feenberg, Andrew (1991) *Critical Theory of Technology*. Oxford: Oxford University Press.

Feenberg, Andrew (1999) *Questioning Technology*. London: Routledge.

Feenberg, Andrew (2002) *Transforming Technology: A Critical Theory Revisited*. Oxford: Oxford University Press.

Film Education (2008) *Creative Rights: Digital Responsibilities*, at: http://www.filmeducation. org/creative_rights/. Accessed 24 December 2008.

Fisher, Ken (2003) 'Is P2P the next 'drug war'?', *Arstechnica*, posted 17 July online at: http://arstechnica.com/news.ars/post/20030717-70.html. Accessed 1 August 2003.

Fisher, Ken (2005) 'MPAA equates pirated DVDs to "drugs on the street"', *Arstechnica*, posted 15 November online at: http://arstechnica.com/news.ars/post/20051115-5580.html. Accessed 2 August 2008.

Fonarow, Wendy (2006) *Empire of Dirt: The Aesthetics and Rituals of British Indie Music*. Middletown, CT: Wesleyan University Press.

Foucault, Michel (1971 [1961]) *Madness and Civilization: A History of Insanity in the Age of Reason*. London: Social Science Publishers.

Foucault, Michel (1974 [1966]) *The Order of Things: Archaeology of the Human Sciences*. London: Tavistock.

Foucault, Michel (1976 [1963]) *The Birth of the Clinic*. London: Social Science Publishers.

Foucault, Michel (1977) 'Nietzsche, genealogy, history', in D. F. Bouchard (ed.), *Language, Counter-Memory and Practice: Selected Essays and Interviews*. Ithaca: Cornell University Press, pp. 139–64.

Foucault, Michel (1980 [1976]) *The History of Sexuality: Volume 1*. London: Penguin.

Foucault, Michel (1991 [1975]) *Discipline and Punish: the birth of the prison*. London: Penguin.

Foucault, Michel (2002 [1969]) *Archaeology of Knowledge*. London: Routledge.

Foucault, Michel (2003) *'Society Must Be Defended': Lectures at the College de France, 1975–1976*. London: Picador.

Frith, Simon (1987) 'Copyright and the music business', *Popular Music*, 7 (1): 57–75

Frith, Simon (1990) *Facing the Music*. London: Mandarin.

Galloway, Alexander (2004) *Protocol: How Control Exists After Decentralization*. Cambridge, MA: MIT Press.

Galloway, Alexander (2005) 'Global networks and the effects on culture', *The Annals of the American Academy*, 597 (January): 19–31.

Ortega Y Gasset, Jose (1930), The Revolt of the Masses, online at: http://www.4literature.net/ Jose_Ortega_y_Gasset/Revolt_of_the_Masses/. Accessed 20 July 2008.

Gates, Bill (1995) *The Road Ahead*. London: Viking.

Gates, Bill (1999) *Business at the Speed of Thought: Succeeding in the Digital Economy*. London: Penguin.

George, Nelson (2003) *Where Did Our Love Go?: The Rise and Fall of the Motown Sound*. London: Omnibus Press.

Gibson, Owen (2008), 'Silicon Valley's hippy values "killing music industry"', *The Guardian*, 29 January, online at: http://www.guardian.co.uk/uk/2008/jan/29/musicnews.music. Accessed 28 September 2008.

Gibson, William (1984) *Neuromancer*. New York: Ace Books.

Giddens, Anthony (1992) *The Transformation of Intimacy*. Cambridge: Polity.

Gitlin, Todd (2003) *The Whole World is Watching: Mass-Media in the Making and Un-Making of the New Left*. Berkeley, CA: University of California Press.

Goethe, Johann Wolfgang von (1989 [1774]) *The Sorrows of Young Werther*. London: Penguin Classics.

Goethe, Johann Wolfgang von (2005 [1808]) *Faust: Part One*. London: Penguin Classics.

Goldstein, Paul (2003) *Copyright's Highway: From Gutenburg to the Celestial Jukebox*. Stanford, CA: Stanford University Press.

Gopal, Ram D., Bhattacharjee, Supid and Sanders, G. Lawrence (2006), 'Do artists benefit from online music sharing?', *Journal of Business*, 79 (3): 1503–33.

Gouldner, Alvin (1976) *The Dialectic of Ideology and Technology: The Origins, Grammar and Future of Ideology*. London: Macmillan.

Gowers, Andrew (2006) *Gowers' Review of Intellectual Property*. Norwich: HMSO.

Grint, Kieth and Woolgar, Steve (1997) *The Machine at Work: Technology, Work and Organization*. Cambridge: Polity.

Gross, Grant (2003) 'Does file trading fund terrorism? Industry execs claim peer-to-peer networks pose more than just legal problems', *IDG News Service*, online at: http://www. interesting-people.org/archives/interesting-people/200303/msg00180.html. Accessed 2 August 2008.

Grosso, William (2003) *Getting Lectured by the MPAA at the Movies*, 28 August, online at: http://www.oreillynet.com/pub/wlg/3716. Accessed 2 August 2008.

Habermas, Jurgen (1971 [1970]) *Towards a Rational Society*. London: Heinemann Educational Books.

Habermas, Jurgen (1972) *Knowledge and Human Interests*. London: Heinemann Educational Books.

Habermas, Jurgen (1976) *Legitimation Crisis*. London: Heinemann Educational Books.

Habermas, Jurgen (1979) *Communication and the Evolution of Society*. London: Heinemann Educational Books.

Habermas, Jurgen (1984) *The Theory of Communicative Action* (Volume One). Cambridge: Polity.

Habermas, Jurgen (1987) *The Theory of Communicative Action* (Volume Two). Cambridge: Polity.

Habermas, Jurgen (1989 [1962]) *The Structural Transformation of the Public Sphere: An Inquiry into a Category of Bourgeois Society*. Cambridge: Polity Press.

Habermas, Jurgen (1990) *Moral Consciousness and Communicative Action*. Cambridge: Polity.

Halbert, Debora (2005) *Resisting Intellectual Property*. London: Routledge.

Hall, Stuart, Critcher, Charles, Jefferson, Tony, Clarke, John and Robert, Brian (1978) *Policing the Crisis: Mugging, the State and Law and Order*. London: Palgrave Macmillan.

Hansen, Mark (2006) *New Philosophy for New-Media*. Boston, MA: MIT Press.

Haraway, Donna (1991) 'A cyborg manifesto: science, technology, and socialist-feminism in the late twentieth century', in *Simians, Cyborgs and Women: The Reinvention of Nature*. New York: Routledge. pp.149–81.

Haraway, Donna (1997) *Modest_Witness@Second_Millennium.FemaleMan ©Meets_Onco Mouse: Feminism and Technoscience*. New York: Routledge.

Hardin, Garrett (1968) 'The tragedy of the commons', *Science*, 162 (3859): 1243–8.

Hardt, Michael and Negri, Antonio (2000) *Empire*. Cambridge, MA: Harvard University Press.

Hardy, Thomas (2007 [1895]) *Jude the Obscure*. London: Penguin Classics.

Haugland, Jan (2003) 'You support terrorism if you download that', *MP3Secular Blasphamy*, posted 15 March 2003 online at: http://blogs.salon.com/0001561/2003/03/15.html. Accessed 2 August 2008.

Heath, Christian and Luff, Paul (1993) 'Disembodied conduct: interactional asymmetries in video-mediated communication', in Graham Button (ed.), *Technology in Working Order: Studies of Work, Interaction and Technology*. London: Routledge, pp. 35–54.

Hegel, Georg Wilhelm Freidrich (1991) *Elements of the Philosophy of Right*. Cambridge: Cambridge University Press.

Henwood, Flis (1994) 'Establishing gender perspectives on information technology: problems, issues and opportunities', in Eileen Green, Jenny Owen and Den Pain (eds), *Gender by Design*. London: Taylor and Francis, pp. 31–49.

Himanen, Pekka (2001) *The Hacker Ethic and the Spirit of the Information Age*. London: Secker and Warburg.

Hine, Christine (2000) *Virtual Ethnography*. London: Sage.

Holahan, Catherine (2008) 'Sony BMG plans to drop DRM', *Business Week*, 4 January 2008, online at: http://www.businessweek.com/technology/content/jan2008/tc2008013_398775.htm. Accessed 18 July 2008.

Holmes, Brian (2003), 'The emperor's sword: art under WIPO', in *World-Information.Org*, December 2003, online at: http://world-information.org/wio/readme/992007035/1078488424. Accessed 1 July 2008.

Howe, Jeff (2004) 'File-sharing is, like, totally uncool', *Wired Magazine*, 12 (5): 11.

Hugo, Victor (1998 [1862]) *Les Miserables*. London: Penguin Popular Classics.

Hull, Geoffrey (2004) *The Recording Industry* (2nd edition). London: Routledge.

Hutchby, Ian (2001) *Conversation and Technology: From the Telephone to the Internet*. Cambridge: Polity.

Huxley, Aldous (1932) *Brave New World*. London: Chatto and Windus Ltd.

Jameson, Fredric (1991) *Postmodernism: Or, the Cultural Logic of Late Capitalism*. London: Verso.

Jobs, Steve (2007) *Thoughts on Music*, posted 6 February, online at: http://www.apple.com/hotnews/thoughtsonmusic/. Accessed 18 July 2008.

Jones, Bradley (2008) *Web 2.0 Heroes: Interviews with 20 Web Influencers*. Indianapolis, IN: Wiley.

Jordan, Tim and Taylor, Paul (2004) *Hacktivism and Cyberwars: Rebels with a Cause?*. London: Routledge.

Kirkpatrick, Graeme (2004) *Critical Technology: A Social Theory of Personal Computing*. Aldershot: Ashgate.

Kirkpatrick, Graeme (2008) *Technology and Social Power*. London: Palgrave.

Kirton, Andrew, Jones, Paul and David, Matthew (2008) *Somewhere over 'In Rainbows'*, paper presented at the 1st ISA Forum, Barcelona, 5–8 September.

Kittler, Frederick (1990) *Discourse Networks, 1800/1900*. Palo Alto, CA: Stanford University Press.

Kittler, Frederick (1997) *Literature, Media, Information Systems: Critical Voices in Art, Theory & Culture*. London: Routledge.

Kittler, Frederick (1999) *Gramophone, Film, Typewriter*. Palo Alto, CA: Stanford University Press.

Kravets, David (2008a) 'Death of DRM could weaken iTunes, boost iPod', *Wired Magazine*: 16 (4), online at: http://www.wired.com/entertainment/music/news/2008/01/rip_drm. Accessed 18 July 2008.

Kravets, David (2008b) 'RIAA appeals Jammie Thomas mistrial', 15 October, online at: http://blog.wired.com/27bstroke6/2008/10/riaa-appealing.html. Accessed 22 December 2008.

Krueger, Alan B (2004) *The Economics of Real Superstars: The Market for Rock Concerts in the Material World*, 12 April 2004, Lunchtime speech, online at: www.irs.princeton.edu. Accessed 1 October 2008.

Krueger, Alan B. and Connolly, Marie (2006) 'Rockonomics: the economics of popular music', in Victor A. Ginsberg and David Throsby (eds), *Handbook of the Economics of Art and Culture*. Amsterdam: North-Holland, pp. 667–720.

Kusch, Martin and Collins, Harry (1998) *The Shape of Action: What Humans and Machines Can Do*. Cambridge, MA: MIT Press.

Latour, Bruno (2005) *Reassembling the Social*. Oxford: Oxford University Press.

Leong, Susanna H. S. and Saw, Cheng Lim (2007) 'Copyright infringement in a borderless world – does territoriality matter? Society of Composers, Authors and Music Publishers of Canada v Canadian Association of Internet Providers [2004] 2 SCR 427', *International Journal of Law and Information Technology*, 15 (1 March): 38–53.

Lessig, Lawrence (2004) *Free Culture: How Big Media Uses Technology and the Law to Lock Down and Control Creativity*. New York: The Penguin Press.

Levi, Steven (1984) *Hackers: Heroes of the Computer Revolution*. New York: Anchor Press.

Levine, Robert (2006), 'Unlocking the iPod', *Fortune Magazine*, 23 October 2006, online at: http://money.cnn.com/magazines/fortune/fortune_archive/2006/10/30/8391726/index.htm. Accessed 18 July 2008.

Lewontin, Richard (1993) *The Doctrine of DNA: Biology as Ideology*. London: Penguin.

Lewontin, Richard (2000) *It Ain't Necessarily So: The Dream of the Human Genome and Other Illusions*. London: Granta.

Liebowitz, Stan J. (2003) 'Will MP3 downloads annihilate the record industry? The evidence so far', in Gary Libecap (ed.), *Advances in the Study of Entrepreneurship, Innovation, and Economic Growth*, 15. Greenwich CT: JAI Press, pp. 681–712.

Liebowitz, Stan J. (2004a) 'The elusive symbiosis: the impact of radio on the record industry', unpublished paper (School of Management, University of Texas at Dallas), online at: www.utdallas.edu/~liebowit/intprop/complpff.pdf. Accessed 1 October 2008.

Liebowitz, Stan J. (2004b) 'Pitfalls in measuring the impact of file-sharing', unpublished paper (School of Management, University of Texas at Dallas), online at: www.utdallas.edu/~liebowit/intprop/pitfalls.pdf. Accessed 1 October 2008.

Light, Donald (2004) 'From migrant enclaves to mainstream: reconceptualizing informal economic behavior', *Theory and Society*, 33 (6 December): 705–37.

Light, Donald and Warburton, Rebecca (2005) 'Extraordinary claims require extraordinary evidence', *Journal of Health Economics*, 24: 1030–33.

Lindsey, Cam (2008) 'Radiohead reveal how successful *In Rainbows* download really was: facts for pay-what-you-want release finally made public', *New Musical Express*, 15 October 2008, online at: http://www.nme.com/news/radiohead/40444. Accessed 12 November 2008.

Litman, Jessica (1991) 'Copyright as myth', *Pittsburg Law Review*, 53: 235–49.

Locke, John (1988) *Two Treatises of Government*. Cambridge: Cambridge University Press.

Love, Courtney (2000) *The Love Manifesto*, online at: http://www.indie-music.com/modules.php?name=News&file=article&sid=820. Accessed 12 September 2008.

Lukács, Georg (1972 [1922]) *History and Class Consciousness*. Cambridge, MA: MIT Press.

Lyon, David (2001) *Surveillance Society: Monitoring Everyday Life*. Milton Keynes: Open University Press.

Lyon, David (2002) 'Everyday surveillance: personal data and social classifications', *Information, Communication & Society*, 5 (2): 242–57.

McCormick, Niel (2008) 'Live Nation: who took a slice of madonna's pie?', *Daily Telegragh*, 1 October 2008, online at: http://blogs.telegraph.co.uk/neil_mccormick/blog/2008/10/01/live_nation_who_took_a_slice_of_madonnas_pie. Accessed 31 October 2008.

McLuhan, Marshall (1962) *The Gutenburg Galaxy: The Making of Typographic Man*. London: Routledge.

McLuhan, Marshall (1964) *Understanding Media: The Extensions of Man*. London: Routledge.

MacKenzie, Donald and Wajcman, Judy (1985) *The Social Shaping of Technology*. Milton Keynes: Open University Press.

MacKenzie, Donald and Wajcman, Judy (1999) *The Social Shaping of Technology* (2nd edition). Milton Keynes: Open University Press.

Marcuse, Herbert (1986) *Reason and Revolution*. London: London.

Marcuse, Herbert (2002 [1964]) *One Dimensional Man*. London: Routledge.

Marie Claire (2007) 'Madonna set to sign new £60m recording contract', in *Marie Claire*, 12 October 2007, online at: http://www.marieclaire.co.uk/news/celebrity/160683/madonna-set-to-sign-new-60m-recording-contract.html. Accessed 31 October 2008.

Marshall, Lee (2005) *Bootlegging; Romanticism and Copyright in the Music Industry*. London: Sage in association with Theory, Culture and Society.

Martin, Peter (1995) *Sound and Society: Themes in the Sociology of Music*. Manchester: Manchester University Press.

Marx, Karl (1995) *Capital: An Abridged Version* (David McLellan, ed.). Oxford: Oxford Paperbacks.

Mason, David, Lankshear, Gloria, Cook, Peter, Coates, Sally and Button, Graham (2001) 'Call centre employees' responses to electronic monitoring: some research findings', *Work, Employment & Society*, 15 (3): 595–605.

Mason, David, Button, Graham, Lankshear, Gloria and Coates, Sally (2002a) 'Getting real about surveillance and privacy at work', in Steve Woolgar (ed.), *Virtual Society? Technology, Cyberbole, Reality*. Oxford: Oxford University Press, pp. 137–52.

Mason, David, Button, Graham, Lankshear, Gloria, Coates, Sally and Sharrock, Wes (2002b) 'On the poverty of apriorism: technology, surveillance in the workplace and employee responses', *Information, Communication and Society*, 5 (4): 555–72.

May, Christopher (2002) *The Information Society: A Sceptical View*. Cambridge: Polity.

May, Christopher (2004) 'Cosmopolitan legalism meets "thin community": problems in the global governance of intellectual property', *Government and Opposition*, 39 (3): 393–422.

May, Christopher (2007a) *The World Intellectual Property Organisation: Resurgence and the Development Agenda*. London: Routledge.

May, Christopher (2007b) *Digital Rights Management: The Problem of Expanding Ownership Rights*. Oxford: Chandos.

May, Christopher and Halbert, Debora (2005) 'AIDS, pharmaceutical patents and the African State: reorienting the global governance of intellectual property', in Amy S. Petterson (ed.), *The African State and the AIDS Crisis*. Burlington: Ashgate, pp. 195–217.

May, Christopher and Sell, Susan (2005) *Intellectual Property Rights: A Critical History*. Boulder, CO and London: Lynne Rienner Publishers.

Mayhew, Leon (1997) *The New Public: Professional Communication and the Means of Social Influence*. Cambridge: Cambridge University Press.

Menn, Joseph (2003) *All the Rave: The Rise and Fall of Shaun Fanning's Napster*. New York: Crown Business.

Merriden, Trevor (2001) *Irresistible Forces: The Business Legacy of Napster & the Growth of the Underground Internet*. Oxford: Capstone Publishing Limited.

Michels, Robert (1962) *Political Parties: A Sociological Study of the Oligarchical Tendencies of Modern Democracy*. New York, NY: Collier Books.

Midgley, Mary (1996) 'One world but a big one', *Journal of Consciousness Studies*, 3 (5–6): 500–14.

Miller, Daniel and Slater, Don (2000) *The Internet: An Ethnographic Approach*. Oxford/ New York: Berg.

Miller, Donald (1989) *Lewis Mumford: A Life*. Pittsburgh: University of Pittsburgh Press.

Mitchell, Stuart (2004) 'Labelled with greed', *The Sunday Times*, Doors Section, 22 February, p. 12.

Moody, Glenn (2002) *Rebel Code: Linux and the Open Source Revolution*. London: Penguin.

Morris, Nigel (2008) 'Music industry to tax downloaders', *Independent*, online at: http://www. independent.co.uk/arts-entertainment/music/news/music-industry-to-tax-downloaders-875757.html. Accessed 13 August.

Moustrous, Alexi and Sabbagh, Dan (2008) 'Music companies to police illegal downloads', *The Times*, 25 July, online at: http://entertainment.timesonline.co.uk/tol/arts_and_entertainment/ music/ article4393540.ece. Accessed 13 August.

MPEG (Motion Picture Expert Group) (1989) *Press Release*, online at: http://www.chiariglione. org/mpeg/meetings/kurihama89/kurihama_press.htm. Accessed 1 July 2008.

Mumford, Lewis (1934) *Technics and Civilization*. London: George Routledge and Sons Ltd.

Mumford, Lewis (1964) 'Authoritarian and democratic technics', *Technology and Culture*, 5 (1): 1–8.

Mumford, Lewis (1967) *The Myth of the Machine: Technics and Human Development*. London: Secker and Warburg.

Mumford, Lewis (1971) *The Myth of the Machine: The Pentagon of Power*. London: Sacker and Warburg.

Murphy, Anthony (2002) *Queen Anne and Anarchists: Can Copyright Survive in the Digital Age?*, Oxford IP Research Centre Seminar, 26 February, online at: http://www.oiprc.ox.ac. uk/EJWP0202.pdf. Accessed 28 September 2008.

Murphy, Raymond (1985) 'Exploitation or exclusion?', *Sociology*, 19 (2): 225–43.

Murphy, Raymond (1988) *Social Closure: The Theory of Monopolization and Exclusion*. Oxford: Oxford University Press.

New Musical Express (2007) 'The Charlatans to give new album away free', in New Musical Express, 1 October 2007, online at: http://www.nme.com/news/the-charlatans/31475. Accessed 31 October 2008.

Oberholzer, Felix and Strumpf, Koleman (2004) 'The effect of file-sharing on record sales, an empirical analysis', unpublished paper (Harvard Business School and Department of Economics, University of North Carolina Chapel Hill), online at: www.unc.edu/~cigar/ papers/FileSharing_March2004.pdf. Accessed 1 October 2008.

Orwell, George (1949) *Nineteen Eighty-Four*. London: Secker and Warburg.

OzJuggler (2007) 'Jack Valenti dies, to critical acclaim', *Kuro5hin: technology and culture, from the trenches*, 28 April 2007, online at: http://www.kuro5hin.org/story/ 2007/4/28/12281/6192. Accessed 1 August 2008.

Pareles, Jon (2002) 'David Bowie, 21st century entrepreneur', *The New York Times*, 9 June 2002: 30.

Pareto, Vilfredo (1991) *The Rise and Fall of Elites: Application of Theoretical Sociology*. Edison NJ: Transaction Publishers.

Peterson, R. A. and Berger, D. G. (1975) 'Cycles of symbol production: the case of popular music', *American Sociological Review*, 40 (2): 158–73.

Plant, Sadie (1998) *Zeros and Ones*. London: Fourth Estate.

Posner, Gerald (2005) *Motown: Music, Money, Sex and Power*. London: Random House.

Poster, Mark (2006) *Information Please: Culture and Politics in the Age of Digital Machines*. Durham, NC: Duke University Press.

Prasad, Akhil and Agarwala, Aditi (2008) 'Whodunit! Assessing copyright liability in cyburbia: positing solutions to curb the menace of copyrighted "file-sharing" culture', *Journal of International Commercial Law and Technology*, 3 (1): 1–12.

Presdee, Mike (2000) *Cultural Criminology and the Carnival of Crime*. London: Routledge.

Reid, Jim (2008) 'Virgin defends file-sharing campaign', *BBC Newsbeat*, posted 3 July 2008, online at: http://news.bbc.co.uk/go/pr/fr/-/newsbeat/hi/technology/ nesid_7486000/7486836.stm. Accessed 10 August 2008.

Reingold, Howard (2000) *The Virtual Community: Homesteading on the Electronic Frontier* (revised edition). Cambridge, MA: MIT Press.

Reiss, Spencer (2006) 'His space', *Wired Magazine*, 14 (7), online at: http://www.wired.com/wired/archive/14.07/murdoch_pr.html. Accessed 1 August 2008.

Ribowsky, Mark (2007) *He's a Rebel: Phil Spector – Rock and Roll's Legendary Producer* (2nd edition). Cambridge, MA: Da Capo Press.

Rojek, Chris (2001) *Celebrity*. London: Reaktion Books.

Rojek, Chris (2006) 'Something for nothing: the controversy over P2P file exchange and its implications for leisure', *Leisure and Society*, 30 (1): 133–48.

Rojek, Chris (2007) *Cultural Studies*. Cambridge: Polity.

Rose, Steven (1997) *Lifelines*. London: Penguin.

Rosen, Sherwin (1981) 'The economics of superstars', *The American Economic Review*, 71 (5 December): 845–58.

Rousseau, Jean-Jacques (1987 [1761]) *Julie, or the New Eloise*. Pennsylvania: Pennsylvania State University Press.

Sabbagh, Dan (2008a) 'Parents to be punished for children's net piracy', in *The Times*, 24 July, online at: http://technology.timesonline.co.uk/tol/news/tech_and_web/article4387283.ece. Accessed 13 August.

Sabbagh, Dan (2008b) 'Downloading illegally? Look out, they're watching you', *The Times*, 24 July, online at: http://www.timesonline.co.uk/tol/news/uk/article4387307.ece. Accessed 13 August.

Sandall, Robert (2007) 'Off the record', *Prospect Magazine*, 137 (August), online at: http://www.prospect-magazine.co.uk/pdfarticle.php?id=9735. Accessed 12 September 2008.

Savage, David and Healey, Jon (2004) 'Supreme Court to hear file-sharing dispute', in *The Los Angeles Times*, 11 December 2004, online at: http://www.latimes.com/technology/la-fi-scotus11dec11.1.3888518.story?page=1&coll=la-headlines-technology. Accessed 17 June 2008.

Shelley, Mary (1998 [1818]) *Frankenstein*. Oxford: Oxford Paperbacks.

Simpson, Aislinn (2008) 'Airport scans for illegal downloads on iPods, mobile phones and laptops', *The Daily Telegraph*, 10 July.

Sklair, Leslie (2002) 'The transnational capitalist class and global politics: deconstructing the corporate-state connection', in *International Political Science Review*, 23 (2): 159–74.

Sloterdijk, Peter (1984) 'Cynicism – the twilight of false consciousness', *New German Critique*, 33 (Autumn): 190–206.

Snapper, John (1999) 'On the web, plagiarism matters more than copyright piracy', *Ethics and Information Technology*, 1 (2): 127–36.

Spender, Dale (2003) *Nattering on the Net: Women, Power and Cyperspace*. Melbourne: Spinefex.

Sterling, Bruce (1993) *The Hacker Crackdown: Law and Disorder on the Electronic Frontier*. London: Viking.

Suchman, Lucy (1987) *Plans and Situated Actions: The Problem of Human-Machine Communication (Learning in Doing)*. Cambridge: Cambridge University Press.

Sweeney, John (2008a) 'Digital media piracy', *The Guardian*, 24 July, online at: http://www.guardian.co.uk/media/2008/jul/24/digitalmedia.piracy1. Accessed 13 August.

Sweeney, John (2008b) 'Illegal filesharing: government hits back at BPI over last-minute letter', *the Guardian*, 31 July, online at: http://www.guardian.co.uk/media/2008/jul/31/digitalmedia.downloads/print. Accessed 13 August 2008.

Teicholz, Nina (2002) 'Privatizing propaganda: Poppy Bush and his cronies rescued Dubya's Iraq policy. Now they're saving his propaganda war', *Washington Monthly*, December 2002, online at: http://findarticles.com/p/articles/mi_m1316/is_12_34/ai_95914085. Accessed 6 August 2008.

Terranova, Tiziana (2004) *Networking Culture: Politics for the Information Age*. London: Pluto.

Thompson, Clive (2005) 'The BitTorrent effect', *Wired Magazine*, 13 (1), online at: http://www.wired.com/wired/archive/13.01/bittorrent.html. Accessed 16 July 2008.

de Tocqueville, Alexis (2008 [1856]) *Ancien Regime and the Revolution*. London: Penguin Classics.

Tönnies, Ferdinand (1988) *Community and Society*. Edison, NJ: Transaction Publishers.

Trollope, Anthony (1994 [1875]) *The Way We Live Now*. London: Penguin Classics.

Turkle, Sherry (1995) *Life on the Screen: Identity in the Age of the Internet*. New York: Simon and Schuster.

Turkle, Sherry (2005) *The Second Self: Computers and the Human Spirit*. Cambridge, MA: MIT Press.

Turner, Adam (2003) 'Software piracy "funding terrorism"', *The Sydney Morning Herald*, 21 March, online at: http://www.smh.com.au/articles/2003/03/21/1047749921225.html. Accessed 10 August 2008.

Turner, Graeme (2004) *Understanding Celebrity*. London: Sage.

Turner, Kathleen (2002) 'Financing terror: profits from counterfeit goods pay For attacks', *Customs Today*, 38 (11 November), online at: http://www.cbp.gov/xp/CustomsToday/2002/November/interpol.xml. Accessed 1 August 2008.

UK Parliamentary Office for Science and Technology (2002) *Postnote: Copyright and the Internet*, London, HMSO.

Vaidhyanathan, Siva (2003) *Copyrights and Copywrongs: The Rise of Intellectual Property and How it Threatens Creativity*. New York: New York University Press.

Valenti, Jack (2004) *Testimony of Jack Valenti President and CEO Motion Picture Association of America, Before the Committee on Foreign Relations, United States of America*, 9 June 2004, online at: http://foreign.senate.gov/testimony/2004/ValentiTestimony040609.pdf. Accessed 1 August 2008.

Vincents, Okechukwu Benjamin (2007) 'When rights clash online: the tracking of P2p copyright infringements Vs. the EC Personal Data Directive', *International Journal of Law and Information Technology*, 15 (3): 270–96.

Virilio, Paul (1984) *War and Cinema: The Logistics of Perception*. London: Verso.

Virilio, Paul (2000) *The Information Bomb*. London: Verso.

Wajcman, Judy (1991), *Feminism Confronts Technology*. Cambridge: Polity.

Wall, David (2007) *Cybercrime: The Transformation of Crime in the Information Age*. Cambridge: Polity.

Walsh, David (2001) 'Hollywood enlists in Bush's war drive', World Socialist Web Site, posted 19 November 2001, online at: http://www.wsws.org/articles/2001/nov2001/holl-n19.shtml. Accessed 2 August 2008.

Wang, Wallace (2004) *Steal This File-sharing Book: What They Won't Tell You About File-sharing*. San Francisco, CA: No Starch Press.

Warner, Timothy (2003) *Pop Music: Technology and Creativity – Trevor Horn and the Digital Revolution*. Aldershot: Ashgate.

Watkinson, John (2001) *The MPEG Handbook*. Oxford: Focal Press.

Weber, Max (1930 [1905]) *The Protestant Ethic and the Spirit of Capitalism*. London: Unwin Hyman Ltd.

Weber, Max (1958). 'The three types of legitimate rule', *Berkeley Publications in Society and Institutions*, 4 (1): 1–11.

Weber, Max (1978) *Economy and Society*. Berkeley, CA: University of California Press.

Weber, Max (1991) 'Bureaucracy', in H.H. Gerth and C. Wright Mills (eds), *From Max Weber*. London: Routledge, pp. 196–239.

Webster, Frank (2006) *Theories of the Information Society*. London: Routledge.

Webster, Juliet (1996), *Shaping Women's Work: Gender, Employment and Information Technology*. London: Longman.

Weinstein, Stuart and Wild Charles (2007) 'The copyright clink conundrum: is Chan Nai-Ming the modern day Josef K.?', *International Review of Law, Computers and Technology*, 21 (3): 285–93.

West, Dave (2007) 'Internet CD shop must pay £41m to labels', *DigitalSpy*, posted 30 May 2007, online at: http://www.digitalspy.co.uk/music/a58428/Internet-cd-shop-must-pay-gbp41m-to-labels.html. Accessed 18 June 2008.

Williams, Chris (2008) 'RIAA filesharing Jammie Thomas wins retrial: judge slams "oppressive" $220,000 damages award', *The Register*, online at: www.theregister.co.uk/2008/09/25/jammie_thomas_again/. Accessed on 22 December 2008.

Williams, Malcolm and May, Tim (1996) *Introduction to the Philosophy of Social Research*. London: Routledge.

Wittgenstein, Ludwig (1953) *Philosophical Investigations*. Oxford: Blackwell.

Winner, Langdon (1985) 'Do artifacts have politics?', in D. MacKenzie and J.Wajcman (eds), *The Social Shaping of Technology*. Milton Keynes: Open University Press, pp. 26–38.

Winston, Brian (1998) *Media, Technology and Society. A History: From the Telegraph to the Internet*. London: Routldege.

Wolfe, Tom (1966) *The Kandy-Kolored Tangerine-Flake Streamline Baby*. London: Jonathan Cape.

Woolgar, Steve (1988) *Science: The Very Idea*. London: Tavistock.

Woolgar, Steve (ed.) (2002) *Virtual Reality? Technology, Cyberbole, Reality*. Oxford: Oxford University Press.

Yar, Majid (2006) *Cybercrime and Society*. London: Sage.

Youngs, Ian (2007) 'Sound of 2007: Enter Shikari', BBC News, 5 January, online at: http://news.bbc.co.uk/go/pr/fr/-/1/hi/entertainment/6193215.stm. Accessed 29 October 2008.

Zhang, Michael X (2002) 'Stardom, peer-to-peer and the socially optimal distribution of music', unpublished paper (School of Management, MIT), online at: http://web.mit.edu/zxq/www/mit/15575/p2p.pdf. Accessed 1 October 2008.

Zimiatin, Evgenii Ivanovich (1987) *We*. New York: Avon.

Zola, Emile (2008 [1885]) *Germinal*. Oxford: Oxford World Classics.

Zeitlyn, David, David, Matthew and Bex, Jane (1999) *Knowledge Lost in Information: Patterns of Use and Non-Use of Networked Bibliographic Resources*. London: Office of Humanities Communications.

Zuboff, Shoshana (1988) *In the Age of the Smart Machines: The Future of Work and Power*. London: Butterworth-Heinemann.

Index